TROUBLESHOOTING WITH SNMP
AND ANALYZING MIBS

Troubleshooting with SNMP and Analyzing MIBS

Louis A. Steinberg

McGraw-Hill
New York   San Francisco   Washington, D.C.
Auckland   Bogotá   Caracas   Lisbon   London
Madrid   Mexico City   Milan   Montreal   New Delhi
San Juan   Singapore   Sydney   Tokyo   Toronto

McGraw-Hill

A Division of The McGraw-Hill Companies

1 2 3 4 5 6 7 8 9 0   AGM/AGM   0 5 4 3 2 1 0

ISBN 0-07-212485-7

The sponsoring editor for this book was Steven Elliot and the production supervisor was Clare Stanley. It was set in Century Schoolbook by D&G Limited, LLC.

Printed and bound by Quebecor/Martinsburg.

Throughout this book, trademarked names are used. Rather than put a trademark symbol after every occurrence of a trademarked name, we use names in an editorial fashion only, and to the benefit of the trademark owner, with no intention of infringement of the trademark. Where such designations appear in this book, they have been printed with initial caps.

This book is printed on recycled, acid-free paper containing a minimum of 50 percent recycled de-inked fiber.

This book is dedicated to my wife, May, whose patience has allowed me to fanatically pursue the understanding and implementations of network management for more than a decade.

CONTENTS

PREFACE

Another book by another geek telling the world how wonderful the Simple Network Management Protocol is. As a reader, you probably want that about as much as you want a routing loop. I promise you, this is neither. *Troubleshooting with SNMP and Analyzing MIBS* gives you specific recommendations for monitoring your network infrastructure. For each technology covered in this book, you'll learn what data to collect and how to interpret it. I'll show you how data becomes information and how information becomes insight.

"What we have here is a failure to communicate." (Strother Martin in the movie *Cool Hand Luke,* 1967). Fortunately, these words no longer ring true in network management. When I started working with the Internet Engineering Task Force (IETF) on the original MIB-1 working group in 1988, that was the case. Communications require a common language— a *protocol*, if you will. At the time, most network equipment was managed by using proprietary protocols. We configured and monitored our gear using vendor-supplied applications. To this day, I still find myself reciting the old IDNX configuration mantra: card3-slot2-port2->card2-slot4-port1.

In the late 1980s, a number of protocols battled to become the common protocol for managing networks: *Simple Gateway Monitoring Protocol* (SGMP), which was the predecessor of SNMP; *Common Management Information Protocol Over Transmission Control Protocol* (CMOT); and even *High Level Entity Management Protocol* (HEMS). In the end, simplicity won—*Simple Network Management Protocol* (SNMP) became the de-facto standard, and communication has improved as a result.

> **NOTE:** *Tom Cikoski, who maintains the SNMP FAQ (http://www. landfield.com/faqs/snmp-faq/part1/), is fond of saying that the "Simple" in SNMP is really a developer's statement. Simple to code does not mean simple to use. In fact, most users don't know or care what the underlying protocol is. I coded some of the earliest SGMP and SNMP implementations (after the protocol authors, of course), and I can attest to the fact that SNMP implementation was a lot easier than my failed attempt to write a CMOT stack. The only tricky part was implementing the encoding language (ASN.1) efficiently—a challenge that both SNMP and CMOT share.*

So, we have a common language with SNMP, but without content this has no value. It might as well be French. Every language requires a grammar; in SNMP's case, that grammar is called the *Structure of Management Information* (SMI). Now we can communicate. The problem is that we don't yet have anything to say. When vendors promise that their equipment "speaks SNMP," your response should be, "Yes, but what can it tell me?" You need to make sure that their products do more than minimally support the required standard instrumentation. Few really do a complete job.

A common language is not useful without content. In networking terms, we need common *Management Information Bases* (MIBs). Once defined, we have a dictionary of words that are understood and can be communicated in our language.

Only one problem—we lack understanding. Have you ever looked a term up in the dictionary and walked away without knowing what the heck it meant? There are piles of MIBs defined in piles of vendor documents and *Requests For Comments* (RFCs). Each MIB defines piles of bits of information, and each of those bits has a unique name and a couple of lines of description. If you were to take the time to read through all of the MIBs, some would make sense and some would not.

If you tried to make sense of all this without help, you would most likely shorten your lifespan by several years and quite possibly end up a candidate for rehab.

> **NOTE:** *Some instrumentation requires description. If I were to tell you that your T1 was experiencing "errored seconds" you might think you understand that this means your T1 frames have CRC errors. The problem is that this counter also increases when we see other errors, like AIS. To know that you have CRC errors on your T1 frames, you have to know to look for an absence of AIS and other things.*
>
> *A good friend of mine, Dave Curado, once looked at a MIB object through SNMP. He understood the basic definition of the object itself, and got back a value like 327. Was this good? He said, "It's like I know how many oranges are on the tree. Is this a good year?" Values without context and interpretation are useless.*

This book solves your problem. My company, NetOps Corporation (www.netops.com), is in the network fault-analysis business. We offer everything from fault-prediction technologies and services to a real-time, inside-out, root-cause analysis tool. In building this infrastructure, we have gained valuable hands-on experience by watching and analyzing real-world problems at the largest ISPs, carriers, trading floors, and Fortune

500 networks. We have plowed though piles of documentation, figured out the meanings, and determined which values are good and which are bad.

Although I won't tell you about the sophisticated analysis techniques that we use, I will tell you how to use SNMP and MIBs: what is important to look at, what it means, why you want to know, and what ranges of values should set off alarms. You can use this information to optimally configure your network management polling and thresholding for basic problems, and just maybe live a normal, rehab-free life.

How to Use This Book

This book is divided into three sections:

- Section 1 is a general overview of SNMP (mostly version 1, the most commonly encountered version) and related topics.

- Section 2 describes how to make use of data to solve various problems, such as fault and performance analysis.

- Section 3 describes the most commonly used MIBs, and gives implementation guidelines for configuring your tools. Key vendor extensions are included, such as those for Cisco and Nortel (Bay Networks) devices. The goal is for you to be able to implement a functional management system by implementing those groups that represent technologies that you use.

Throughout the book, I sometimes digress off the main point, offering anecdotal evidence to support what I am saying. When I do so, my comments are set off as notes. Feel free to skip these rantings if you prefer to read quickly.

Who Should Read This Book?

This book is written primarily for engineers who are involved in the configuration and implementation of monitoring and debug tools. Anyone responsible for the design, configuration, or the use of network monitoring systems such as HP's OpenView, IBM's NetView/6000, Micromuse's Netcool, CA's Unicenter, Castlerock's SNMPc, and even MRTG will find this book helpful. If you use these or similar tools, and are frustrated by the lack of useful information they provide, your problem may well be one of configuration. If you run a test infrastructure, you similarly need to know what problems to look for. Finally, if you are a vendor building a new box, you must be aware of the objects that describe real-world problems and account for them in your design.

If you are configuring tools to watch a network, use this book as a template. Look up those technologies that you use, verify that your vendor minimally supports the standards, and use Section 3 as a guide for modeling your systems. The MIB objects listed in the third section are likely to be among the ones that you will want to monitor first. I will provide suggested thresholds for red, orange, and yellow alerts. You may need to adjust these thresholds for your infrastructure, but experience has demonstrated that they are generally correct. You should focus on those thresholds that I define as "red."

Note that this is not a guide for sophisticated analysis, predictive management, or true root cause diagnosis. Such a work would take many volumes and require disclosing trade secrets. This is a simple thresholding scheme to be used for fault detection. The debug phase of a problem will commence when one or more of these objects is found to exceed a threshold, and is followed by the fix phase. Because this book suggests looking at one object at a time, most of what is provided herein describes fault states or capacities.

NOTE: *Some folks take offense when told that monitoring objects like CPU utilization, error rates, etc are capacity measurements. In general, I define capacities to be anything that is tested against thresholds to determine congestion (such as discards), volumes used or remaining (CPU utilization, memory, buffers), or top consumers (by address, protocol, etc). Even corruption rates can be thought of as a capacity, as they are compared against acceptable corruption levels). If it tells you what but not why something is happening, and it isn't a state variable, it's probably a capacity measurement.*

While I'm at it, I'll define the cause of a problem as the answer to the question "why?" Root cause analysis occurs when you no longer need to ask why something is happening, and allows you to proceed from the debug stage to implement a fix. Measuring network performance (or application performance) allows you to detect a symptom. If things are slow, the question to be answered is "why are they slow?" Topology based analysis may yield a partial answer by pointing to a suspect device. That's certainly a where and a part of a why. Additional analysis might reveal that packets are being dropped by a router, causing TCP to time out and retry. That's a causal analysis as well, but not a root cause. Root cause is complete when you know why the drops happen (buffer congestion, misconfiguration of the device, exception paths exercised by unexpected options, etc) and actually makes the problem go away.

If you are considering deployment of a new technology, you will likely want to test it first in a lab environment. The problem is that most of us can create a microcosm of a planned deployment, but knowing what to look for can be tricky. It's easy enough to use packet generators to push traffic through the testbed, but what do you look for, other than dropped packets, excessive response times, and perhaps a lack of smoke from the exhaust fans? Test environments can use simple monitoring tools to watch for the "orange" or even "yellow" thresholds and check device behavior. If it doesn't look good in the lab, expect your problems to scale up with your production deployment.

Vendors building new implementations of network technologies can also make use of the information provided here. You should reference this book twice. In the early design phase, you will want to know what kinds of problems people really have (and look for). The instrumentation herein will provide you with an understanding of the problems most feared. Make these areas of your design robust, and make sure that you instrument these problems well. Once you have a prototype, you will want to stress test the robustness of your design. You should be extremely sensitive to these, perhaps even more so than the yellow thresholds define.

In short, collect and interpret this data. It's needed to effectively manage networks in a real-world environment. This makes it an important part of your deployed infrastructure.

ACKNOWLEDGMENTS

Gratefully acknowledged are the efforts of the entire team at NetOps, particularly analysts Fuat Baran, David Fiore, and Joseph Riccobono. Kevin Castner served as a reviewer, attempting to keep me honest. Drs. Jeff Case and Craig Partridge took it upon themselves to introduce me to network management years ago; you may blame them, but I offer my thanks.

Readers should assume that all value in this book comes from those who assisted me and that the errors are my own.

FOREWORD

I started working on network management in 1988, when I joined a small group developers that held meetings in a small conference room at a small comapany called Advanced Computing Environments (later renamed to InterOp, Inc). Back then I worked for a not so small company (IBM) that had just agreed to build the next generation backbone of a small network called NSFNet (later called the Internet backbone). The dozen or so folks around that conference table represented the network management area for a small standards body called the Internet Engineering Task Force. While discussions of the SGMP, HEMS, and CMOT protocols each took their turn, our primary goal was to define a common set of managed objects (MIB) that each vendor would support. Our cardinal rule was simple; nothing could be proposed until it had already been prototyped and used somewhere. This "useful in the real world" approach was designed to avoid the common standard bodies mistake of specifying something that didn't make sense to build.

Network management has come a long way since then. The Internet has seen explosive growth, SNMP has become widely adopted, and the number of standard MIBs has similarly increased. I have personally come a long way since then. I no longer need to bridge the worlds of IBM and the IETF, a role that led to my singular distinction of being the first person to attend an IETF meeting wearing a suit.

With this book, I attempt to return to the fundamental reason for network monitoring. The basic need is not for protocols and parameters but rather to collect and interpret information. Everything else is designed to support this goal. By identifying which objects are most useful to watch for a range of technologies, and further describing how to interpret their values, I hope to have a book that is truly "useful in the real world."

Lou Steinberg
New Fairfield, CT

1

Optimizing Your Environment

Introduction

To make good use of your support tools, you need devices that are well-instrumented. Unmanaged hubs are out; the first time you spend hours debugging a problem with one, you will wish you spent the extra $100 for a box that tells you details about what is happening. Vendors with weak support of the MIBs are out, too. You are spending a lot of money on your infrastructure. You have the right to expect it to be maintainable.

All things being equal, choose your vendors based on their willingness to make your support costs lower by offering better instrumentation. If you like a product with instrumentation gaps, negotiate discounts on your maintenance agreements until you are fully supported. Similarly, make sure that your maintenance agreement allows you to declare instrumentation bugs as critical, so you aren't left in the dark when you find that a supported object is broken.

NOTE: *You might not dump a vendor based on manageability alone, but I did when I ran an outsourced networking business for IBM. When I figured out the support costs (additional engineers, cost of downtime, etc.), the obvious technology choice was bad for our business. Even major technology vendors with good records of providing instrumentation fall short in some areas. Cisco fails to fully support all of the MIB objects deemed Mandatory in the standards space. This leaves you blind about portions of the instrumentation that Cisco claims to support. Nortel (Bay routers) tends to have wonderful instrumentation in its private extensions, but fails to map much of it to the equivalent name in the standard location. Its data is generally available, but you can't apply your standard models so your configuration effort is increased.*

Okay, you have a well-instrumented infrastructure. Let's further assume that it all speaks SNMP. Be willing to monitor it. You can choose to collect some data only when needed, but that means you can't use much of the instrumentation to *decide* that you have a problem. This is the primary flaw in trap-directed or value-based polling, in which more data is collected only after you know that there is something wrong. If you don't detect the problem, you won't be able to do much about it. Sure, you can look at a dozen objects on each box and ignore the others, but you are flying blind. You can also drive on an interstate highway with your eyes closed. I don't suggest either. You need information to detect and debug problems. Information requires data. You can't interpret what you didn't collect.

NOTE: *By now, most of you will have peeked at Section 3 to get an idea of what this book offers. If you think about it in the context of a large network, your next objection is likely to the volume of data that I suggest you collect. Reread the previous paragraph.*

Typical polling volume concerns center around two issues: bandwidth consumed on the network and additional load on the devices being monitored. I can respond with one solution, namely PDU-packing. As you have learned, an SNMP GET REQUEST generally takes far fewer than 64 bytes. The protocol itself allows you to get more than one MIB object within the request and without the overhead of another entire message. This is called PDU-packing. Because the packet would probably have been padded to 64 bytes anyway, the second, third and likely more start by consuming padding bits and always have high wire efficiency.

You agree, but anyone who has watched their router's CPU while walking the route table knows the impact that SNMP has on the devices being monitored. True, but the high cost of polling (on the device) is generally divided between the processing of the received packet and parsing the encoding protocol. PDU-packing lets you collect data from a number of MIB objects for about the same cost as collecting one.

For proof, I refer you to the data collection that NetOps has been doing for more than five years. We use SNMP to watch 50–100 MIB objects *per second* on each device we monitor, without loading the devices or the network. With PDU-packing, those 50–100 objects are collected via a single GET message, which elicits a single GET-RESPONSE. We send one *packet per second* (PPS) to each target, and get one back. Polling with this granularity is really useful only if you have a sophisticated analysis engine, but you can see how polling can be non-intrusive.

You might still object that a large infrastructure could contain thousands of devices, resulting in thousands of pps. You might also note that the packets we send and receive with this level of PDU packing are generally well over 64 bytes long. Both are true, and we address this by distributing our low-impact pollers. I would counter that you are unlikely to need the granularity that we do (for this simple detection problem), so your task is likely easier than ours, and mine has been proven possible by existence.

You have the instrumentation and are willing to collect data from it. All that remains is to pick the right element-monitoring tools. Flexibility in configuration is paramount here, so many of the applications provided by technology hardware vendors fall short. These applications tend to be uniquely focused on configuration management, and are less adept at fault monitoring. A notable exception was the Spectrum platform from Cabletron, but they have announced that it will become a separate business. If you are running a mission-critical infrastructure of any size, you probably have already installed a management platform tied to your most important application: trouble ticketing. Most of these platforms have simple facilities that allow you to add new objects to monitor and basic alert-level thresholds. Some even offer the capability to pack PDUs and to distribute polling loads.

One area worthy of mention is the new group of end-user experience tools. Rather than monitoring the health of individual elements, these applications attempt to detect user-visible problems by emulating user transactions or by monitoring real user transactions. They typically alert on loss of connectivity and on degraded performance. Although valuable as a high-level detection and reporting system, it is only slightly better than waiting for the phones to ring. These monitors provide little data as to *why* there is a problem—only that one exists. This represents problem-detection at its highest level, with a minimal set of debug data (and even less debug information).

NOTE: To be fair, these tools are valuable. They can identify communities of users impacted by a single problem, are unbiased, and find integration problems that element monitoring systems might miss. Some also attempt to locate the device at fault topologically. True root-cause analysis requires more, so to debug the failure we end up with the same old requirements of data collection and interpretation.

The basic philosophy underlying this book is that you need to understand the health of your infrastructure, one element at a time. This understanding forces you to interpret collected data, which in turn drives your data-collection requirements. Collecting data without analyzing it adds no value. Analysis without sufficient data is flawed.

Introduction to SNMP & MIBs

This section provides a general overview of the *Management Information Bases* (MIBs) that make up our content, the language of *Simple Network Management Protocol* (SNMP), and the grammar imposed by *Abstract Syntax Notation 1* (ASN.1) encoding rules. It is by no means complete, but aims to familiarize the reader with basic concepts. We will first discuss the MIB data to be communicated. Next, an overview of ASN.1 describes the encoding rules under which we operate. We then study the SNMP protocol itself, which uses encoded fields to ultimately transfer MIB data. Then, we analyze the shortcomings of SNMP. We end with some words of advice on choosing vendors for your system.

MIBs

An MIB describes instrumentation that is/should be/must be supported, and assigns a unique identifier string to each of these points. In SNMP, the MIB is a tree structure in which all instrumentation points (called objects) reside at the leaves. Each *Object Identifier*

(OID) describes the path to walk from the "root" of the tree to a specific leaf. In traversing the tree, one takes a series of steps based on the "child" nodes available at any given point, with each step further refining the information expressed to that point. The branches are locally ordered with numbers from left to right.

An MIB is primarily a naming convention to uniquely describe a single data point. In Figure 1-1, for example, to identify that we are discussing the color of pants, one names the path `clothes.pants.color`. Note that this name is different from `clothes.shirt.color`, which describes a similar but different object. Also note that by convention the root node is named. Because we number the branches from left to right under each node, `clothes.shirt.color` can be referred to as *1.1.2* or `clothes(1).shirt(1).color(2)`. The object representing style of shoes worn is named by `clothes(1).footware(3).shoes(1).style(2)` or *1.3.1.2*. This format that uses a string of numbers or their text equivalents, separated by periods, to represent steps walking through the MIB tree is referred to as *dotted decimal notation*. Again, objects are found only at a leaf of the tree. If a node has children, it cannot name an object in an SNMP MIB. In addition, each path provides the only way to reach each child (that is, there is a one-to-one correspondence between each path and each child). In other words, no child has more than one parent (see Figure 1-2).

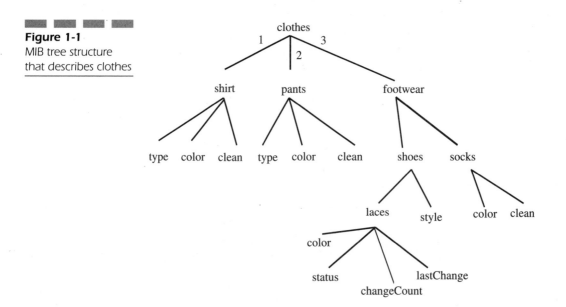

Figure 1-1
MIB tree structure
that describes clothes

Figure 1-2 demonstrates an MIB that is not legal in SNMP. The path `clothes.footware.shoes.style` names an MIB object that can also be reached by `clothes.footware.socks.style`.

NOTE:　*Timothy left the house today dressed for school. If I wanted to describe how he was dressed, I might use the MIB objects in Figure 1-1. Like all parents, I care about how clean his clothes are, the style of clothes (are those shorts being worn in winter?), the colors of his outfit, and whether or not his shoelaces are tied (an dynamic object whose state has been known to revert back to untied spontaneously).*

Most of the objects in Figure 1-1 represent states such as color, style, or the state of shoelaces. In a network MIB, these might be the state of an interface, power supply, or BGP peer. I purposely added objects such as `clothes(1).pants(2).clean(3)` *to demonstrate an object with a more dynamic value. This object can be expressed as a number ranging from 1 through 10, with 1 being freshly washed and 10 requiring an EPA-approved Hazardous Materials team to handle disposal and the requisite environmental impact study.*

The MIB further defines the attributes of each leaf node, such as the allowable value ranges and instantiation. We have already

Figure 1-2
An illegal SNMP MIB.
Each child node
can have only
one parent.

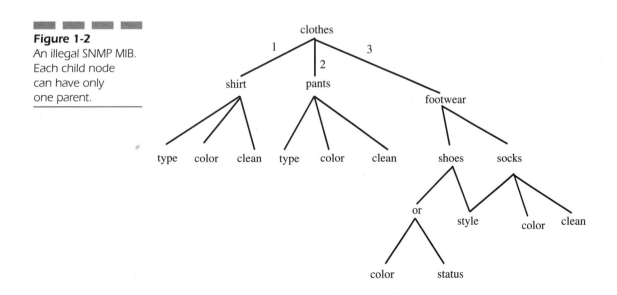

discussed the concept that objects such as `clothes.footware.shoes.laces.status` have state. It might be defined as an INTEGER, where the value 1 indicates tied and a value of 2 means untied (the value 0 is never assigned to an enumerated INTEGER). The object `clothes.footware.shoes.laces.changeCount` is a Counter that shows the number of times `clothes.footware.shoes.laces.status` changed state (shoelaces were untied and retied) today, while `clothes.footware.shoes.laces.lastChange` measures seconds (or 100ths of seconds called TimeTicks—another convention under SNMP) since the shoelaces last changed state. The object `clothes.footware.shoes.style` should be an enumerated INTEGER. Some MIB designers might choose to use a printable text string because the style variations could be complex to enumerate.

NOTE: *MIB designers would do well to avoid printable strings, called DisplayStrings, whenever possible. DisplayStrings are nice to print to a console, but are almost impossible to parse and monitor with automated tools (one minor syntax change in the next software release and all is lost). Some vendors have products with tables of these strings to instrument log files. These MIBs are useless to automated tools, increasing the cost of monitoring your infrastructure.*

Once the concept of MIB naming conventions is understood, most people become confused by instances and tables. We'll start by exploring instantiation.

An MIB object names a particular attribute of a system, but doesn't specify which copy, or instance, we are discussing. By naming the OID `clothes.footware.shoes.laces.status`, we clearly understand that the object is the state of a shoelace. On which shoe? We need to combine an instance of a shoelace with the object that fully specifies the data we seek. If a footId instance were defined to be an integer with an enumerated value of 1 for left and 2 for right, one could specify `clothes.footware.shoes.laces.status.2` to indicate the state of the lace on the right shoe. Note that instances are generally of type INTEGER, but can be represented by most constructs.

For example, in networking we might identify an object in the ARP table (such as an IP address) and use the MAC address as the instance. Fetching the value of a particular IP address associated with MAC address mac1 is done by doing a GET of the object named by ipAddr.mac1 (I'll avoid writing the full object name until we discuss the tables later in this chapter).

Some objects have only one instance possible. By convention, we assign (bind) an instance of 0 to these objects. The variable clothes.pants.clean does not need to specify an instance because only one pair at a time is worn. We refer to this object as clothes.pants.clean.0. Other objects are difficult to identify with a single instance. SNMP allows for objects to be uniquely named by binding more than one instance to the OID, so that the object is unambiguous.

Only two key points remain. The first is that if a node has children, SNMP does not allow it to have instances. In other words, only fully specified objects at the leaves of the MIB tree can be bound to instances. The second is that an instance must uniquely identify one and only one representation of an object.

In my examples, a child's right shoelace state was named with the object clothes.footware.shoes.laces.status.2. This makes sense only because I know that I am talking about a specific child. If I were to ask a teacher whether that child's right shoelace was untied, I would need to identify both the footId and the child in her class. If Timothy were assigned a unique childId of 123, I could use that as his instance. Thus, I would ask about clothes.footware.shoes. laces.status.2.123 to indicate the state of the right(2) shoelace on Timothy(123). As the MIB designer, I could have also chosen to reverse the order of the instances; it really doesn't matter as long as my MIB clearly specifies the order.

Only tables remain to be explained. Tables are simply a different conceptual representation of the objects at the leaves. As in all cases, the MIB itself remains a tree structure. Mapping between these structures causes no small amount of confusion.

A table defines the intersection of columns and rows to uniquely identify the value in some cell. If you consider that the columns can represent objects, the rows specify unique instances. Figure 1-1 should help make this clear. The shoelaces subtree can be represented as a shoelaces table. Each column matches an object previously described, with the addition of objects (columns) for the instances. We walk the MIB tree to an object such as changeCount and get the value associated with a single row. The pair of instances childId.footId are enough to identify a distinct row, so we can get the value of lastChange for childId5-123 and footId5-2. Note that neither of these instances alone identifies a unique row, so both are necessary as Table 1-1 indicates.

ASN.1 and the SMI

Abstract Syntax Notation 1 (ASN.1) is a generalized encoding format defined by the *International Standards Organization (*ISO) and adopted by SNMP. Its *Basic Encoding Rules* (BER) are used to specify how bits are placed on the wire. The encoded SNMP message is sometimes referred to as a *Protocol Data Unit* (PDU).

The basic concept behind ASN.1 is that every encoded item, whether an OID, octet string, an integer, or other, is written as three concatenated fields:

Table 1-1
The intersection of columns and rows identify cell values (see Figure 1-3)

childId	footId	color	status	changeCount	lastChange
123	1	red(2)	1	2	190
123	2	red(2)	2	9	2396
124	1	white(1)	1	1	4589
124	2	blue(3)	1	1	4589

1. The first field is referred to as the type. It is one-byte wide and specifies if, for example, this object is an INTEGER. Types can be globally defined or specific to a single application.

2. The second field is the length. Length identifies the size of the value field in bytes, and is itself of variable length.

3. The final field is referred to as the value field, and contains the encoded value.

This *type-length-value* is generally referred to as a TLV of a construct. Types are assigned to an object in an MIB by defining the object whose SYNTAX is the type being assigned. For example, if an MIB object is defined to be of type INTEGER (encoded as `0x02`) and has a one-byte value of 26 (`0x1a`), the hex TLV encoding would be `02 01 1a`.

NOTE: *Encoding formats have their own idiosynchrasies. Not only is each octet encoded in an OID only allowed a range of 0–127 (the high order bit is set to indicate that the dotted decimal field is continued in the next byte), but the encoding of* `iso(1).org(3)` *is downright goofy. OID encodings, by definition, combine the first two octets into a single value by multiplying the first byte by 40 and adding the second. This happens only on the first two bytes, and generates much less efficiency than confusion. The MIB object* `sysUpTime` *is one of the shortest OIDs that can be encoded in standard space. It indicates the number of TimeTicks that a device has been up, and is represented by the numeric string 1.3.6.1.2.1.1.3.0. This is encoded on the wire as 43.6.1.2.1.1.3.0.*

I have no idea why the encoding rules are so complex and exception laden. My only is based on the fact that the "I" in ISO stands for International. Given the unlikely task of making delegates from countries like England and France agree on anything, they settled on rules that made thing equally unpalatable for all!

Note that zero is a valid length, and is often used with a type of NULL as a kind of a placeholder. Other common types used in

SNMP include OCTET_STRING, OBJECT_ID, COUNTER, GAUGE, DisplayString (a textual convention format of an OCTET STRING), TimeTicks, SEQUENCE, and SEQUENCE_OF. The last two types are interesting because their value field contains one or more other constructs, each with its own TLV. Figure 1-3 demonstrates this.

For convenience, I might choose to define the construct in Figure 1-4 as the following:

```
SEQUENCE {
      INTEGER            status;
      TimeTicks          lastChange;
}
```

A SEQUENCE defines a fixed set of constructs and the order in which they appear. A SEQUENCE_OF behaves similarly, only it allows the SEQUENCE to be repeated any number of times. This is used primarily in defining objects that exist in tables, which are a SEQUENCE_OF rows. Note that the length field of a SEQUENCE or SEQUENCE_OF is the total length of the TLVs contained within its value.

As described earlier, objects in a table can be thought of as the headings of columns, with one column for each defined OID. Rows are the instantiation of the table, allowing a cell (object) to be uniquely identified by specifying the column and then the row. Mapping this to our tree structure is the trick.

Figure 1-3

A SEQUENCE
construct defined

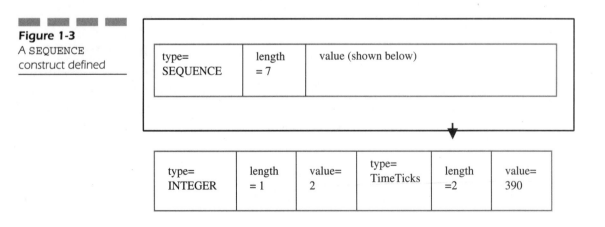

Assume that the table in Table 1-1 is to be a subtree of the cloth's MIB named `lacesTable`. Each row in `lacesTable` is a SEQUENCE that defines the order and content of the table's columns. That is, a row could be named `LacesEntry` and be defined as follows:

```
LacesEntry:= SEQUENCE {
        INTEGER        childId;
        INTEGER        footId;
        INTEGER        color;
        INTEGER        status;
        Counter        changeCount;
        TimeTicks      lastChange;
};
```

`LacesEntry` is now a complex object that defines the columns of lacesTable. It really only looks like a single row. What is now needed is a SEQUENCE_OF this row, allowing it to be repeated in its entirety any number of times. This is done by describing an object whose name is `lacesEntry` (note the difference in capitalization) and whose SYNTAX is that of type `LacesEntry`. The subtree `lacesTable` is now simply a SEQUENCE_OF lacesEntry objects. The result is that every defined table in every MIB has an OID that represents its entries as a SEQUENCE_OF before actually naming the objects we seek to access. The definition of the table would also name the index or indices used to identify a specific entry (row). The `lastChange` object on Timothy's right foot can now be defined as follows:

```
clothes(1).footware(3).shoes(1).lacesTable(2).lacesEntry(1).lastC
    hange(6).2.123
```

The *Structure of Management Information* (SMI) is a companion document to the standards describing the MIBs and the SNMP protocol. Its function is to define the basic subset of ASN.1 that is permitted for use by SNMP and MIB designers. Some useful "application-specific" objects are defined, such as TimeTicks and Counters, but much of the document restricts usage and implementation for the sake of simplicity. Numeric values and strings that are unbounded in size under ASN.1 definitions are limited here. Only a subset of the ASN.1 primitives are permitted (such as

INTEGER and OCTET STRING). For those building SNMP instrumentation, it is important to first understand encoding limitations and ranges. If you plan to simply use a tool that gathers MIB data via SNMP, you need to understand only a few basic things:

1. Counters are unsigned numbers that increase, but never decrease. The only time they are permitted to go backward in an MIB is when they wrap (that is, count up past 2**32 −1) or are cleared (which requires all counters to be reset along with sysUpTime).

2. INTEGERs are signed numbers, limited in the number of bits they hold.

3. DisplayStrings are simply OCTET STRINGS that, by convention, are printable ASCII characters, also limited in length.

4. Gauges are rarely used (in fact, they are coded the same way as unsigned INTEGERs); they act like counters that have the capability to count down. Most numeric objects can be readily coded as INTEGERs or Counters.

5. OPAQUE is a type best avoided. It allows for the sending of constructed objects, but at the expense of general interoperability.

Two significant versions of the SMI have been defined. SMI version 1 was a part of the original SNMP specification. (SMIv2) applies to all SNMP implementations (including newer implementations of SNMP version 1) and primarily added support for unsigned integers, 64-bit counters, and standardized ways to manipulate table rows. SMIv2 provides the standard encoding requirements for all new MIBs.

SNMP

We have now reviewed how data is described by an MIB, and some of the basic encoding constructs and formats. This equates to our content and our grammar. The last item is the language itself.

Three versions of the SNMP protocol are generally discussed. Version 1 is the de facto standard of the industry, and is widely supported. A second version, SNMPv2, was defined years later to address some of the shortcomings of version 1. The primary goal of SNMPv2 was to enhance authentication and security, although other features were also added. Unfortunately, there was significant disagreement within the working group. Multiple competing versions of SNMPv2 were proposed and the working group disbanded without ever producing a single specification that users and industry could adopt. The goals of SNMPv2 still had merit. The *Internet Engineering Task Force* (IETF), a standards body that defines such things for the Internet community, is again trying to meet them with a new protocol, SNMPv3. At the time of this writing, only SNMPv1 is in widespread use. As a result, this overview will concern itself with version 1 only.

SNMPv1 defines five different types of messages; all but TRAP are formatted identically. Figure 1-4 shows the format of the basic encoded SNMPv1 PDU.

The fields named in Figure 1-4 are the following:

version This integer indicates the version number of the SNMP protocol in this PDU. For our purposes, we are describing version 1, which requires a value of 0 in this field.

Figure 1-4
Format of basic
encoded SNMPv1
PDU

```
PDU:= {
        INTEGER           version;
        DisplayString     community;
        INTEGER           type;
        INTEGER           requestId;
        INTEGER           errorStatus;
        INTEGER           errorIndex;

        SEQUENCE OF {
          SEQUENCE {
            OBJECT IDENTIFIER     oid;
            ANY                   value;
          };
        };
};
```

community   This `DisplayString` is generally thought of as the equivalent of a password. Its original purpose was to define a "view" of the agent. Some views may well have authentication or access components (read-only or read-write). If not a supported view for the request, access is denied. It is equally valid to use community to provide access to a subset of the objects such as a particular VLAN.

type   This field indicates the type of SNMPv1 message. Supported types for this format are `GetRequest`, `GetNextRequest`, `GetResponse`, and `SetRequest` (see Figure 1-5 for a TRAP message format).

A `GetRequest` is a query for one or more specific MIB objects. `GetNextRequest` is similar to a `GetRequest`, except that it fetches the next instance in the MIB tree (described in detail below). SetRequest is used to set specific values into MIB objects, which may control the device's behavior or cause an action. Collectively, these three types are referred to as "requests." `GetResponse` returns an indication of success or failure for any of the three request types. It additionally contains one or more values in response to a `Get` or `GetNext` request and is generally referred to as simply a response or reply. Managers are entities that generally send request messages, and agents are entities that respond to requests.

requestId   This integer is a number that is placed in each request message by the manager and is returned in the response message by the agent. Managers typically place unique request values in this field and use the field on a response to match it with a specific request.

	REQUESTED OID	RETURNED OID	VALUE
Table 1-2 *A walk of all shoelace* *color instances*	clothes.footwear.laces.color.0	clothes.footwear.laces.color.123.1	2
	clothes.footwear.laces.color.123.1	clothes.footwear.laces.color.123.2	2
	clothes.footwear.laces.color.123.2	clothes.footwear.laces.color.124.1	1
	clothes.footwear.laces.color.124.1	clothes.footwear.laces.color.124.2	3
	clothes.footwear.laces.color.124.2	clothes.footwear.laces.status.123.1	1

errorStatus This integer is always set to 0 in a request. Response messages fill in 0 to indicate no error. If the agent encounters any error other than an authentication failure, it returns a value of `TooBig(1)`, `NoSuchName(2)`, `BadValue(3)`, `ReadOnly(4)`, or `GenError(5)`. The protocol requires that when a nonzero errorStatus is returned, the response PDU must be identical to the request, with only two exceptions: the type field contains a value indicating `GetResponse` and the error fields (`errorStatus` and `errorIndex`) are set appropriately. The first error encountered during processing controls the choice for the error fields.

An indication of `TooBig` means that either the request or response message exceeded the maximum PDU size that this agent supports. Agents are required to support PDUs that are up to 484 bytes long because that PDU becomes a 512-byte message when it is wrapped in UDP/IP for transmission. Early Internet routers often fragmented messages that were larger than 512 bytes, leaving the reassembly of the fragments to the agent. The 484/512 -byte minimum was chosen to accommodate those agents that did not wish to support IP reassembly. Today, most agents support a maximum PDU size of approximately 1500 bytes.

`NoSuchName` indicates that a requested `object.instance` did not exist in the MIB. This could be the result of a tree traversal that walked off a nonexistent branch. Other causes include invalid instances, requested access to an object that is defined to be not-accessible, and failure to walk the MIB tree to a leaf node.

`BadValue` and `ReadOnly` are returned only in response to a `SetRequest`. The former indicates that a set tried to apply a value that was unacceptable to the agent. Primary causes of this are out of range values and unsupported types. The latter indicates that an attempt was made to write to an object that is defined to be read-only.

A `GenError` is a general failure of an agent to process a request. It is most commonly sent when the agent is temporarily unable to access a needed resource, such as allocating memory.

errorIndex The `errorIndex` integer is a pointer within a `GetResponse` PDU that indicates, in the order of the requested varbinds, which was the first to experience a failure. It points by providing an index into the varbind list and is set to a value of 0 whenever errorStatus is 0. This field also contains a 0 when the failure was not caused by a specific varbind. For this reason, it is generally nonzero when the errorStatus field contains NoSuchName, BadValue, or ReadOnly. It is always set to 0 in a request.

SEQUENCE OF The SEQUENCE_OF object is identical to the SEQUENCE object (see below), except that the entire value field may be repeated zero or more times. This is used to return groups of information without knowing the number of items in advance.

SEQUENCE This construct is a type whose value field contains other ASN.1 objects. One or more objects may be declared as contained within this field (see Figure 1-4). The contained objects occur exactly once and in the same order that they are defined.

In this message format, the SEQUENCE contained within the SEQUENCE_OF holds an object and instance, followed by a value. This pairing of instantiated objects with values is referred to as a varbind, which is short for *variable binding.*

Note that the type PDU that wraps the entire message is an implicit SEQUENCE.

OID The object identifier within the PDU names an object being retrieved or set. It contains an encoded form of the dotted decimal OID and instance.

value The value field holds the information associated with the OID and may be of any type. On a GetRequest, it is typically set to a type of NULL as a placeholder. A SetRequest fills this field in with the value that the agent is to apply to this OID. In a response message, this field contains the value being set or retrieved.

In an earlier note, the topic of PDU packing was referenced. A PDU is "packed" when the SEQUENCE_OF field contains more than one varbind (OID/value pairs). This has value for two reasons. By filling a request with more than one varbind, one gains substantial efficiency. This technique also permits groups of varbinds to be fetched or set at the same time.

Consider that a message within a manager must be assembled, encoded, padded to the minimum size, and transmitted. Padding consumes network resources and adds no value. In the agent, the message must be received (using a high-priority device driver), decoded, disassembled, and the values must be retrieved or set. The process is then reversed for a response. Adding additional varbinds to a manager's request initially consumes padding bytes, requiring no additional bytes on the wire. Later, varbinds do grow the PDU in size, but by much less than another encoded PDU. In addition to message length, packing a PDU also results in fewer messages to be encoded/decoded, transmitted/received, and processed. When large volumes of data are to be transferred, this results in substantial resource savings for both the manager and agent. Note that a single PDU requesting multiple varbinds results in a single response PDU with multiple varbinds.

The second advantage afforded by PDU packing is that all objects are fetched or set "atomically." In a GetRequest, this results in a single snapshot of all values at the same moment in time. A SetRequest requires that all of the objects be successfully set together and that none of them be set if any one fails. Setting multiple related objects together clearly adds value when creating or filling complex structures.

One final efficiency afforded by the protocol is that response messages contain varbinds in the same order as the corresponding request. Those building SNMP protocol engines may make use of this requirement to enhance internal performance.

The GetNext request type walks the MIB tree, including instances, searching for the next accessible instance after the named OID. The type of tree walk is referred to as a "depth first search" or a lexicographical walk. This traversal simply means that one continues down the tree, taking the first available (leftmost) branch at each node. If already at a leaf node, the tree is walked towards the root until another downward path exists. At that point, the next path (one to the right of the path followed upwards) is followed down, with successive steps again taking the first available path. The response OID returned matches the response value and not the OID in the original request.

GetNext walking allows one to iterate and get all instances of a single object by using the last returned instance in the next fetch. The starting instance may be left off or set to zero (e.g. "get me the next instance of OID foo.bar after the zeroth instance of that object"). Once all instances are exhausted, the GetNext operator will either return an entirely different OID or a NoSuchName error if the end of the MIB has been reached. Objects with multiple instances walk the outermost one first, followed then by inner instances.

Entire tables can be fetched via GetNext, though not with great efficiency. The first instance of the first object is retrieved as before. A GetNext of the color.0 object in Figure 1-3 would result in an OID of color.123.1 and a value of 2. A GetNext of OID color.123.1 would then return OID color.123.2. Subsequent fetches would return values for OIDs color.124.1, color.124.2, and then status.123.1 (the next column in the table). Note that when combined with packed GetNext PDUs, entire rows can be fetched in a single request, enhancing performance and ensuring a consistent snapshot within a row.

A walk of all shoelace color instances shown in Table 1-1 follows, including the final walk to the next object. Recall that Table 1-1 represents a subtree within Figure 1-1. See Table 1-2.

Table rows are manipulated via SetRequests. A row can be created but left inactive by setting a new instance of a rowStatus

Figure 1-5
TRAP message format

```
TRAP:= {
          INTEGER             version;
          DisplayString       community;
          INTEGER             type;
          OBJECT IDENTIFIER   enterprise;
          IP ADDRESS          agentAddress;
          INTEGER             genericTrapType;
          INTEGER             specificTrapType;
          TimeTicks           timestamp;

          SEQUENCE OF {
            SEQUENCE {
              OBJECT IDENTIFIER     oid;
              ANY                   value;
            };
          };
        };
```

object to inactive. Once adequately completed, setting the same object to the "active" state enables the row. Row removal occurs when the manager sets a `rowStatus` instance to the "deleted" state.

SNMP TRAPs

SNMP TRAPs are unsolicited messages sent by an agent to a manager. They generally provide information about serious problems without waiting for the manager to discover the issue via polling. A TRAP format is similar to the other PDUs, and is described in Figure 1-5.

Those fields named in Figure 1-5 that differ from the other PDU types are as follows:

version   Identical to the description for Figure 1-4.

community   Identical to the description for Figure 1-4.

type   This integer indicates the type of SNMPv1 message. TRAP is the only supported type for this format.

enterprise   This OID names the entity under whose authority the TRAP is being sent. It is generally either a dotted decimal string representing MIB-2, another standard MIB (such as the frame relay MIB), or an enterprise identifier that identifies the agent's vendor and often product version numbers.

agentAddress   `AgentAddress` contains the IP address of the device that this trap refers to. Note that this may differ from the device that sent the TRAP if the sender alerts the manager to a problem elsewhere.

genericTrapType   The `genericTrapTypes` are the standard reason codes for sending an alert. SNMP defines TRAPs for cold start (hard reboot), warm start, link down, link up, authentication failure, EGP neighbor loss, and a special "enterprise-specific" trap for all other causes. If a value other than enterprise-specific (6) is used, the enterprise field should point to MIB-2.

specificTrapType   The integer in `specificTrapType` allows the agent to further identify a reason code. This field is generally filled with a zero if a standard type (not enterprise-specific) is sent in the generic field, and is up to the enterprise to define otherwise.

NOTE: *Most agents and many platforms assume that if the* `genericTrapType` *is enterprise-specific, the enterprise plus* `specificTrapType` *pair uniquely identifies the trap. This is often the case, but is not required to be true.*

timestamp   The timestamp field contains the `sysUpTime` value—a measure in TimeTicks, or 100ths of a second, of how long the management software has been running on the device referred to by `agentAddress`. This is usually the amount of time since boot, but it could be the time that the SNMP process has been running or the time since statistics were last reset.

SEQUENCE OF   This list of varbinds is similar to the list described under Figure 1-5. In the case of a TRAP, one can optionally include "interesting varbinds" that further clarify the error condition being described. Unlike a response PDU, a TRAP may choose to provide no varbinds. In that case, the value portion of this field is empty.

SEQUENCE   Identical to the description for Figure 1-5.

OID   Identical to the description for Figure 1-5.

value   Identical to the description for Figure 1-5.

Some extensions to version 1 of the SNMP protocol have been proposed, primarily in the areas of authentication and a new type called `GetBulk`. The latter attempted to provide a more efficient mechanism to retrieve large tables and to avoid inconsistencies that can be introduced when tables change while they are being walked. These extensions have not been widely adopted.

Shortcomings of SNMP

Even given the inherent simplicity and power of SNMP and the MIBs, some areas can be improved. As one who has coded a number of SNMP implementations and who regularly uses SNMP to collect data, I offer these insights into its shortcomings.

The SMI

I have encountered a number of issues with the *Structure of Management Information* (SMI), including integers, gauges, constructed objects, and length encoding.

Integers The SMI is too restrictive. SMI version 2 provides us with 64-bit counters to cope with high rates of change on ever-faster networks. This extension is useful, as is the addition of an unsigned 32-bit integer. Unfortunately, the unsigned integer is encoded to look like a gauge, whose properties technically differ from integers (as discussed below). In addition, no provision was made for 64-bit integers of any kind. Integers often serve as bit-masks, and the increasing port density of access gear, coupled with native 64-bit support in most modern operating systems, suggests that 64-bit unsigned integers is both reasonable and useful.

Gauges Gauges have always been confusing. At the original MIB-1 working group meetings, we debated the meaning of this object for extended periods. The original definition was that gauges increase or decrease by 1 (different from an INTEGER) and stop when they reach either 0 or maximum limit. This differs from counters, which increase only by 1 and wrap at their maximum value. Because gauges do not wrap in either direction, the intention was for them to stick permanently when a limit was reached. For example, the upper limit is considered infinity. Adding to it does not change its value. As a result, subtracting from the upper limit (or adding to the lower limit) must also not change its value.

If you tried to increase 10 steps beyond the upper limit, and then decrease by 2, you wouldn't want the gauge to reflect a value of 2 less than the limit. Gauges were defined to stick unless reset.

Constructed Objects Constructed objects should be allowed. These are objects that contain other objects. With such a concept, one could fetch an entire table row or even a table with nothing more than a simple GET request. The SMI actually permits a type called OPAQUE, which is intended to wrap objects that are otherwise not permitted. Unfortunately, use of this type is strongly discouraged, and few managers will allow you to specify the format of data encoded with an OPAQUE object.

Length Encoding The SMI made a big mistake when they disallowed an ASN.1 length encoding format called indefinite length. Objects that are SEQUENCEs or IMPLICIT SEQUENCEs can be easily assembled into buffers with lengths deemed indefinite. Doing so means that we use a special pattern (two bytes of zeros) to flag the end of this field. It's true that this adds some complexity to the protocol engines in that they need to do pattern stuffing and stripping. That effort is simple when compared to the building of PDUs containing many varbinds today; we can't simply write the data into a buffer and send it. Before adding an object to a SEQUENCE, we need to specify the total size of this and all future objects that will be added. We need to repeat this for every embedded SEQUENCE. Buffers can't be assembled until all of their components are independently analyzed, an act that consumes significant resources.

MIBs

Some issues you may run into with MIBs include unsupported MIB objects and poorly implemented objects.

Unsupported MIB Objects Standard MIBs are poorly implemented. Some vendors don't seem to understand that MANDATORY objects MUST be supported. Returning a value of 0 only is slightly better than a NoSuchName error, and many vendors fail to even do users that courtesy. I have yet to find a complete, correctly implemented example of MIB-2, and it is the most basic of the standard MIBs.

Poorly Implemented Objects   Some vendors define extensions or changes to the MIB that make it useless. Cached values, those that incorrectly hold their values for extended periods and then suddenly leap forward, imply that there are dramatic bursts in errors that really don't exist. Bay/Nortel router MIBs do this with a number of objects, Cisco does it to a lesser extent. Other vendors prefer to build MIB objects and tables filled with `DisplayStrings`. These are nice to print out, but terrible for automated tools. Some devices actually hide information from management tools, presenting red/green status instead of numeric values. These are the automotive equivalent of "idiot lights" that replace dashboard gauges.

One of the most poorly implemented standard objects is `sysUpTime`. It is supposed to measure the time over which the management statistics have been collected (how long the management entity has been running). If any standard managed object is reset, they should all be reset and `sysUpTime` set back to 0. Implementations that allow standard objects to be cleared without resetting `sysUpTime` are broken. Failure to do this makes a single counter reset impossible to distinguish from a counter wrap.

SNMP

Even SNMP itself has a few issues, although these are primarily the result of the way the protocol is used. Commonly encountered problems occur with TRAPs, authentication, and the error index.

TRAPs   SNMP TRAPs have proven themselves to be useful, largely due to the robustness of the infrastructures they run over. Most networks seem capable of delivering most TRAPs, even in the face of the problems they identify. This is important because many management platforms do basic interface status and reachability testing only, and use TRAPs to detect more specific errors.

SNMP rides over UDP/IP, a choice that was made intentionally. Connection-oriented and reliable protocols such as TCP require additional overhead to establish a session. The protocol designers felt that this overhead might increase the failure rate of the management commands issued to correct problems when significant losses are encountered, precisely the time when network management is needed most. UDP offered a simpler mechanism, and using response packets to acknowledge requests lets a manager time out and resend requests as desired.

TRAPs are different. The basic philosophy that "no news is good news" assumes that bad news can be delivered. A device that hard fails might be unable to send a trap to alert the management platform. High error rates can corrupt TRAP PDUs. A link that fails might choose to forward the "link down" message through a path that uses the failed link, as routing might not converge immediately. Clearly, TRAPs can be lost. As a result, only a limited set were defined initially, and the understanding was that managers should use TRAPs to direct their polling attention, but should always poll to detect all types of problems; this is the only way to be sure.

A working group later attempted to define a way for managers to poll for TRAPs. With this, all messages were either reliably delivered or the manager would time out the polls and understand that connectivity was lost. This was presented in RFC1224, but never reached the standards track.

The fact is that most critical TRAPs are delivered. Adding layers of mid-level managers that poll agents and trap to the enterprise manager can enhance the robustness of an infrastructure. Such an architecture places the trap generator closer to its destination and doesn't rely on a failing device to originate failure messages.

Authentication   Most people implementing networks believe that community strings are passwords. They are not. Although it is true that they do limit access, they are not intended to be secure. Specifically, community strings are easily captured and reused. For this reason alone, many people shy away from permitting write access (SetRequest) via SNMPv1. Those that do must employ filters and other techniques to prevent unauthorized SNMP traffic from being destined to their infrastructure.

These filters are well-advised for another reason. Even without knowing the community string, SNMP can be used to affect a denial of service attack. The processing overhead required to parse large numbers of PDUs is significant. A comprehensive access strategy is the best defense.

Most early SNMP implementations had placeholders for an authentication field. Although ignored in "modern" SNMPv1 agents, authentication was a driving force behind the need for later versions.

Error Index Perhaps the single most disappointing limitation of the protocol itself is the presence of only one error indicator. Heavily packed PDUs that contain any errors result in no useful information. Although understandable with an SNMP `SetRequest` (you wouldn't want to set only half the objects that control an action), this limitation is unnecessary with a `GetRequest`.

The simplest solution is to allow an agent to correctly respond to a `GetRequest` with all available varbinds that precede the first failing OID. No sense in failing to answer varbinds 1–10 if number 11 is the first to encounter an error. A more complete solution would have been to eliminate the `errorIndex` field and place an `errorStatus` next to each varbind. The percentage increase in overhead is minimal (it actually saves one field if the request contains only a single varbind). The result is that all available information can be returned on each `GetRequest`.

I have implemented both of these variations on the protocol in an environment that uses significant levels of PDU packing to monitor large volumes of objects. I found that these techniques substantially reduce the periods in which polling coverage is impacted by vendors generating `NoSuchNames` on required objects. Each PDU that fails must be rebuilt with the offending object eliminated and resent, only to find the next error. This can be improved.

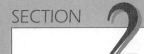

Introduction to Using MIB Data

Introduction

Network managers collect MIB data for a variety of purposes. Monitoring and debug is an obvious application, as is projecting future capacity and performance needs. Other valuable uses exist, but are often overlooked. These missed opportunities include enhanced availability measurements and even fault prediction. This section discusses the application of MIB data and suggests ways to facilitate its collection.

Let's begin by describing a common progression of MIB data analysis. This order offers incremental complexity; each step also provides an additional level of value. Once a basic monitoring infrastructure is in place, many choose to measure effectiveness by computing availability. The section entitled "Measuring Infrastructure Availability: The Real Numbers" provides detail on how to generate an accurate and useful set of values. "Capacity Planning Versus Fault Analysis" and "Performance Analysis Versus Fault Analysis" then discuss capacity planning and performance analysis, respectively. An overview of each topic is followed by a review of commercially available solutions.

In "Perfomance Analysis Versus Fault Analysis," an enhanced level of fault analysis is explored (forming the basis for Section 3) and is followed by fault-prediction analysis in "Fault Prediction."

Once these analysis techniques are understood, "Configuring Your Management Platform" provides insight regarding the configuration of a management platform to gather this information. Finally, "Centralized Versus Distributed Data Collection" concludes with a discussion of centralized versus distributed polling and methods used to gather the data for analysis.

Measuring Infrastructure Availability: The Real Numbers

The growing popularity of measuring availability represents an evolutionary step in network and systems management. In the early days of networking, the goal was merely to detect a catastrophic outage and begin working on a fix. The operations mindset became one of "probe and test," in which tools pinged boxes and looked for any that failed to respond (pings are ICMP-based reachability tests). Over time, commercial versions of homegrown "probe and test" applications emerged, which enhanced the user interface with pretty maps and colors. This was followed by debug tools that specialized in packet capture (protocol analyzers and RMON-like probes), by capacity-planning tools, and then by availability tracking. Unfortunately, availability measurement took its cue from the still popular "probe and test" methods by merely pinging infrastructure devices and recording the response drops and latency.

There are a number of problems that arise when pings are used to measure availability. As a metric, availability should be used to quantify the extent to which the infrastructure performs for the users. Users access databases, web sites, email, and applications. Any measurements that claim high availability during periods of poor connectivity to these services are clearly flawed. Infrastructures have built-in redundancy that must also be accounted for in computing availability. Just because IP routes around degraded areas in a network's core does not mean that the degradation should be ignored; it increases failure risk (if you really didn't care about the loss of redundancy, your CFO probably wants to know why you purchased redundant equipment). Real availability measurements primarily look at the end user's experience, but must account for loss of redundancy. Useful measurements not only include metrics, but also offer insight as to why the numbers are poor when problems are seen. Using this definition, pings fail to provide what is required.

You may use pings to measure availability. Why does it fail these criteria? First, ICMP Echo Requests are not user data and cannot reflect the user's experience. Some problems are induced or aggravated by packets of particular sizes. Ping tests generally fail to account for normal size and data distributions. Some problems expose equipment and line sensitivities to specific patterns that occur randomly in user data. The odds of your choosing such a pattern with ping are slim. The use of "synthetic transactions" that test the applications natively can help, but they still may not expose the above.

Second, reachability tests also fail to validate that *users* are able to reach resources they need, only that your test tool can reach these systems. Routing problems, filters, high loss levels, and similar problems may all conspire to make systems unreachable to your users while they remain reachable by your measurement tools. Distributing the collection points closer to the users may help reduce this problem, but not eliminate it.

Third, ICMP and other protocols can be prioritized or deprioritized by the infrastructure, so their accuracy is always questionable.

Finally, pings offer little to no data about the cause of a problem, only that one might exist.

NOTE: *When I ran a large network outsourcing business within IBM, we did use ping drops and latency to measure ourselves. I can tell you from experience that this method wasn't accurate. Routing and filtering problems kept some customers off the air for extended periods or prevented them from reaching specific resources. The NOC-based pings did not reflect this.*

Understanding the flaws in the measurement process allowed us to affect the results. When ping response times were poor, we were able to improve numbers simply by upgrading the performance of the box doing the pings (taking the measurements). We fully understood that our Bay routers treated pings as high priority, whereas Cisco treated them as low priority. We even knew that some IBM routers would answer pings to the address of an interface that was hard down. Mark Twain wrote of "lies, damn lies, and statistics." Our measurement qualified because only the measurement improved; not the user experience.

So what should be used to measure *real* availability? The answer is a combination of box availability, path availability (a user's ability to reach the desired services), and service availability. We'll examine each in turn.

Box Availability   Box availability can include box response, a ping-like component in which the measurement system looks for percentage of queries that were answered. This number is further reduced by the percentage of total interface seconds that were operationally down. For example, if a box has three interfaces, one of which is down for 10 seconds, the interface availability over a 60-second interval is as follows:

interface availability= $100 - ((\Sigma$ downtime_for_interface_i)/ (interval $\times$ interfaceCount))

interface availability= $100 - ((1 \times 10)/(60 \times 3))$

interface availability= $100 - {}^{10}/_{180}$

interface availability= 99.94%

You should weight the box responses about three times stronger than the interface status, though this ratio may be adjusted based on the number of interfaces in the box and the presence of redundant paths from the measurement point. Systems with large numbers of interfaces will suggest better interface availability by averaging in a large `interfaceCount`. All packets traverse the common system, so losses there have roughly twice the impact of losses on any single interface. The factor of 3 assumes that there is an average of six interfaces on a typical box and is derived by dividing the typical `interfaceCount` by 2.

If the percentage of box responses is 92.25% and the interface availability is 99.94%, then the box availability can be shown as follows:

box availability= $(3 \times$ box response rate + interface availability)/4

box availability= $(3 \times 92.25 + 99.94)/4$

box availability= 94.17%

Note that by distributing the collection of these metrics close to the targets, you can avoid mistaking dropped and errored packets between the NOC and a target for that target's inability to respond. In short, distributed SNMP polling engines that monitor `ifOper-Status` (and count responses that time out) on each interface can be used to accurately measure box availability.

Path Availability Next, we need to account for path availability. The goal of path availability is to accurately reflect the percentage of *user traffic* that fails to reach its destination. Rather than attempt to emulate user traffic or try to count lost pings, you use MIB data in the routers and switches to accurately reflect the percentage of packets that are not being forwarded. There is no need to worry about mimicking user payload patterns, routing errors, filters, etc.; you look at the results of actual data.

Path availability is actually computed at each box. For each interface, you sum the total increase (represented as Δ) of input and output errors, plus the total increase of input and output discards (ΔifInErrors + ΔifOutErrors + ΔifInDiscards + ΔifOutDiscards). This number is the total increase in *interface drops* over your measurement period. To this, add the increase in all system level packet discard and error counters (everything from ipInHdrErrors to ipOutNoRoutes). We now have the incremental total number of packets that failed to traverse the box. Over the same measurement period, you sum the increase in good and dropped packets received by each interface (ΔifInNUCast + ΔifInUcast + *interface drops)*. This represents the total number of packets that the box handled. Note that the count of packets transmitted is not included. On any box designed to forward data, counting packets on both reception and on transmission would result in twice the number of messages handled. This is not the case with end-stations; systems hosting user applications should add the increase in transmitted packets because most of these will be originated locally. It is a simple matter to compute path availability on any box (where each interface *i* is analyzed) over an interval with the following formula:

$$path\ availability\ (box) = 100 - (100 \times (\Sigma\,(\Delta\ interface\_drops.i) +$$

$$\Delta\ system\_packet\_discards + \Delta\ system\_packet\_errors)\backslash$$

$$\Sigma\,(\Delta\ interface\_drops.i + \Delta ifInNUCast.i + \Delta ifInUcast.i))$$

Note that we stick to using the packet and error counters defined in MIB-2, and not those provided in vendor extensions and protocol or transmission groups. The reason for this is MIB-2 defines at each layer generic counters representing packets dropped due to errors in decoding or parsing (called errors), and packets dropped even though they had no errors (discards). Vendor and transmission group extensions serve to better refine the causes of packet drops, but ultimately duplicate the totals from the MIB-2 counters.

> **NOTE:**   *Notice that I summed the individual changes in each counter, rather than simply adding the total counter values and subtracting the previous total. The reason for this is that the individual counters wrap when they exceed their maximum values (typically $2^{32} - 1$). Each counter must be individually compared with its previous value; if the new count is less than the previous, and the object* sysUpTime *has not reset during the measurement interval, then you must assume that the value has advanced through $2^{32} - 1$ and continued counting up from 0.*
>
> *In choosing measurement intervals, you must be careful to ensure that counters cannot wrap through and exceed their current value in the time allotted. The sample interval should be the lesser of just under one-half the period in which the counter can wrap and the measurement interval over which availability is being computed. If the period over which you intend to compute availability exceeds the maximum sample interval, take several samples. The total change in counter value is the sum of the individual counter changes.*
>
> *Other things I like to account for when measuring increases in counter values include the following:*
>
> **1.** *Filter out absurd values in the deltas because some vendors may have inaccurate counts or may allow individual counters to be reset without clearing* sysUpTime. *For each counter, decide in advance what the maximum reasonable change is over your measurement interval. If that is grossly exceeded, remember the newly provided value for the delta in the next interval and assume that the absurd increase for this interval is 0.*
>
> **2.** *Ignore the delta operation if* sysUpTime *indicates that the counters were cleared during this measurement interval. As previously discussed, remember the current value for the next delta.*
>
> **3.** *Verify that the total packet count is large enough to be statistically meaningful. If I received only two packets and one contains an error, it might not make sense to claim a 50% error rate.*

You may also notice that I ignore traffic originated by a packet for-warding box, such as routing updates and network management responses. It is possible that these locally generated packets have been counted in the output drops but were not included in the total packets received. These should be relatively small and have little impact on the result, although you may choose more complex algorithms to account for them. Purists will also choose to not count packets inbound or drops in either direction on any loopback interface.

Service Availability   The final component of an accurate, real availability measurement is service availability. Some choose to tie this to service performance, others to whether the service simply responds or not within a reasonable period. Service measurements are fairly new, but seem to be following the path that was previously set by infrastructure management. Network managers tested applications to see if they existed, began to gather data for capacity planning, and are now studying ways to measure performance. As before, more sophisticated fault analysis (*why* is it breaking?) have largely been overlooked.

Service availability can be thought of as analogous to interface availability, in which each application is being tested to see if it is running. This can be done via synthetic transactions that mimic user access (locally because you don't want to measure possible path availability here) or by local monitoring applications and scripts. Several new standards that track MIBs—including RFCs 2788 (*Network Services Monitoring MIB*), 2287 (*Definitions of System-Level Managed Objects for Applications*), and 2564 (*Application Management MIB*)—may be of use here.

As with interface availability, service availability simply measures the percent of time that the required services were available to the users. You should measure these as close to the (servers running the) applications as possible, so as not to confuse path or box availability problems with the service. Assume that application_a represents some application numbered from 1 to `applicationCount`:

$$service\ availability\ =\ 100 - ((\Sigma\ downtime\_for\_application\_a)\backslash$$

$$(interval \times applicationCount))$$

Total Infrastructure Availability Now that box, path, and service availability have been computed, a true measure of availability is feasible. We will assume the traditional infrastructure architecture of access devices feeding distribution devices, which, in turn, feed core devices. Such an architecture is shown in Figure 2-1.

Users connect directly to access devices, which may be modems, Frame Relay PVCs, or LAN ports. They are aggregated at a distribution layer, which ties together multiple segments or user connections. The distribution layer typically feeds a highly redundant core, which represents the backbone. Servers, unlike users, typically connect directly to the distribution layer.

Assuming no redundancy, a failure at the access layer totally isolates a user or small group of users. A distribution layer failure totally isolates a group of users or access to a group of services. When measuring availability to a specific user or of a specific service, access and distribution layer outages are total. When discussing the availability of the total infrastructure, these outages affect only a portion of the whole and should be accounted for accordingly. This is done by computing the average availability for each box at the access layer.

A simple failure in the core may offer degraded performance or a lack of redundancy, but it should not isolate users from services. Core failures only have $\frac{1}{2}$ the standard impact, assuming that a redundant infrastructure will not partition with roughly 50% of its boxes down and that you are using a fault-tolerant routing protocol.

Figure 2-1

Traditional infrastructure in which access devices feed distribution devices that feed core devices

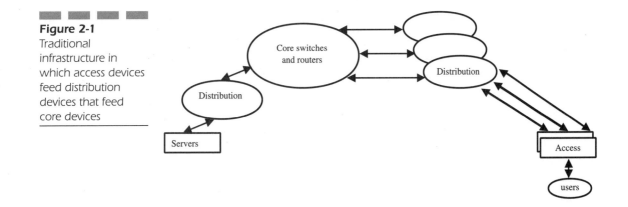

Readers wishing to compute real availability for an entire infrastructure must first compute availability at each device. This is done by multiplying the various forms of availability and scaling, as appropriate. For example, if an access device has a box availability of 90% and a path availability of 80%, the real availability (without accounting for services) is $.9 \times .8 = .72$ or 72%.

The following steps are used to compute the real availability of an entire infrastructure:

1. If applications (services) are to be considered as a part of this analysis, take the average service availability of all those measured on each server. You may choose a weighted average if some services are more important to your business than others. Multiply this by the box availability and again by the path availability measured on that same server. Average this number for each server that is hosting applications. Call this result Sa and assign a value of 100% if services are not being measured.

2. For each box at the access layer, multiply the box availability times the path availability. Average this for each box at the access layer. Call this result Aa and assign a value of 100% if the access layer is not being considered (some service providers choose to not include access devices).

3. For each box at the distribution layer, multiply the box availability, B, times the path availability. If access devices have redundant paths into the distribution layer, landing on different distribution boxes, the impact of a single box failure is a loss of redundancy only. In this case, you may use an enhanced box availability of $(0.5 + B/2)$. Multiply this by the number of access boxes (or users) that share this distribution device. Average this number for all distribution layer devices, and divide the result by the total number of access boxes (or users). Call this Da.

4. For each box in the core, determine the box availability B. Next, compute enhanced box availability of $0.5 + B/2$. Average this number for all core devices and call the result Ca.

5. Compute real infrastructure availability $= Sa \times Aa \times Da \times Ca$.

Note that we may compute enhanced box availability to account for redundancy, but never discount the impact of path availability. Box failures may be routed around, but path availability measures the loss of data for packets that actually chose to traverse the path.

NOTE: *Congratulations! You have accurately computed the real availability of your infrastructure and service layer. It's important to make good use of this information.*

System monitoring and debug is generally driven by the need for self-preservation. You run a NOC or monitoring system to manage crises and tactically keep your infrastructure alive.

Capacity measurement and planning is driven by an understanding that crisis avoidance is better than crisis management. A deeper belief in this premise will lead you to implement fault prediction as well. Properly followed, this will fundamentally shift the way in which you view infrastructure management.

Availability measurements are too often used as tools to beat up the organization collecting them. That leads to a natural desire to get a "good" number instead of the real number. Real availability measurements should answer the question "How do I improve?". We have generated what I described earlier as useful availability, as you can inspect the individual availability terms to see where any availability may be falling short of your goal. This leads to steps that can actually improve your results.

Focusing solely on the availability number and not the terms from which it was derived can be quite disappointing. In some environments, a real availability of over 95% is actually quite acceptable. Consider a simple example containing a server, two access and distribution layers, and a core. Assume that service availability, S_a, is 99.96%, allowing only 15 minutes per day when the application is not available. Assume that the access layer (A_a) runs at 99.8% availability because the local telco loop is often only guaranteed to be better than 99.7% for each of the two tail circuits. If the distribution layer availability, D_a, and the core availability,

Ca, each run a clean 99.99%, the total availability is 99.7%. This may not sound impressive, but it is accurate.

Capacity Planning Versus Fault Analysis

The most common form of MIB data analysis is capacity planning. This is done by sampling MIB objects at regular intervals and trending the results forward. Sample intervals vary, but are typically 5 to 30 minutes. Analysis of this information is limited; most capacity tools graph their data and allow the user to visually determine how close to maximum he is. This clearly doesn't scale—each router and switch might have hundreds of metrics such as CPU utilization, system and card memory, port utilization, and port error rates. Objects may also include second-order effects such as Ethernet collision levels. Some tools use basic curve fits to estimate when various capacities will be exhausted. Some define health metrics by averaging or combining these capacities and thresholding the result. In any case, capacity-planning tools are characterized by their infrequent sampling and simple thresholding of one or few metrics to determine when additional resources will be needed.

This is a valuable thing to do. Hardware upgrades and new circuits take time to order and install. By accurately determining when current resources will not suffice, you can arrange to buy additional capabilities before your infrastructure runs out of steam. This may or may not be cost-effective, but at least there are few surprises.

■ ■

NOTE: It is important that you focus first on capacity-tracking and notification tools, rather than on those that offer periodic reporting. The former run continuously and alert you to overutilization and congestion, whereas the latter generate graphs and reports that must be studied for signs of problems. The goal is to study only those capacity reports that are likely to be valuable. Having to glean nuggets of value from reports on a regular basis doesn't scale, and is a process that is likely to be abandoned as soon as you get busy. I've seen dozens of network managers that purchased infrastructure health-reporting tools who receive piles of daily and weekly (or worse, real-time, web-based) reports that never get read. One suggested that the only way he could ever get value from his filing cabinet full of color charts and graphs would be to wallpaper his house. Pick your event-notification platform first and integrate capacity events with it.

Once proper notification is in place, you should use reporting and analysis tools on areas that regularly show up as capacity "hot spots." Utilization patterns based on time of day and day of the week can be extremely valuable.

One client noticed daily congestion problems just after midnight. The performance bottleneck was consuming not only link capacity, but also eating router CPU and memory (the result of large access control lists). The result was high latency and loss, resulting in extremely long database synchronization.

If she were simply managing to capacity events, my client would have increased her bandwidth and upgraded her routers. She didn't. By studying the capacity reports, she noticed that her average utilization was reasonable, but that certain traffic flows spiked on weekdays shortly after midnight. By using a protocol analyzer, she determined that several departments were doing automated backups of their servers, and that the default settings on the backup tools had all of them start at midnight. My customer managed her capacity problem by having the departments stagger the start of backups.

I refer to this phenomenon as the "lunch effect." At many large companies, utilization peaks are seen around 9:00 A.M. (when employees first show up in the morning) and again when they return from lunch at about 1:00 P.M. Checking email and the web seem to be standard actions of arriving employees. This is a natural peak that you should build an infrastructure to accommodate. ISPs have different peaks. Those servicing home users see natural peaks at around 7:00 P.M. (just after dinner) and again from 10:30 P.M. to 1:00 A.M. (power users).

The combination of scalable capacity-detection/alerting tools that direct you to capacity reports can be powerful. Together, they will help you optimize your resources and avoid congestion.

Available Capacity Planning and Analysis Tools Capacity-planning tools make for poor fault-analysis systems. By their very nature, those systems that detect utilization problems assume that high levels of resource consumption is sufficient to require corrective action (add more capacity). Fault-analysis tools are optimized to detect improper conditions and to facilitate understanding about *why* those conditions exist. Capacity monitors assume that *what* is sufficient, and therefore collect lower data volumes, offer little interpretation of that data, and generally utilize few vendor-specific metrics. True, infrastructure exhaustion may cause failures but real fault analysis seeks to know *why* the infrastructure is being consumed.

Capacity-planning and analysis tools are available from a number of sources. The following list is a sample of what's available at the time of publication, and the author's opinions of the roles they best serve.

- Management Platforms as Capacity Monitors

  Most network-management platforms offer basic polling, thresholding, and notification functions, along with the capability to collect and graph data for trending purposes. Notification can be as simple as turning an icon red or sending an automated page. Unfortunately, the vast majority of platforms require the user to develop capacity models for each class of monitored device or technology. These models describe what to monitor and how to test the results. Users without the time or experience to define such models are reduced to using native "probe and test" facilities. Section 3 of this book lists the objects that you should configure your platform to poll, many of which represent capacities (CPU, port and media utilization, drops, buffers, etc.). Simple platforms range from Castle Rock's SNMPc to CA's Unicenter Framework. HP OpenView offers more function, but still has a limited understanding of what to collect out-of-the-box. More sophisticated platforms, such as Spectrum, include more complete libraries to measure capacities of a number of infrastructure elements.

  No matter which platform is chosen, this should be your primary notification tool.

- NetHealth (Concord)

  NetHealth is one of the best known capacity reporting tools. It produces web-based reports that highlight problem areas based on predefined models and thresholds (but offers some level of customization). The user interface and reports are optimized to cover reasonably large groups of devices, but it remains an analysis and reporting tool. It cannot notify in real time of problems, making it most effectively used as a tool to diagnose small domains of devices once alerting tools have found a commonly congested area. Given that Concord prices are based on the number of devices monitored, this is also the best way to optimize tool costs.

- EnterprisePro (INS/Lucent)

  INS, recently purchased by Lucent, developed *EnterprisePro* (EPro) as a direct competitor to NetHealth. Some differences exist in the bundling of service offerings, but many of the Concord comments apply. Differences are primarily in the area of service-availability reports.

- Trend SNMP (DeskTalk)

  DeskTalk took a completely different approach to capacity reporting and analysis. They use a moderately high-volume polling engine to collect SNMP data and store it in an SQL database. This allows them to provide a platform upon which they, and others, can build reporting tools. Key limitations are the lack of out-of-the-box usability and the performance problems inherent in centralized storage of larger data sets (including network bandwidth, memory, CPU, and disk consumption). The main advantage of this approach is that it maximizes flexibility of the applications, whether developed by the user or provided by third parties. This solution is primarily favored by power users of open (standards-based) reporting tools, though much of it can be duplicated by platforms that act as data repositories.

- Eye of the Storm (Prosum)

  Prosum's offerings primarily focus on capacity reporting with real-time alerting. Unlike pure reporting tools, Prosum offers real-time notification of bottlenecks that integrates with most enterprise managers. Although lacking the flexibility of Trend or the sophistication of EPro, Prosum provides a middle ground approach that doesn't require the user to assemble this function using his platform's native components.

- RMON1

  RMON defines a set of SNMP MIB objects that instrument data collected on a network segment. In addition, it provides a basic set of packet capture filters. Some of the instrumentation provides error rates, which are mainly useful as a capacity measurement as they don't indicate why the errors are occurring. RMON also provides a set of utilization metrics, such as the top users of a segment's bandwidth. Although the packet-capture capabilities offer some value as a debugging tool, RMON1 is generally used as a capacity-reporting tool. RMON2 provides similar data, with additional metrics that detail application utilization. A number of vendors supply RMON collectors (called probes) and the application software needed to manage them.

  One major drawback of using RMON is the need to place remote probes on every monitored segment. Systems that collect and interpret SNMP data directly from each monitored device don't require this additional hardware deployment.

- MRTG/RRD Tool

  Multi Router Traffic Grapher (MRTG) is a popular software package that is often used to graph capacities and bandwidth utilization. It is relatively simple to configure, and it produces near real-time graphs that can be directly posted in an in-ternal web site. MRTG is freely available as a download from CAIDA.org. Think of MRTG as a reporting tool with almost no thresholding or native intelligence. It is now being replaced by the database-central RRD tool.

Perfomance Analysis Versus Fault Analysis

One aspect of infrastructure management that has recently gained in popularity is performance analysis. Applications are measured, directly or indirectly, to determine response time and satisfaction levels of the end users. Three developments are likely to accelerate this trend: *Virtual Local Area Networks* (VLANs), *Application Service Providers* (ASPs), and *Service Level Agreements* (SLAs).

VLANs, especially those provided by outsource Network Service Providers, allow you to share a common infrastructure while appearing to be on a single flat LAN. The result is that you have essentially hidden the shared infrastructure, which makes it extremely difficult to monitor. Elements still degrade and fail, of course, and will impact the service that you experience. Without the ability to do element management, all you can do is monitor the impact at your virtual layer.

The emerging field of application outsourcing to an ASP encourages users to measure the performance of the virtual service. The entire infrastructure is ignored by design. Users simply pay for access to a service and ignore issues of transport and delivery. The abstraction of services again drives measurement to that which is visible: the reachability and performance of the service itself. Nothing else can be seen.

SLAs define the contractual agreements between you and your service provider. Because few providers wish to open their systems to customer monitoring, SLAs tend to be defined as a combination of availability and delay thresholds. Failure to meet these thresholds often results in penalties, so service providers monitor for compliance. *Network Service Providers* (NSPs), *Internetwork Service Providers* (ISPs), and ASPs all provide SLAs as a natural way to measure their deliverables. This adoption is driving the acceptance of performance-measurement tools, which leads to their commonplace status in the enterprise.

NOTE: *One common mistake is to allow your vendor to define the SLA measurement criteria and to track his own performance. Sadly, this is becoming commonplace. Vendors define simplistic measurements, using tools such as ping to measure delay, and then tell you if they failed their own test. I once likened this to the IRS allowing you to interpret the tax code and then audit yourself for compliance.*

As in capacity planning, performance monitoring can be done to generate real-time alerts, or as a part of regular reporting. Reporting is of limited use unless it is highly summarized or targeted by alerts— there is simply too much to report on. They must be read to add value, and this process doesn't scale. Reports also tend to contain substantially more information than is reviewed in real time as they hold the equivalent of a day's or a week's alerts, all summarized in one place. This results in more to review in a single sitting than is seen at any given moment in an alert-based system.

So how are performance measurements taken? They are either measured directly by observing and timing delays between user requests and received responses, or they are emulated by using a technique called synthetic transactions. One of the earliest measurement tools was the "expert sniffer" by Network General (now called Network Associates). This debug tool would watch delays in application connections, referred to as sessions or flows, and highlight those that appeared to be excessive. As a debug tool, this worked well. As a monitoring or reporting system, it suffered from the need to constantly cover all segments. Some newer systems attempt to do this by placing probes near the centralized servers, but even those can be distributed in a modern multi-service environment. Synthetic transactions can reduce this problem, but not eliminate it. Accurate measurements require the systems emulating users to also be distributed to points near the users. As mentioned earlier, synthetic transactions also suffer from the fact that they only approximate what users are doing and the ways in which they do it. Even still, performance measurements using emulated user activities are a natural extension to the distributed application response testing suggested earlier.

Those infrastructure managers who have lost visibility into their elements generally seek to compensate by measuring business impact. If you no longer have the ability to quickly isolate and fix problems, it becomes increasingly important to understand who is being affected by performance problems. Often referred to as business impact reporting, some tools even attempt to assign financial costs. This is similar to measuring availability grouped by communities of interest, only it lacks the detail explaining *why* there is a problem, which requires a traditional debug activity.

It is again important to remember that performance measurement is not fault management. Performance management tends to be reporting-centric, it abstracts out the elements in the infrastructure, and can be used to determine that "something may be wrong here." It is driven by an abstract view of services and users, making it most useful when the infrastructure simply isn't viewable. Real-time performance monitoring fails to provide more than cursory pointers to the existence of problems, and deepens a dependency on element monitoring to diagnose their root cause.

Following is a list of tools commonly used for measuring performance, along with the author's opinion of their key capabilities:

- EnterprisePro (INS/Lucent)

  Although listed previously as a capacity-planning tool, the integration of technology from its VitalSigns acquisition allowed INS to add performance-reporting features. Data is gathered via software distributed to each desktop that measures the performance of actual transactions. The results are reported periodically, without integration to popular alerting platforms. The top-level screens clearly summarize both service degradation and affected users by community.

- S3 (Nextpoint)

  Nextpoint was an early leader in performance measurement and reporting via synthetic transactions. Its tool is a programmable platform that enables the user to define the transaction and set thresholds, although a library of popular applications is pre-built. S3 is primarily a reporting tool because its integration with other platforms is light.

- Netscout

  Netscout probes add session or flow-tracking to traditional RMON probes. Their application software can analyze the results and look for both congestion and performance issues. This is designed primarily as a reporting tool.

- NetFlow (Cisco)

  Recent router and switch software releases from Cisco support flow-based transaction logging on some hardware. Referred to as

NetFlow, these transactions are logged and analyzed remotely from the box sending flow data. Several third-party capacity and performance analysis tools exist that accept NetFlows, though users are cautioned to carefully plan the amount of network bandwidth this system requires. Failure to do so could result in flow updates affecting performance when the network is most congested.

- Trinity (Avesta/Visual)

Avesta, recently purchased by Visual Networks, has focused on measuring performance degradation and outages and mapping that back to business impact. Its model allows the user to collect basic data regarding service levels and assign cost metrics to the applications and user communities. This is simply a reporting and costing tool. Visual has long focused on capacity and performance reporting for Frame Relay and ATM pipes, but appears to broadening its view.

- Unicenter (Computer Associates)

Computer Associates (CA) has taken a different route to performance by tightly integrating it with its Unicenter TNG platform. Reporting facilities are typical for an Enterprise Network Management System, but the company tends to excel in the area of real-time detection. Using a concept called "neugents," it baselines state, capacity, and performance metrics to learn normal behavior (tied to time of day, etc.). It can then detect when measured values, such as performance, deviate from expected and alert the user.

This tight integration of performance measurement with a platform's core detection and alerting abilities is valuable, but it comes with a price. Baselining tells you only when something is different, not *why* behavior is unexpected. Deviations can be both good and bad, but the assumption here is that a problem exists. Even if there is a problem, you start with little or no data to assist in its debug. This situation is typical for performance-measurement tools, but a lowering of the value proposition typically delivered by management platforms.

Analyzing MIB Data to Enhance Fault Detection

This book opened by stressing the need to interpret data, rather than simply collect, graph, and react to basic failure states. Happily, some tools do exactly that. Most of them use the term "root cause analysis," but apply it to things as diverse as locating the epicenter of a failure (topology analysis) and element level *depth perception*. This section looks at the way MIB data is analyzed and interpreted by a number of common tools.

Before we begin, it's important to understand the motivations behind fault management. Network Operations Centers generally operate in a crisis mode; they detect problems and drive them to resolution. A typical fault moves through the three distinct phases, shown in Figure 2-2.

Completing each phase as quickly as possible optimizes crisis management, and ensures that total outage duration is minimized. Availability is boosted by throwing resources at each step in the process.

This technique may be obvious, but it is one of the least efficient in terms of both resource consumption and overall availability. The following includes discussion of the time typically spent at each phase. This comes from both years of experience and the analysis of trouble tickets from a number of large infrastructures with service-impacting outages.

Figure 2-2
Phases of NOC fault management

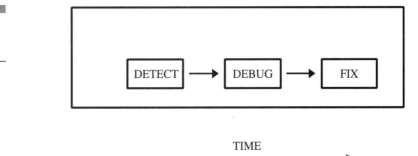

Detect Phase Detection is central to most NOC environments. As discussed, the approach used by most tools is to "probe and test." This effectively does reachability sweeps. On large infrastructures (more than 500 monitored devices), management platforms attempt to minimize traffic by testing infrequently. The result is a common sweep time of 40 minutes, which results in a mean time to detect failures of 20 minutes. Worse still, many less obvious problems go undetected. A strategy that monitors and analyzes data from significantly more MIB objects, at a greater frequency, can both close the detection time and increase the ability to see problems that are currently missed.

NOTE: I once did an outage analysis on a major phone company's outsource network business. The results were incredible. The service advertised was IP connectivity, but most of the problems that were detected and resolved were Frame Relay failures (the underlying transport). Given that major ISPs typically experience routing problems, packet corruption, queue drops, etc., the lack of these tickets raised eyebrows. It wasn't until I looked at the number of problems reported by users that self-cleared or resulted in a "no trouble found" closure that I understood what was happening. They didn't know how to look for the issues they were encountering. Detection of Frame Relay outages was well understood and their monitoring systems reflected that. Other problems required either user complaints or a total reachability failure for detection. Worse, with no data from detection, second-level support engineers rarely found the cause of problems. Users complained that things were "slow," but that didn't provide enough of a starting point to do diagnosis. Good detection requires that you know what you are looking for and that you find it quickly.

Debug Phase The debug phase depends heavily on the accuracy and completeness of detection. If detection simply finds that things are "not answering" or "slow," time spent on debug is greatly increased. NOCs often rely on more skilled support engineers to assist with this.

Debug can take as little as a few minutes and as long as a few hours. If the on-call engineer isn't readily available, time is lost while he is found, updated, and obtains remote connectivity. Typical debug times are 45 minutes for moderately complex problems with reasonable detection data. If detection was incomplete, the engineer needs to finish that phase first. Engineering debug tools are typically designed to only look at one element at a time (in depth). In contrast, NOC tools are optimized to monitor many devices simultaneously, making them better candidates for detection.

Consider the converse: if NOC detection tools can provide too little data and lengthen debug cycles, they can also be enhanced to provide extra information and shorten this phase. Detection tools that collect and analyze hundreds or thousands of MIB objects per device can reduce or eliminate debug time by merging debug into detection. This results in fewer panic calls to third-level support, increased availability, and a higher accuracy rate (tools can inspect more data than a person, leading to more precise solutions).

Accuracy is key to the debug phase because incorrect guesses greatly lengthen the duration of an outage. During debug of a complex problem, an engineer generally observes a limited data set and guesses at a cause. This theory is then tested by looking for supporting symptoms. Once considered likely, the engineer advances to the fix stage, where actions are taken to resolve or mitigate the problem. If the theory was wrong, the attempted fix doesn't work (hopefully, it didn't make things worse). It must then be backed out and the debug phase restarted. This controlled iteration can consume significant amounts of time. Accuracy eliminates waste.

NOTE: *The obvious problems aren't always as they appear. One particularly tricky debug session was started without enough data. We clearly had a routing protocol problem because packets were being forwarded to systems that should not have received them. We spent a lot of time trying to fix the wrong problem.*

As luck would have it, we had t1 cards with defective memory. The cards held a cache of the routing table. Values written to the card could be immediately read back, but tended to change over time. This placed junk in the forwarding table. It wasn't until we had more data, changes in routing behavior without any routing updates, that we began to properly debug the error.

Fix Phase   The fix phase involves taking actions based on the findings of the debug phase (*"what is the problem?"*) and the engineer's knowledge and experience. It may involve bringing in an expert in a particular technology, such as telco or routing protocols. The fix for a problem might be remotely implemented by issuing a command to change a device configuration or it could require physically replacing hardware. In all cases, fixes require specific actions on specific elements.

Time spent on fix implementation cannot be improved through analysis, although false steps can be avoided. Physical replacement times are generally aided by sparing and remote access policies. These account for a small percentage of the problems seen on most infrastructures. Much more common is the need to react to a changing environment—new or failing protocols, unexpected traffic, and externally induced instability can often be repaired remotely. A new class of tools, active management, can take automated actions that quickly and accurately implement remote fixes. Of course, this simply increases the dependency on a complete and accurate diagnosis during debug.

NOTE: Active management with insufficient analysis can hurt. Imagine a simplistic manager that is programmed to reboot any router that runs out of resources. Now consider the impact of a large routed environment. A route flap could consume significant resources in a relatively short period of time. If this triggered a reboot, it could destabilize routing on adjacent routers, which might also then be candidates for reboots. As the boxes come back up, they will again dedicate large amounts of resources to initial routing updates. This could again cause the boxes to reboot, continuing the cycle. Simplistic analysis and actions are to be avoided in active environments.

It's clear that an NOC should do more than just "probe and test." By gathering MIB data frequently, you can cover a broader problem set and detect issues quickly. You enter the debug phase armed with details that lead to accurate diagnosis and shorten the outage. You might even be able to take an automated action that self-corrects the problem. How sophisticated should the NOC and their analysis tools be?

The answer lies not in the level of sophistication, but in time. The NOC remains focused on tactically taking those actions that ensure availability. Sophisticated fault detection and near-term (within 24 hours) fault prediction reasonably fall into its mission. Longer-term analysis, planning, and fault prediction should be the focus of an Engineering group.

The first step to sophisticated analysis is collection. You can't analyze what you don't collect. You need tools that look at everything of value on every monitored system. Section 3 defines those MIB objects of value for various technologies. There is far too much data to simply collect, graph, and read. You need tools capable of understanding the information that you gather. These tools need to interpret the data. If they offer a deeper understanding by diagnosing combinations of symptoms, you maximize their value.

The following examples demonstrate the importance of collecting, analyzing, and interpreting data that is often overlooked by simplistic tools:

- Cisco routers have an object (`locIfOutResets`) that counts the number of times each interface was reset. Monitoring this object and interpreting the results can lead to both detection and diagnosis of configuration problems. By default, Cisco enables a protocol called keepalives on each port. When a serial line has keepalives enabled, it sends a keepalive message every 10 seconds. It also expects to receive a keepalive from the remote end every 10-second interval. If three intervals pass without receiving keepalives, the router assumes a problem with the interface and resets the port. If `locIfOutResets` increments every 30 seconds on a serial interface, odds are that the local end has keepalives enabled and the remote end does not (or connectivity is lost). To observe a pattern that repeats every 30 seconds, this MIB object should be checked at least every 15 seconds on each port. Frequent collection and interpretation allows a tool to detect and diagnose this problem quickly and completely.

- Most routers and switches instrument their percentage of CPU utilization. This capacity is well worth monitoring, but as a symptom of a larger problem. Rather than viewing this as merely a single data point, consider that some task consumes CPU cycles at any moment. Knowing that the CPU is high has value to a planning group. Knowing *why* the CPU is high now has immediate value to an NOC. Because CPU utilization spikes rapidly, this object should be sampled every few seconds. Next, sample every task, process, and activity that might consume CPU resources. By correlating the CPU spikes with utilization spikes from each possible cause, you can rapidly determine which cause is driving the resource utilization. The items that are correlated with the CPU must each be sampled every few seconds as well; it does little good to say that a symptom appeared to be active in the same 10-minute window that the CPU appeared high. What is important is that a specific activity tracks instantaneous CPU movement. High-volume collection, correlation, and interpretation can quickly yield answers to why the resource is being consumed.

■ A key measurement for any router is the rate at which packets are being discarded because no valid next hop exists in the IP forwarding table. The counter `ipOutNoRoutes` should be monitored every few seconds to look for signs of instability. If you simultaneously monitor the rate at which each BGP peer is sending routing updates to this box (`bgpPeerInUpdates`), you can correlate these objects. Any peer whose high update rates seems to track forwarding failure rates is very likely destabilizing routing locally. Again, each instance of each MIB object should be sampled every few seconds to allow for accurate correlation. The result is quick detection of a commonly overlooked problem, complete with diagnosis.

The last two examples not only collect and interpret MIB objects, but first attempt to correlate symptoms with each instance of objects representing possible causes. This second by second correlation, called MicroCorrelation™, allows the debug phase to be almost eliminated. (MicroCorrelation™ is simply the name my company applies to the correlation of value spikes in data. Because symptoms instrumented in MIB objects may only exist for a second or two, correlating related symptoms or causes must be done on a second-by-second basis.)

This approach complements MacroCorrelation, in which high-level events are correlated (e.g., syslog messages with time of day). Micro-Correlation™ engines can feed their diagnosis into a MacroCorrelation engine for further analysis, summarization, and location of the geographic location of a problem's origin. This analysis is sophisticated, but yields significant *depth perception* and value. Accurate diagnosis in real-time results from this convergence of the detect and debug phases.

Figure 2-3 provides an illustration of this. In this graph, we have overlaid the rates at which ethernet frames experience more than one collision for different ports on the same box. Simple analysis suggests a level of congestion; there are reasonable levels of frames being deferred more than once. Sophisticated analysis says much more. The collision rates tend to track each other second by second. Note that the levels of collisions, although not identical, tend to move together. This would have been missed had the levels simply been sampled periodically. Interpretation of the correlation leads to one of several likely conclusions:

1. The ports are joined together at layer 2, perhaps through a bridge or switch.

2. The ports connect to congested LANs and the traffic we are sending is being flooded to both. This is most likely if the device we are monitoring is a switch and the traffic is multicast or

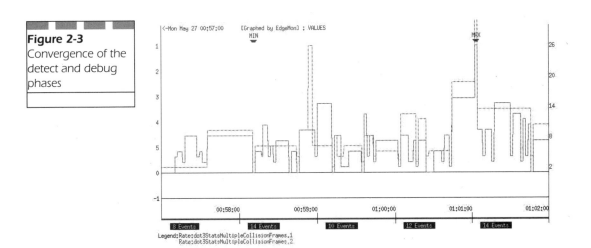

Figure 2-3
Convergence of the detect and debug phases

broadcast at layer 2. By overlaying `ifOutNUCast` rates, we can support or dismiss this possibility.

The correct answer turned out to be item 1. Users had bridged together two LAN segments without realizing the impact (the segments were on different router ports), as shown in Figure 2-4. Variations in the levels were due to the fact that both router ports were not always transmitting at the same time.

Which vendors offer analysis capabilities within their tools? The following list again reflects the author's opinion as to how many of the popular tools perform today.

- Netcool (Micromuse)

  Netcool, the flagship product from Micromuse, is a rules-based system that does real time fault monitoring. At its core is a database that is programmed to remove redundant events. Into this system, Micromuse takes alarm feeds from hundreds of sources. The result is a centralized collection of alarms, from which the duplicates have been stripped with total event counts provided. Micromuse does offer some data collection through SNMP polling features, with simple thresholding and alarming. These can be thought of as another source of events.

  The philosophy behind Netcool is that sufficient alarm data exist in various formats, distributed around the enterprise on devices and consoles. Although it is true that many sources of alarm

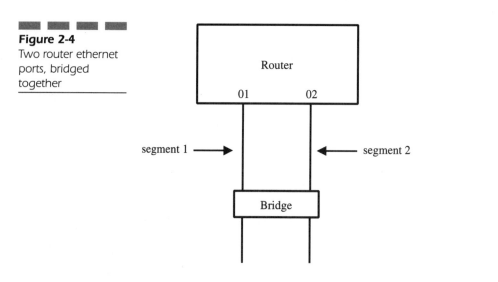

Figure 2-4
Two router ethernet ports, bridged together

information exist, Netcool is only as intelligent as the events fed into it. Its limited Precision application includes topology-based root cause, in which Netcool attempts to identify a device or port that is causing problems with others. For example, a failure to communicate with box a might be due to the fact that you also cannot communicate with box b, and box a is reachable only via box b.

Micromuse has begun to discuss the concept of automating actions in the fix phase of problems, through new rules and applications.

- Spectrum (Cabletron/Aprisma)

Aprisma, a recent spinoff from Cabletron, produces the popular Spectrum enterprise management platform. In addition to standard platform features, Spectrum offers a degree of MacroCorrelation. Rules can be defined that create relationships between monitored objects, and those results can be tested against thresholds. Data volumes are not sufficient to allow for MicroCorrelation, and the platform does not come programmed with rules for this. Pre-built MacroCorrelation models are available, which test for device-specific indications of failures. This offers some level of detection enhancement over other platforms. Topologically aware rules can also be created, which attempt to identify the origin of a failure.

- eNMS (Tavve)

Tavve has combined distributed data collection and reporting with an engine that does alarm filtering/deduplication, similar to Netcool. Tavve also offers basic topology analysis that identifies the element or component causing problems. None of these concepts is unique, but Tavve's packaging provides a convenient combination of features.

- inCharge (System Management ARTs)

SMARTS offers a relatively sophisticated platform that detects problems based on a proprietary matching of symptoms to observations. As such, it is a MacroCorrelation engine, primarily capable of doing topological analysis to determine the port, interface, or box that is the origin of a problem. This makes it a reasonable fault-detection tool, but complex diagnosis leading to why a failure occurs is left to others in the debug phase.

- PRIISMS (ION Networks)

  ION offers a platform, PRIISMS, capable of implementing automated actions via distributed control points (Network boxes). These actions might include notification, additional data gathering, or even implementing fixes. ION's focus on active management during the fix implementation stage is unique, and early in this field. Automated actions during the debug and fix stage have the potential to restore service very quickly.

  The platform itself requires intelligent diagnosis, analysis during the debug phase, before corrective actions can be automated. Without a clear understanding of the problem, implementing automated fixes has the potential to make things worse. PRIISMS also relies on the user to define many of the action routines and associate them with diagnoses.

- OpenRiver (Riversoft)

  Riversoft claims to provide automated actions through a facility they refer to as "Interventionless." In fact, their platform today seems to primarily focus on basic statistics collection and topological analysis of failures. Topological analysis provides an understanding of where an outage is centered, but not why an element is failing. Given that automation of the fix stage generally requires understanding about why there is an outage, there are likely few such automated actions available.

- NerveCenter (Veritas)

  Veritas purchased NerveCenter, a popular MacroCorrelation engine. NerveCenter plugs into the event stream of management platforms, such as OpenView, and allows the user to create rules that involve the behavior of multiple MIB objects. Both NerveCenter and the underlying platforms lack the data volume to provide MicroCorrelation™, but the rules can be used to both eliminate duplicate alarms and to enhance detection of certain problems.

- Visionary (NetOps Micromuse)

  NetOps' Visionary is a distributed MicroCorrelation™ engine. It dramatically increases monitoring coverage and reduces typical detection time when compared with traditional platforms and tools. As an element-centric diagnostic tool, Visionary provides information about *why* devices are not behaving properly. In doing so, it completes most or all of the debug phase in real time. The resulting events should then be sent to a topological or MacroCorrelation analysis system, capable of evaluating findings across elements. Visionary also sends analyzed events to automated action tools, which can then implement fixes or gather more data. When properly integrated into a larger system, Visionary becomes the intelligence layer (*depth perception*) that improves detection, accuracy, and helps shrink outage durations. NetOps has recently announced its acquisition by Micromuse, and intergrated Visionary with Netcool.

Fault Prediction

MIB analysis can provide more than real-time diagnosis. When sensitized, MicroCorrelation ™ and related analysis can be used to "predict" problems that are not yet visible to end users. The trade-off is a larger volume of event data and a higher incidence of false alarms.

There are five basic principles behind fault prediction:

1. Many outages build slowly over time. Traffic increases, circuit quality degrades, routing convergence takes longer as tables build, hardware error-rates increase, and power supplies get loaded. These problems result in slowly increasing levels of drops, errors, and performance degradation.

2. Robust protocols and infrastructures are designed to hide small levels of failures. TCP and SPX time out dropped packets and resend, protocol window sizes adjust, misordered packets are buffered, etc. Networks, systems, and applications commonly have problems that the infrastructure users don't notice.

3. Instrumentation exists that describes small problems. There are thousands of MIB objects defined in hundreds of MIBs that count nearly every type of drop, corruption, and resource usage. The data is out there, hidden in the standard MIBs and vendor extensions resident on each device. Nearly all of these devices speak SNMP version 1.

4. Analysis of the available data lets you see problems while they are small and are still being hidden from the users. If you can model the devices, collect enough data, reduce it to a manageable set, correlate and analyze the objects, and interpret the results, you can accurately distinguish noise from real events. Section 1 discussed the concepts of accessing the MIB instrumentation via SNMP. This section shows that sophisticated rules-based systems can perform the second-by-second correlation of value spikes returned by these objects, and interpret the results. Section 3 will provide you with suggestions of what specific objects to monitor. What remains is building the tools to manipulate the data, and the rules to analyze and interpret it. This early stage fault detection looks to users like fault prediction, as you see the problem long before they do.

5. Once a problem has been identified, actionable steps must be defined and implemented. Too many organizations, schooled in a crisis management approach, see problems coming and delay taking action. The result is that the problems continue to grow and ultimate crisis is not averted.

NOTE: *Step 5 can be compared to driving one's car toward a tree. Sophisticated tools and sensors might tell you that a problem is approaching, but it's up to you to either hit the brakes or turn the wheel. My telling you that you are going to crash won't prevent a disaster.*

NetOps had one client that simply didn't understand the importance of this step. For more than six months, we told them that they had routers whose stability was exposed by a large unstable routing cloud. System resource consumption was being driven to extreme levels, and they would not survive a major event. Our suggested fix was to limit the number of direct peers on each box. Rather than fix the problem, this customer wanted proof that things couldn't be left alone. They got it. One day, a router was rebooted and it never came back. It had enough resources to slowly bring up each of its routing peers, but it couldn't handle trying to connect them all at once. As a result, it would boot halfway, run out of resource, crash, and reboot. This cycle continued until it was brought up in complete isolation. This same customer later complained that implementing fault prediction had done nothing to make their infrastructure better.

The whole secret behind fault prediction is to recognize that it requires the same sophisticated analysis as fault diagnosis. Only the sensitivities change.

In Figure 2-2, we described the phases that an NOC goes through in addressing problems. Figure 2-5 shows the life cycle of the problem itself with the phases added.

Most network managers focus on boosting availability by decreasing the time from $t2$ to $t5$. Fault prediction applies the detection $(t2-t3)$ and diagnosis $(t3-t4)$ times *before* $t2$. You detect and debug using the same techniques, simply more sensitized. Specifically, thresholds for detection are set to a level that the NOC would typically ignore as not service-impacting. This level of detection should be used to alert Engineering of a possible future problem.

One cost of sensitive analysis is that higher volumes of data need to be compared against different thresholds than the NOC

Figure 2-5
The life cycle of the
problem in phases

predict	detect	debug	fix	
t1	t2	t3	t4	t5

time

t1= early symptoms appear

t2= symptoms degraded, impact felt by user

t3= NOC alerted to problem

t4= NOC completes diagnosis

t5= fix complete

desires. To eliminate duplicate data collection, the monitoring tools should be able to simultaneously look for both sensitive and severe levels on each monitored object. Fortunately, the analysis need not be in real time. Predictive detection lets Engineering run analysis jobs periodically and still be ahead of problems.

The other significant cost of this sensitized analysis is in the false alarm rate. Detecting and extrapolating problem causes based on weak symptoms can lead to significant levels of inaccurate diagnosis. The cure for this is to implement detection and analysis tools that sanity-check their own results. One good way to do this is to eliminate suspect data with sanity thresholds. Another trick is to look for indications of each specific fault over long periods of time. Although it might be weak, if a problem is real it should tend to occur frequently.

Correctly implemented, this early stage fault detection leverages the monitoring infrastructure already in place for crisis detection and diagnosis. It repeats these tasks periodically in a more sensitized manner, looking for weak indications of failure. False alarms can be minimized by technology, but the more predictive (and sensitive) you get, the more likely you will need skilled engineers checking the results. This may not be easy to do, but it is possible and does yield a substantial return. NetOps has been providing similar fault-prediction services for years.

Configuring Your Management Platform

We have explored the importance of collecting and analyzing large volumes of MIB data for use both in real-time fault detection/ analysis and prediction. Your management infrastructure should be designed to support these goals and to provide other needed services.

In general, a management platform, or "ecosystem," should support core services. It hosts or integrates with a robust trouble-ticketing system. It serves as a repository for configuration and inventory data. It is vital to track what resources are failing, who is responsible for fixing them, and their current status. It is equally vital to know what resources are available, and where, to implement quick workarounds. This requires having updated circuit ids, hardware counts and serial numbers, software and operating system release levels, "remote hands" access numbers, and vendor-maintenance information available at a moment's notice. It is helpful to also have histories of each circuit or part if it has previously experienced problems. Cards and circuits that repeatedly show unexplained errors, however infrequently, should be replaced as a matter of course.

Your platform should provide real-time detection, analysis, and alerting of faults. To accomplish this, you need to design your infrastructure to accommodate data collection and interpretation. The following pages will discuss the need to distribute the monitoring and collection of data to accomplish this task, perhaps independently of your traditional management platform.

Even with distributed monitoring and collection, it is important that you at least perform periodic reachability tests to each critical system directly from your primary platform. The management infrastructure is typically driven by exceptions, with the belief that "no news is good news" (see the discussion of SNMP TRAPs in Section 1). If the distributed monitoring tools should fail, it's possible that the NOC would never know. Standard "probe and test" applications that come with most platforms will suffice for this activity. Turn off autodiscovery, ignore the fact that sweep times will be long, and program the platform to explicitly watch each critical system.

The only portions of your system that you should be dependent on are the hardware and software running in the NOC itself. NOC infrastructures must have high availability. This means installing redundant power, telco, cooling, backup wiring through multiple closets, etc. Most large NOCs are staffed, so the odds of noticing a failure in the local application are reasonably good. Contrast this with the possibility of knowing that an application on a remote server failed when its disk crashed.

NOTE: *Previously, I mentioned several areas of infrastructure that are commonly overlooked. Connectivity from your NOC to your network should be diversely routed. If you exit your building, make sure that you have multiple circuits. You should also verify that the phone company doesn't place them on the same fiber (ask for* *"diverse routing"). Ensure that the pairs leave your building through different conduits. Route redundant paths inside your building through different wiring closets so that a single hub failure or fire doesn't isolate your NOC. If you are in a cold climate, the windows in your machine room should be operable (in case of a cooling system failure). Visualize infrastructure failures and design around them.*

Make sure that you also monitor and test the exception paths in the management infrastructure. Many network designers include remote terminal servers, connected to console ports, which are accessible via modem. The intent is to allow "out of band" control if the remote device is not reachable. This works well unless the modem fails. The phone company, without notice, can easily disconnect lightly used or unused phone numbers. Your NOC will never know that the dial access won't work until it is needed. When we built the NSFNet backbone, we also built a tool that dialed and connected to each modem once a month. It was rare to get through a test without finding at least one modem that was offline.

If not careful, it's easy to build other infrastructure dependencies into NOC tools. One common error is to configure NOC systems so they require network-based name resolution to operate, such as DNS. More than once, I've witnessed large operations centers humbled by a failure that isolates them from this service.

The key point to remember is that you need to build a high availability infrastructure for your NOC. You need to rely on it. You should then test it periodically. Even after this is done, constantly test for direct connectivity to all critical systems. You can't rely on remotely distributed management components to tell you when they fail, and they are unlikely to have the same level of infrastructure redundancy and human interaction as the systems in your NOC.

Distributed monitoring is desirable, though it shouldn't be relied on solely. The same holds true for tools that actively manage elements; you need to keep a level of direct control. There is no reason to rely only on intermediate managers to implement fixes, especially when the network itself is suspect. This simply creates a single point of failure when you most likely need your infrastructure to perform.

Once you have basic monitoring, alerting, and trouble tickets in place, you can add more sophisticated analysis. Start with the elements and build up. Watch everything all the time. Poll cycles vary, depending on the object and how you plan to analyze it, but consider monitoring things of importance every few seconds or minutes. Use the results to feed a MicroCorrelation™ analysis engine that can correlate and interpret data within an element to shrink both detection and diagnosis. The same data collectors can checkpoint sensitized thresholdings of the same raw events for predictive analysis later. Don't confuse real-time NOC data with that gathered for capacity planning or predictive analysis, even if they share the same collectors.

Pass the results of MicroCorrelation™ to a MacroCorrelation engine that accounts for inter-device (element) behavior, time of day, and events logged from non-SNMP sources. Some platforms have this ability natively, so this is simply a matter of writing the rules you need. If yours does not, consider adding a third-party correlation engine. If no such function is available, you should at least identify the element level rules that are likely to identify widespread effects (e.g., reception of high levels of broadcast traffic), and differentiate them from faults likely to be seen on one device only. Widespread effects should be tagged or colored as warnings only; they indicate areas being affected by a problem instead of the individual system at fault.

The output of this analysis should be given to an engine that is topologically aware. The intent is to remove redundant alarms based on reachability and containment. The result then goes to the display or notification level.

Figure 2-6 shows this layered approach. Those layers marked *centralized* are best performed by the enterprise manager or in the NOC.

NOTE: ***How to Present Fault Data*** *A matter of great debate continues to be how to best present fault data via a GUI. Text, icons, 3D views, and tables all have their proponents. All work fine for the top-level view of notifying someone that a fault has been detected. My opinion is as follows:*

- *Text was and is the standard setter. The phone company has been running networks for years by printing alerts as text on large*

Figure 2-6
The layered approach
to MIB data analysis

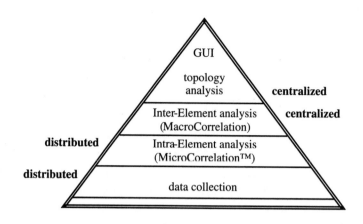

screens. *Understanding why is simple; you can convey much more information in a line of text (color, time, system, and error) than you can with a colored icon.*

■ *Topology icons are the easiest to train less-skilled operators on. The maps they overlay also have a degree of executive appeal (no correlation intended). The level of summarization involved results in icons imparting the least amount of information from a high level. 3D versions of this offer little more than pretty pictures over 2D icons.*

■ *Grids can be used to show relationships. Less real estate limits the amount of information displayed. What's gained is the ability to map geography to services or impact, such as groups of systems to affected applications. These relationships are primarily of value to more skilled engineers.*

What about web-based GUIs? Sure, they work fine. Just remember that the primary motivation for web-based access is to share the information with remote users. Then, recall that your second-level support engineer may want very different data than the NOC operator, so there may not be much information to share. On-call support engineers often need to access their tools remotely, making them ideal candidates for web-based systems. They will primarily want to display the status of a single element and control its configuration. They will also want to read and update trouble tickets.

Your NOC needs to access the same trouble tickets, but has a need to see summarized views of the entire infrastructure. Whether or not the NOC views need to be accessed remotely is a function of your organization's skills and processes.

Centralized Versus Distributed Data Collection

Previously, we described how to use second-by-second MicroCorrelation™ to shrink the duration of outages. We also discussed the application of this technique to fault prediction. We strongly suggest that this data-collection and element-level analysis be distributed. Why? In a word: volume. If you want to automate effective, accurate, root cause diagnosis at the element level, you need lots of data. You can't analyze what you didn't collect.

The fact is that correlations based on topology, from radically different sources of information (e.g., syslog versus SNMP), and those between elements should be done in a centralized location. They require high-level views of the infrastructure that would be hard to accurately distribute and maintain. Element-level analysis requires only a view of each element and can be effectively distributed widely. Fortunately, the volume of information passed upward in Figure 2-6 reduces quickly between layers.

This book began by stating that the cost of high-volume data collection can be resolved by efficiently packing multiple queries for objects into a single packet. That is true, to a point. Consider an element level analysis engine. Assume that there are 1000 targets to be monitored, 400 of which are large core or distribution devices. The balance is smaller access devices. The large devices each probably have 1000 objects worth collecting, with an average of 100 in any given second. PDU packing might allow you to send and receive only one packet per second to each device, but the packets will be roughly 1200 bytes each. This results in 400pps in and out, or an aggregate of 800pps. These packets consume 960,000 bytes per second, or 7.7Mbps. Assume 300 bytes per small device, polled every two seconds, and you need an additional 1.4Mbps over 300pps. Few management platforms would accept the impact of 1,100pps, and few NOCs would want to continuously consume three T1s worth of data to backhaul the traffic.

Now, assume that there are 10 logical domains, with the targets evenly distributed. By locally polling in each of those domains, we end up collecting 110pps (55pps each way) and consuming under 0.9Mbps. If the local domains are serviced by 100Mbps ethernets, these volumes could be acceptable. If not, more domains can be added.

Experience suggests that most of the collected data is not significant enough to analyze, so it can be locally discarded. The balance, perhaps one percent, can be analyzed for indications of problems by a MicroCorrelation™ engine. That engine might detect a problem worth reporting to the next layer 0.5% of the time. Each of our 10 domains could send its raw data on detected problems to a centralized MacroCorrelation engine. Unlike SNMP polling, this notification data wouldn't require packets of the same size to be returned. The total raw data volume would then be = .01 (1% analyzed) × .005 (0.5% triggers an event) × .5 (unidirectional data flow) × 0.9Mbps = 22.5 bits per second. The MacroCorrelation engine doesn't need all of the raw data, only averages over time, so an estimate of three bytes per second is undoubtedly excessive. Distribution of polling and element analysis dramatically reduces the data flow to the NOC.

One positive side effect of distributing data collection is that it can be locally archived. This aids in storage issues related to holding data in anticipation of predictive analysis. It also provides an historical view of what occurred if the network becomes temporarily partitioned. The more collection domains, the more likely that you will capture relevant data while the NOC was isolated from remote systems. Another benefit is that this architecture lends itself to redundancy and automated failover.

 # Summary

I've lost count of the number of network managers that have complained to me of poor problem detection. These are people who have generally invested significant resources in platforms (OpenView or Spectrum) and capacity-planning tools (RMON or NetHealth). Some have implemented simple correlation to remove duplicate alarms (generally using NetCool). They are surprised that their ability to detect and manage problems seems little improved. In fact, they are getting exactly what they asked for—simplistic detection and no interpretation.

If you find yourself in such a situation, I suggest the following. First, implement distributed application response testing. You can set performance thresholds, but the primary goal is to detect significant faults. This will test both the key elements of your infrastructure as well as their integration with each other. Tie this to your real-time alerting system. If not already done, add alarm reduction to your real-time system. This is done by eliminating duplicate alarms, often through topology analysis. Next, add serious element analysis. Understand that networks don't break; individual components do. Networks aren't fixed; problems on individual elements are. To really zero in on problems, you need to know the true root cause. Deep element analysis strengthens fault detection while adding interpretation; a combination I call *depth perception*. Finally, add planning tools. Capacity planning and reporting can be tactically pointed at domains indicating periodic congestion and should always be run against key choke points in your design. Real-time capacity detection can almost always be seen by enhancing the configuration of your platform. Fault prediction should be run against key elements in your infrastructure (whose outage is most likely to impact availability, as defined earlier).

Introduction to Monitoring MIB Objects

Introduction

This section suggests, by technology, what MIB objects to monitor and what to look for. For each technology that you implement, you should seriously consider watching the set listed below. Each recommended object has the following attributes:

Name: Textual name of the leaf node for this object

MIB: Where to look for authoritative definition of the object

OID: Object Identifier that uniquely names this object

Instantiated by: Additional information regarding instance, 0 for objects with only one instance

Description: Brief overview of what this object represents

Returns: ASN.1 type of returned value.

Suggested poll period: How frequently to collect each instance of this object

Preprocessing: How to manipulate the returned value prior to thresholding; *rate* suggests testing the increase per second, *delta* simply tests the change between polls, and *none* suggests no preprocessing

Threshold comparison: Type of test to apply on the preprocessed value returned by this object against the suggested thresholds

symbol	comparison against thresholds
!	not equal to
>	greater than
<	less than
=	equal to

Threshold: Suggested levels for alarm: (Red), caution (Orange), and warning (Yellow). The thresholds may need to be tuned for your environment, but these offer a reasonable starting point.

No such list can hope to be current, and this may not fully complete the set of objects that you should monitor. Please think of these as suggested guidelines. Your needs may vary, but these objects and parameters represent those currently used by NetOps Corp in its technology deployments. Some have been adjusted for an environment in which MicroCorrelation™ may not be possible.

MIB-2

```
Name: sysUpTime                        MIB: RFC-1213
OID: 1.3.6.1.2.1.1.3


Instantiated by: 0


Description:


Time since the network management portion of this device has been
last initialized. Usually indicates last reset or boot. This should
be reset when counters are cleared, although few vendors implement
it properly.


Returns: timeticks                     Suggested poll period: 60
Preprocessing: none                    Threshold comparison:  <


Red threshold: 25000   Orange threshold:    Yellow threshold:
```

```
Name: ipInHdrErrors                    MIB: RFC-1213
OID: 1.3.6.1.2.1.4.4


Instantiated by: 0


Description:


The number of IP datagrams that contained errors or unsupported
options in their IP header. Generally indicates checksum failures,
but can have other meanings. Some vendors, including Cisco,
increment this object when TTL is exceeded, so traceroutes can
affect it.
```

Returns: counter   Suggested poll period: 9

Preprocessing: rate   Threshold comparison: >

Red threshold: 100   Orange threshold: 50   Yellow threshold: 25

Name: ipInAddrErrors   MIB: RFC-1213

OID: 1.3.6.1.2.1.4.5

Instantiated by: 0

Description:

The number of packets received that have illegal or unsupported IP addresses. Some vendors increment this counter when they receive packets destined for 0.0.0.0, an old-style local segment broadcast.

Returns: counter   Suggested poll period: 9

Preprocessing: rate   Threshold comparison: >

Red threshold: 10   Orange threshold: 0   Yellow threshold:

Name: ipInUnknownProtos   MIB: RFC-1213

OID: 1.3.6.1.2.1.4.7

Instantiated by: 0

Description:

The number of IP packets received whose layer 4 protocol (e.g. TCP, UDP) is unknown to this device. Note that these are packets destined to this device and not simply forwarded by it at layer 2 or 3.

Returns: counter   Suggested poll period: 9

Preprocessing: rate   Threshold comparison: >

Red threshold: 0   Orange threshold: Yellow threshold:

Name: ipInDiscards   MIB: RFC-1213
OID: 1.3.6.1.2.1.4.8

Instantiated by: 0

Description:

The number of IP packets received successfully by this device and
then dropped during input processing, even though they did not
contain errors. This is often the result of either resource
limitations or traffic shaping, but can also be caused by filters.

Returns: counter   Suggested poll period: 9
Preprocessing: rate   Threshold comparison: >

Red threshold: 10   Orange threshold: 0   Yellow threshold: 210

Name: ipOutDiscards   MIB: RFC-1213
OID: 1.3.6.1.2.1.4.11

Instantiated by: 0

Description:

The number of IP packets received successfully by this device and
then dropped during output processing, even though they did not
contain errors. This is often the result of either resource
limitations or traffic shaping, but can also be caused by filters.

Returns: counter   Suggested poll period: 9
Preprocessing: rate   Threshold comparison: >

Red threshold: 10   Orange threshold: 3   Yellow threshold: 1

Name: ipOutNoRoutes   MIB: RFC-1213
OID: 1.3.6.1.2.1.4.12

Instantiated by: 0

Description:

The number of IP packets dropped by this device due to a lack of a
path to the destination address. This may indicate periods of
routing non-convergence.

Returns: counter   Suggested poll period: 6
Preprocessing: rate   Threshold comparison: >

Red threshold: 100   Orange threshold: 50   Yellow threshold: 0

Name: ipReasmFails   MIB: RFC-1213
OID: 1.3.6.1.2.1.4.16

Instantiated by: 0

Description:

The number of IP packets that were dropped because of a failure to
reassemble them into full packets. This may indicate either a lack
of local resources or packet loss within the infrastructure. The
fact that fragmentation occurs at any great volume may also be of
concern.

Returns: counter   Suggested poll period: 9
Preprocessing: rate   Threshold comparison: >

Red threshold: 10   Orange threshold: 0   Yellow threshold:

Name: ipFragOKs   MIB: RFC-1213
OID: 1.3.6.1.2.1.4.17

Instantiated by: 0

Description:

The number of IP packets that were successfully fragmented into
smaller datagrams, presumably to route over an interface with a
lower MTU. The fact that fragmentation occurs at any great volume
may be of concern.

Returns: counter   Suggested poll period: 6
Preprocessing: rate   Threshold comparison: >

Red threshold: 100   Orange threshold: 50   Yellow threshold: 10

Name: ipFragFails   MIB: RFC-1213
OID: 1.3.6.1.2.1.4.18

Instantiated by: 0

Description:

The number of packets that were dropped because of a failure to
fragment them into smaller datagrams. This often indicates a lack
of local resources. The fact that fragmentation occurs at any great
volume may also be of concern.

Returns: counter   Suggested poll period: 9
Preprocessing: rate   Threshold comparison: >

Red threshold: 10   Orange threshold: 0   Yellow threshold:

Name: ipRoutingDiscards   MIB: RFC-1213
OID: 1.3.6.1.2.1.4.23

Instantiated by: 0

Description:

The number of route table entries that were dropped, even though
they contained no errors. This may indicate a lack of local
resources, but can also be caused by routing policies.

Returns: counter   Suggested poll period: 9
Preprocessing: rate   Threshold comparison: >

Red threshold: 50   Orange threshold: 10   Yellow threshold: 0

Name: tcpAttemptFails   MIB: RFC-1213
OID: 1.3.6.1.2.1.6.7

Instantiated by: 0

Description:

The number of TCP sessions to or from this box that failed to reach
the ESTABLISHED state. This should be a rare event, and may
indicate improperly configured filters, local configuration or
resource errors, or a security incident.

Returns: counter   Suggested poll period: 11
Preprocessing: rate   Threshold comparison: >

Red threshold: 5   Orange threshold: 0   Yellow threshold:

Name: tcpEstabResets   MIB: RFC-1213
OID: 1.3.6.1.2.1.6.8

Instantiated by: 0

Description:

The number of TCP sessions that unexpectedly reset, due to the
receipt of a TCP header with the RST bit set. This often indicates
infrastructure instability, but can also be caused by applications
that do not terminate cleanly. Some mail (SMTP) clients, in
particular, create this error.

Returns: counter   Suggested poll period: 11
Preprocessing: rate   Threshold comparison: >

Red threshold: 5   Orange threshold: 0   Yellow threshold:

Name: tcpRetransSegs   MIB: RFC-1213
OID: 1.3.6.1.2.1.6.12

Instantiated by: 0

Description:

The total number of retransmissions on all TCP sessions terminating
at this box. Retransmissions are generally the result of
unacknowledged packets, suggesting either packet discards or
corruption.

Returns: counter   Suggested poll period: 11
Preprocessing: rate   Threshold comparison: >

Red threshold: 5   Orange threshold: 0   Yellow threshold:

Name: tcpInErrs   MIB: RFC-1213
OID: 1.3.6.1.2.1.6.14

Instantiated by: 0

Description:

The total number of TCP packets, received by this device, which had
errors preventing their delivery. The most common error is a
checksum failure, indicating data corruption. Note that these are
messages destined to, not merely forwarded by, this entity.

Returns: counter   Suggested poll period: 6
Preprocessing: rate   Threshold comparison: >

Red threshold: 5   Orange threshold: 0   Yellow threshold:

Name: tcpOutRsts   MIB: RFC-1213
OID: 1.3.6.1.2.1.6.15

Instantiated by: 0

Description:

The number of TCP sessions reset by this device. Sessions resets occur when the sending station sets the RST bit in the header of a TCP packet. These create tcpEstablishedRsts at the remote end.

Returns: counter   Suggested poll period: 6
Preprocessing: rate   Threshold comparison: >

Red threshold: 5   Orange threshold: 0   Yellow threshold:

Name: udpNoPorts   MIB: RFC-1213
OID: 1.3.6.1.2.1.7.2

Instantiated by: 0

Description:

The total number of UDP packets received by this box with a destination port number, indicating that they are to be passed to an unsupported application. In volumes, these needlessly consume local and network resources. Common causes are environments rich in Microsoft WINS (Windows Name Service) traffic, and some proprietary market data protocols. This traffic is often delivered unintentionally to numerous devices by sending it to a broadcast or multicast address.

Returns: counter   Suggested poll period: 9
Preprocessing: rate   Threshold comparison: >

Red threshold: 50   Orange threshold: 25   Yellow threshold: 5

Name: udpInErrors   MIB: RFC-1213
OID: 1.3.6.1.2.1.7.3

Instantiated by: 0

Description:

The total number of UDP packets, received by this device, which had errors preventing their delivery. Note that these are messages destined to, not merely forwarded by, this entity.

Returns: counter	Suggested poll period: 9
Preprocessing: rate	Threshold comparison: >

Red threshold: 50   Orange threshold: 25   Yellow threshold: 5

Name: snmpInBadCommunityNames   MIB: RFC-1213
OID: 1.3.6.1.2.1.11.4

Instantiated by: 0

Description:

The number of SNMP messages received by this device that had unsupported community strings. Community strings in SNMPv1 indicate a MIB view, and are generally used as trivial passwords. Increases in this value are often the result of misconfigured managers (possibly running autodiscovery), although security incidents can also be at fault.

Returns: counter	Suggested poll period: 3
Preprocessing: rate	Threshold comparison: >

Red threshold: 5   Orange threshold: 0   Yellow threshold:

Name: snmpInASNParseErrs   MIB: RFC-1213
OID: 1.3.6.1.2.1.11.6

Instantiated by: 0

Description:

The number of SNMP PDUs received by this device that could not be parsed due to errors in their ASN.1 encoding. This is generally caused by defective software.

Returns: counter   Suggested poll period: 3
Preprocessing: rate   Threshold comparison: >

Red threshold: 5   Orange threshold: 0   Yellow threshold:

Name: icmpInMsgs   MIB: RFC-1213
OID: 1.3.6.1.2.1.5.1

Instantiated by: 0

Description:

The total number of ICMP messages received by this device. Some
amount of ICMP may be expected, but bursts at high levels often
indicate a problem.

Returns: counter   Suggested poll period: 10
Preprocessing: rate   Threshold comparison: >

Red threshold: 10   Orange threshold: 5   Yellow threshold: 1

Name: icmpInErrors   MIB: RFC-1213
OID: 1.3.6.1.2.1.5.2

Instantiated by: 0

Description:

The total number of ICMP messages received by this device that
could not be processed due to errors. These are generally caused by
corruption.

Returns: counter   Suggested poll period: 4
Preprocessing: rate   Threshold comparison: >

Red threshold: 10   Orange threshold: 1   Yellow threshold:

Name: icmpInDestUnreachs   MIB: RFC-1213
OID: 1.3.6.1.2.1.5.3

Instantiated by: 0

Description:

The total number of ICMP destination unreachable messages received
by this device. This often indicates either routing convergence
problems or misconfigured applications that attempt connections to
inaccessible addresses.

Returns: counter   Suggested poll period: 3
Preprocessing: rate   Threshold comparison: >

Red threshold: 10   Orange threshold: 5   Yellow threshold:

Name: icmpInTimeExcds   MIB: RFC-1213
OID: 1.3.6.1.2.1.5.4

Instantiated by: 0

Description:

The total number of ICMP TTL Exceeded messages received by this
device. In small volumes, this is often the result of traceroutes.
Larger volumes may indicate routing instability or loops.

Returns: counter   Suggested poll period: 10
Preprocessing: rate   Threshold comparison: >

Red threshold: 10   Orange threshold: 5   Yellow threshold:

Name: icmpInSrcQuenchs   MIB: RFC-1213
OID: 1.3.6.1.2.1.5.6

Instantiated by: 0

Description:

The total number of ICMP source quenches received by this device. In large volumes, this may indicate a need to tune traffic characteristics (e.g., via a TCP slow-start algorithm) or to upgrade the capacities of remote systems.

Returns: counter   Suggested poll period: 4
Preprocessing: rate   Threshold comparison: >

Red threshold: 10   Orange threshold: 1   Yellow threshold:

Name: icmpInRedirects   MIB: RFC-1213
OID: 1.3.6.1.2.1.5.7

Instantiated by: 0

Description:

The total number of ICMP redirects received by this device. This may indicate routing instability, or the misuse of static and default routes.

Returns: counter   Suggested poll period: 3
Preprocessing: rate   Threshold comparison: >

Red threshold: 10   Orange threshold: 1   Yellow threshold:

Name: icmpOutMsgs   MIB: RFC-1213
OID: 1.3.6.1.2.1.5.14

Instantiated by: 0

Description:

The total number of ICMP messages sent by this device. Some amount of ICMP may be expected, but bursts at high levels often indicate a problem.

Returns: counter   Suggested poll period: 10
Preprocessing: rate   Threshold comparison: >

Red threshold: 10   Orange threshold: 3   Yellow threshold:

Name: icmpOutErrors   MIB: RFC-1213
OID: 1.3.6.1.2.1.5.15

Instantiated by: 0

Description:

The total number of ICMP messages that could not be sent by this
device due to errors in the message. This is unusual and may
indicate a local configuration or hardware problem.

Returns: counter   Suggested poll period: 4
Preprocessing: rate   Threshold comparison: >

Red threshold: 10   Orange threshold: 1   Yellow threshold:

Name: icmpOutDestUnreachs   MIB: RFC-1213
OID: 1.3.6.1.2.1.5.16

Instantiated by: 0

Description:

The total number of ICMP destination unreachable messages sent by
this device. This often indicates either routing convergence
problems or clients with misconfigured applications that attempt
connections to inaccessible addresses.

Returns: counter   Suggested poll period: 3
Preprocessing: rate   Threshold comparison: >

Red threshold: 10   Orange threshold: 5   Yellow threshold:

Name: icmpOutTimeExcds   MIB: RFC-1213
OID: 1.3.6.1.2.1.5.17

Instantiated by: 0

Description:

The total number of ICMP TTL Exceeded messages sent by this device.
In small volumes, this is often the result of traceroutes. Larger
volumes may indicate routing instability or loops.

Returns: counter   Suggested poll period: 10
Preprocessing: rate   Threshold comparison: >

Red threshold: 10   Orange threshold: 5   Yellow threshold:

Name: icmpOutSrcQuenchs   MIB: RFC-1213
OID: 1.3.6.1.2.1.5.19

Instantiated by: 0

Description:

The total number of ICMP source quenches sent by this device. In
large volumes, this may indicate a need to tune client traffic
characteristics (e.g. via a TCP slow-start algorithm) or to upgrade
the capacity of this device.

Returns: counter   Suggested poll period: 4
Preprocessing: rate   Threshold comparison: >

Red threshold: 10   Orange threshold: 1   Yellow threshold:

Name: icmpOutRedirects   MIB: RFC-1213
OID: 1.3.6.1.2.1.5.20

Instantiated by: 0

Description:

The total number of ICMP redirects sent by this device. This may
indicate routing instability, or the misuse of static and default
routes on other directly accessible systems.

Returns: counter   Suggested poll period: 3
Preprocessing: rate   Threshold comparison: >

Red threshold: 10   Orange threshold: 1   Yellow threshold:

Name: ifOperStatus   MIB: RFC-1213
OID: 1.3.6.1.2.1.2.2.1.8

Instantiated by: ifNumber

Description:

Indicates the state of each interface. Should be tested on those
interfaces that are marked administratively "up." Note that some
vendors, including Bay/Nortel routers, may not mark interface state
to "down," even when the physical media are disconnected.

Returns: integer   Suggested poll period: 10
Preprocessing: none   Threshold comparison: =

Red threshold: 2   Orange threshold: 3   Yellow threshold:

Name: ifInOctets   MIB: RFC-1213
OID: 1.3.6.1.2.1.2.2.1.10

Instantiated by: ifNumber

Description:

Counts the number of bytes received by this interface. Thresholds provided are a percentage of the total interface bandwidth (as described by ifSpeed). Note that ifSpeed must be accurately set on some devices and is in units of bits. Also note that for half-duplex interfaces, the combination of ifInOctets plus ifOutOctets yields the value to be thresholded.

Returns: counter   Suggested poll period: 300
Preprocessing: rate   Threshold comparison: >

Red threshold: 90%   Orange threshold: 80%   Yellow threshold: 70%

Name: ifInOctets   MIB: RFC-1213
OID: 1.3.6.1.2.1.2.2.1.10

Instantiated by: ifNumber

Description:

Counts the number of bytes received by this interface. Thresholds provided are a percentage of the total interface bandwidth (as described by ifSpeed). Note that ifSpeed must be accurately set on some devices and is in units of bits. Also note that for half-duplex interfaces, the combination of ifInOctets plus ifOutOctets yields the value to be thresholded. This second test specifically looks for underutilized interfaces, which may suggest a routing problem.

Returns: counter   Suggested poll period: 300
Preprocessing: rate   Threshold comparison: <

Red threshold: Orange threshold: Yellow threshold: .05%

Name: ifOutOctets   MIB: RFC-1213
OID: 1.3.6.1.2.1.2.2.1.16

Instantiated by: ifNumber

Description:

Counts the number of bytes sent on this interface. Thresholds provided are a percentage of the total interface bandwidth (as described by ifSpeed). Note that ifSpeed must be accurately set on some devices and is in units of bits. Also note that for half-duplex interfaces, the combination of ifInOctets plus ifOutOctets yields the value to be thresholded.

Returns: counter	Suggested poll period: 300
Preprocessing: rate	Threshold comparison: >

Red threshold: 90%   Orange threshold: 80%   Yellow threshold: 70%

Name: ifOutOctets   MIB: RFC-1213
OID: 1.3.6.1.2.1.2.2.1.16

Instantiated by: ifNumber

Description:

Counts the number of bytes sent on this interface. Thresholds provided are a percentage of the total interface bandwidth (as described by ifSpeed). Note that ifSpeed must be accurately set on some devices and is in units of bits. Also note that for half-duplex interfaces, the combination of ifInOctets plus ifOutOctets yields the value to be thresholded. This second test specifically looks for underutilized interfaces, which may suggest a routing problem.

Returns: counter	Suggested poll period: 300
Preprocessing: rate	Threshold comparison: <

Red threshold: Orange threshold: Yellow threshold: .05%

Name: ifInUcastPkts   MIB: RFC-1213
OID: 1.3.6.1.2.1.2.2.1.11

Instantiated by: ifNumber

Description:

Counts the number of unicast packets received by this interface.
Thresholds here should be computed as a percentage of the interface
speed (converted to bytes) divided by the typical packet size. Note
that for half-duplex interfaces, the combination of ifInUcastPkts
plus ifOutUcastPkts yields the value to be thresholded.

Returns: counter   Suggested poll period: 300
Preprocessing: rate   Threshold comparison: >

Red threshold: 90% Orange threshold: 80% Yellow threshold: 70%

Name: ifOutUcastPkts   MIB: RFC-1213
OID: 1.3.6.1.2.1.2.2.1.17

Instantiated by: ifNumber

Description:

Counts the number of unicast packets sent on this interface.
Thresholds here should be computed as a percentage of the interface
speed (converted to bytes) divided by the typical packet size. Note
that for half-duplex interfaces, the combination of ifInUcastPkts
plus ifOutUcastPkts yields the value to be thresholded.

Returns: counter   Suggested poll period: 300
Preprocessing: rate   Threshold comparison: >

Red threshold: 90% Orange threshold: 80% Yellow threshold: 70%

Name: ifInNUcastPkts   MIB: RFC-1213
OID: 1.3.6.1.2.1.2.2.1.12

Instantiated by: ifNumber

Description:

Counts the number of non-unicast (multicast plus broadcast) packets received by this interface. Thresholds here should be computed as a percentage of the interface speed (converted to bytes) divided by the typical packet size. Note that for half-duplex interfaces, the combination of ifInUcastPkts plus ifOutUcastPkts yields the value to be thresholded. This object will depreciate should RFC 1573 become a standard, and is replaced by IfInMulticast Pkts and IfInBroadcast Pkts.

Returns: counter	Suggested poll period: 300
Preprocessing: rate	Threshold comparison: >

Red threshold: 25%   Orange threshold: 20%   Yellow threshold: 10%

Name: ifOutNUcastPkts   MIB: RFC-1213
OID: 1.3.6.1.2.1.2.2.1.18

Instantiated by: ifNumber

Description:

Counts the number of non-unicast (multicast plus broadcast) packets sent on this interface. Thresholds here should be computed as a percentage of the interface speed (converted to bytes) divided by the typical packet size. Note that for half-duplex interfaces, the combination of ifInUcastPkts plus ifOutUcastPkts yields the value to be thresholded. This object will depreciate should RFC 1573 become a standard, and is replaced by IfOutMulticast Pkts and IfOutBroadcast Pkts.

Returns: counter	Suggested poll period: 300
Preprocessing: rate	Threshold comparison: >

Red threshold: 25%   Orange threshold: 20%   Yellow threshold: 10%

Name: ifInErrors   MIB: RFC-1213
OID: 1.3.6.1.2.1.2.2.1.14

Instantiated by: ifNumber

Description:

Counts the number of packets received by this interface that contained errors at the MAC layer (layer 2). This is generally the result of corruption.

Returns: counter   Suggested poll period: 5
Preprocessing: rate   Threshold comparison: >

Red threshold: 10   Orange threshold: 6   Yellow threshold: 2

Name: ifOutErrors   MIB: RFC-1213
OID: 1.3.6.1.2.1.2.2.1.20

Instantiated by: ifNumber

Description:

Counts the number of packets that could not be sent on this interface because of errors at the MAC layer (layer 2). This is unusual, and may indicate a hardware problem.

Returns: counter   Suggested poll period: 5
Preprocessing: rate   Threshold comparison: >

Red threshold: 10   Orange threshold: 6   Yellow threshold: 2

Name: ifInDiscards   MIB: RFC-1213
OID: 1.3.6.1.2.1.2.2.1.13

Instantiated by: ifNumber

Description:

Counts the number of packets that were dropped inbound on this interface (at the MAC layer), even though they were not in error. This generally indicates a local resource problem on the hardware, but can also be the result of filters.

Returns: counter   Suggested poll period: 5
Preprocessing: rate   Threshold comparison: >

Red threshold: 20   Orange threshold: 10   Yellow threshold: 1

Name: ifOutDiscards   MIB: RFC-1213
OID: 1.3.6.1.2.1.2.2.1.19

Instantiated by: ifNumber

Description:

Counts the number of packets that were dropped outbound on this
interface (at the MAC layer), even though they were not in error.
This generally indicates a local resource problem on the hardware
or media, but can also be the result of filters.

Returns: counter   Suggested poll period: 5
Preprocessing: rate   Threshold comparison: >

Red threshold: 20   Orange threshold: 10   Yellow threshold: 1

Name: ifInUnknownProtos   MIB: RFC-1213
OID: 1.3.6.1.2.1.2.2.1.15

Instantiated by: ifNumber

Description:

Counts the number of packets received by this interface and then
dropped because they specified an unsupported layer 3 protocol.
These are generally non-unicast packets that were not meant to be
delivered to this device. These packets consume both device and
infrastructure resources.

Returns: counter   Suggested poll period: 10

Preprocessing: rate   Threshold comparison: >

Red threshold: 5   Orange threshold: 0   Yellow threshold:

802.1d Bridges

Name: dot1dStpTopChanges   MIB: RFC-1493

OID: 1.3.6.1.2.1.17.2.4

Instantiated by: 0

Description:

The total number of topology updates received by this box. Occasional updates are normal, but higher levels suggest flapping interfaces and an unstable infrastructure.

Returns: counter   Suggested poll period: 6

Preprocessing: rate   Threshold comparison: >

Red threshold: 5   Orange threshold: 0   Yellow threshold:

Name: dot1dStpRootCost   MIB: RFC-1493

OID: 1.3.6.1.2.1.17.2.6

Instantiated by: 0

Description:

The cost, in hops, to the root node. Changes in cost suggest that the path to the root node is changing. This is generally unexpected and may indicate infrastructure instability or a need to fix the root node elsewhere.

Returns: integer   Suggested poll period: 5
Preprocessing: delta   Threshold comparison: !

Red threshold: Orange threshold: Yellow threshold: 0

Name: dot1dStpRootPort   MIB: RFC-1493
OID: 1.3.6.1.2.1.17.2.7

Instantiated by: 0

Description:

The port used to reach the root node. Changes indicate that the
path to the root node is not fixed. This is generally unexpected
and may indicate infrastructure instability.

Returns: integer   Suggested poll period: 7
Preprocessing: delta   Threshold comparison: !

Red threshold: Orange threshold: Yellow threshold: 0

Name: dot1dTpLearnedEntryDiscards   MIB: RFC-1493
OID: 1.3.6.1.2.1.17.4.1

Instantiated by: 0

Description:

The number of entries dropped from the 802.1 forwarding table, even
though they were considered valid. This should happen rarely or it
may indicate a need to increase the memory allocated to the table.

Returns: counter   Suggested poll period: 29
Preprocessing: delta   Threshold comparison: >

Red threshold: 10   Orange threshold: 0   Yellow threshold:

Name: dot1dBasePortDelayExceededDiscard MIB: RFC-1493
OID: 1.3.6.1.2.1.17.1.4.1.4

Instantiated by: dot1dBasePort (port number)

Description:

The number of packets dropped by this port because they remained
inside of the bridge for too long. This may indicate a resource
problem within the box or a need to upgrade congested interfaces to
a higher speed.

Returns: counter   Suggested poll period: 4
Preprocessing: rate   Threshold comparison: >

Red threshold: 10   Orange threshold: 5   Yellow threshold: 0

Name: dot1dBasePortMtuExceededDiscards   MIB: RFC-1493
OID: 1.3.6.1.2.1.17.1.4.1.5

Instantiated by: dot1dBasePort (port number)

Description:

The number of packets dropped by this port because they exceeded
the configured maximum size. This is unexpected and generally
indicates a configuration error.

Returns: counter   Suggested poll period: 4
Preprocessing: rate   Threshold comparison: >

Red threshold: 10   Orange threshold: 5   Yellow threshold: 0

Name: dot1dStpPortState   MIB: RFC-1493
OID: 1.3.6.1.2.1.17.2.15.1.3

Instantiated by: dot1dStpPort (port number)

Description:

The current state of this port. This should be tested on ports that are expected to be up and not blocked (if unsure, only test the red threshold for broken).

Returns: integer   Suggested poll period: 3
Preprocessing: none   Threshold comparison: =

Red threshold: 6   Orange threshold: 2   Yellow threshold: 1

Name: dot1dStpPortForwardTransitions   MIB: RFC-1493
OID: 1.3.6.1.2.1.17.2.15.1.10

Instantiated by: dot1dStpPort (port number)

Description:

The number of times this port has transitioned from learning to the forwarding state. This should be monitored on all ports that are expected to always be enabled (connected to routers or servers).

Returns: counter   Suggested poll period: 30
Preprocessing: delta   Threshold comparison: !

Red threshold: Orange threshold: 0   Yellow threshold:

FDDI

Name: fddimibMACCurrentPath   MIB: RFC-1512
OID: 1.3.6.1.2.1.10.15.73.2.2.1.8

Instantiated by: SmtIndex.MacIndex

Description:

The currently configured path, as determined by MAC. Note that acceptable values are a function of your specific topology.

Returns: integer   Suggested poll period: 2
Preprocessing: none   Threshold comparison: =

Red threshold: 1   Orange threshold: Yellow threshold:

Name: fddimibMACDupAddressTest   MIB: RFC-1512
OID: 1.3.6.1.2.1.10.15.73.2.2.1.13

Instantiated by: SmtIndex.MacIndex

Description:

If set to fail(3), there were two stations on the ring using the same MAC address the last time a test was run. This is generally a configuration problem.

Returns: integer   Suggested poll period: 600
Preprocessing: none   Threshold comparison: =

Red threshold: 3   Orange threshold: Yellow threshold:

Name: fddimibMACErrorCts   MIB: RFC-1512
OID: 1.3.6.1.2.1.10.15.73.2.2.1.24

Instantiated by: SmtIndex.MacIndex

Description:

The number of layer 2 frames that were found by this MAC to be in error. This is generally due to data corruption between this MAC and its upstream neighbor.

Returns: counter   Suggested poll period: 45
Preprocessing: rate   Threshold comparison: >

Red threshold: 100   Orange threshold: 50   Yellow threshold: 10

Name: fddimibMACLostCts   MIB: RFC-1512
OID: 1.3.6.1.2.1.10.15.73.2.2.1.25

Instantiated by: SmtIndex.MacIndex

Description:

The number of frames stripped from the ring due to format errors.
This may indicate serious corruption or noise between this MAC and
its upstream neighbor.

Returns: counter   Suggested poll period: 45
Preprocessing: rate   Threshold comparison: >

Red threshold: 100   Orange threshold: 50   Yellow threshold: 10

Name: fddimibMACRMTState   MIB: RFC-1512
OID: 1.3.6.1.2.1.10.15.73.2.2.1.28

Instantiated by: SmtIndex.MacIndex

Description:

The current state of the MAC Ring Management (RMT) state machine.

Returns: integer   Suggested poll period: 5
Preprocessing: none   Threshold comparison: <

Red threshold: 2   Orange threshold: 7   Yellow threshold:

Name: fddimibMACDaFlag   MIB: RFC-1512
OID: 1.3.6.1.2.1.10.15.73.2.2.1.29

Instantiated by: SmtIndex.MacIndex

Description:

Ring Management detects another MAC on the ring using the same
address (frames destined to this MAC are already marked as
received). This is generally a configuration problem.

Returns: integer   Suggested poll period: 5
Preprocessing: none   Threshold comparison: =

Red threshold: 1   Orange threshold: Yellow threshold:

Name: fddimibMACUnaDaFlag   MIB: RFC-1512
OID: 1.3.6.1.2.1.10.15.73.2.2.1.30

Instantiated by: SmtIndex.MacIndex

Description:

The upstream neighbor detects another MAC on the ring using the
same address (frames destined to this MAC are already marked as
received). This is generally a configuration problem.

Returns: integer   Suggested poll period: 5
Preprocessing: none   Threshold comparison: =

Red threshold: 1   Orange threshold: Yellow threshold:

Name: fddimibMACFrameErrorFlag   MIB: RFC-1512
OID: 1.3.6.1.2.1.10.15.73.2.2.1.31

Instantiated by: SmtIndex.MacIndex

Description:

Flag indicating that the current frame error ratio exceeds its
preset threshold for this MAC.

Returns: integer   Suggested poll period: 4
Preprocessing: none   Threshold comparison: =

Red threshold: 1   Orange threshold: Yellow threshold:

Name: fddimibMACMAUnitdataAvailable   MIB: RFC-1512
OID: 1.3.6.1.2.1.10.15.73.2.2.1.32

Instantiated by: SmtIndex.MacIndex

Description:

A flag indicating whether or not Ring Management believes that this MAC is available.

Returns: integer   Suggested poll period: 10
Preprocessing: none   Threshold comparison: =

Red threshold: 1   Orange threshold: Yellow threshold:

Name: fddimibMACNotCopiedCts   MIB: RFC-1512
OID: 1.3.6.1.2.1.10.15.73.3.1.1.3

Instantiated by: SmtIndex.MacIndex

Description:

The number of frames addressed to this MAC but dropped due to a failure to copy to local buffers. This often indicates a resource problem on this card.

Returns: counter   Suggested poll period: 10
Preprocessing: rate   Threshold comparison: >

Red threshold: 10   Orange threshold: 5   Yellow threshold: 0

Name: fddimibPORTCurrentPath   MIB: RFC-1512
OID: 1.3.6.1.2.1.10.15.73.5.2.1.7

Instantiated by: SmtIndex.PORTIndex

Description:

The currently configured path as seen by this port. Acceptable values are a function of your specific topology, but this test looks for unexpected changes in state.

Returns: integer

Preprocessing: delta

Suggested poll period: 10

Threshold comparison: !

Red threshold: 0   Orange threshold: Yellow threshold:

Name: fddimibPORTLCTFailCts   MIB: RFC-1512

OID: 1.3.6.1.2.1.10.15.73.5.2.1.14

Instantiated by: SmtIndex.PORTIndex

Description:

The number of consecutive times the link confidence test has
failed. This may indicate corruption on or connectivity failure
within the ring.

Returns: counter

Preprocessing: rate

Suggested poll period: 1

Threshold comparison: >

Red threshold: 10   Orange threshold: 0   Yellow threshold:

Name: fddimibPORTLerEstimate   MIB: RFC-1512

OID: 1.3.6.1.2.1.10.15.73.5.2.1.15

Instantiated by: SmtIndex.PORTIndex

Description:

The current estimated, long-term link error rate. This is similar
to a telco bit error rate, and is expressed as 9 for 1 bit error in
10**9 bits sent. Note that many ports shut down if this value
reaches 7.

Returns: integer

Preprocessing: none

Suggested poll period: 600

Threshold comparison: <

Red threshold: 8   Orange threshold: 9   Yellow threshold: 10

Name: fddimibPORTLemCts   MIB: RFC-1512
OID: 1.3.6.1.2.1.10.15.73.5.2.1.17

Instantiated by: SmtIndex.PORTIndex

Description:

The total number of errors observed by the Link Error Monitor.

Returns: counter   Suggested poll period: 5
Preprocessing: rate   Threshold comparison: >

Red threshold: 500   Orange threshold: 100   Yellow threshold: 10

Name: fddimibPORTConnectState   MIB: RFC-1512
OID: 1.3.6.1.2.1.10.15.73.5.2.1.20

Instantiated by: SmtIndex.PORTIndex

Description:

The current state of this port. Note that acceptable values are a
function of your specific topology.

Returns: integer   Suggested poll period: 1
Preprocessing: none   Threshold comparison: <

Red threshold: 2   Orange threshold: 4   Yellow threshold:

Name: fddimibSMTCFState   MIB: RFC-1512
OID: 1.3.6.1.2.1.10.15.73.1.2.1.20

Instantiated by: SmtIndex

Description:

A flag indicating the current configuration of this entity as seen by Station Management (SMT). Acceptable values are a function of your specific topology and equipment, but this test looks for unexpected changes in state.

Returns: integer   Suggested poll period: 5
Preprocessing: delta   Threshold comparison: !

Red threshold: 0   Orange threshold: Yellow threshold:

Name: fddimibSMTRemoteDisconnectFlag   MIB: RFC-1512
OID: 1.3.6.1.2.1.10.15.73.1.2.1.21

Instantiated by: SmtIndex

Description:

A flag indicating that this station was remotely disconnected from the ring.

Returns: integer   Suggested poll period: 5
Preprocessing: none   Threshold comparison: =

Red threshold: 1   Orange threshold: Yellow threshold:

Name: fddimibSMTPeerWrapFlag   MIB: RFC-1512
OID: 1.3.6.1.2.1.10.15.73.1.2.1.23

Instantiated by: SmtIndex

Description:

A flag indicating that SMT believes this station is in a PEER_WRAP state (peer wraps back to this station). Acceptable values are a function of your topology.

Returns: integer   Suggested poll period: 5
Preprocessing: none   Threshold comparison: =

Red threshold: 1   Orange threshold: Yellow threshold:

Frame Relay

Name: frCircuitState   MIB: RFC-2115
OID: 1.3.6.1.2.1.10.32.2.1.3

Instantiated by: IfNumber.Dlci

Description:

The current state of this PVC. Note that the first instance
describes the interface number (the same value as used in the
interfaces table), and the second instance is the DLCI of the PVC.

Returns: integer   Suggested poll period: 9
Preprocessing: none   Threshold comparison: =

Red threshold: 3   Orange threshold: 1   Yellow threshold:

Name: frCircuitReceivedFECNs   MIB: RFC-2115
OID: 1.3.6.1.2.1.10.32.2.1.4

Instantiated by: IfNumber.Dlci

Description:

The total number of FECNs received on this PVC. This indicates
congestion along the forward path.

Returns: counter   Suggested poll period: 8
Preprocessing: rate   Threshold comparison: >

Red threshold: 50   Orange threshold: 25   Yellow threshold: 0

Name: frCircuitReceivedBECNs   MIB: RFC-2115
OID: 1.3.6.1.2.1.10.32.2.1.5

Instantiated by: IfNumber.Dlci

Description:

The total number of BECNs received on this PVC. This indicates
congestion along the reverse path (outbound on this PVC).

Returns: counter   Suggested poll period: 8
Preprocessing: rate   Threshold comparison: >

Red threshold: 50   Orange threshold: 25   Yellow threshold: 0

Name: frCircuitReceivedDEs   MIB: RFC-2115
OID: 1.3.6.1.2.1.10.32.2.1.18

Instantiated by: IfNumber.Dlci

Description:

The total number of frames received along the forward path that was
marked as "discard eligible." This indicates that the traffic in
the reverse direction (inbound) is exceeding its committed
information rate (CIR). If sustained, the CIR may need to be
increased.

Returns: counter   Suggested poll period: 8
Preprocessing: rate   Threshold comparison: >

Red threshold: 25   Orange threshold: 15   Yellow threshold: 1

ATM

Note that both the IETF and the ATM Forum defined ATM MIBs.
These objects reflect those originally found in RFC-1695, the
IETF's MIB.

Name: aal5VccCrcErrors   MIB: RFC-2515
OID: 1.3.6.1.2.1.37.1.12.1.3

Instantiated by: IfNumber.VccVpiIndex.VccVciIndex

Description:

The total number of packets assembled from AAL5 ATM cells that had CRC errors. This often indicates corruption on the circuit.

Returns: counter   Suggested poll period: 7
Preprocessing: rate   Threshold comparison: >

Red threshold: 30   Orange threshold: 20   Yellow threshold: 0

Name: aal5VccSarTimeOuts   MIB: RFC-2515
OID: 1.3.6.1.2.1.37.1.12.1.4

Instantiated by: IfNumber.VccVpiIndex.VccVciIndex

Description:

The total number of packets that could not be reassembled from AAL5 cells due to timeouts. This tends to indicate packet loss along the circuit.

Returns: counter   Suggested poll period: 7
Preprocessing: rate   Threshold comparison: >

Red threshold: 25   Orange threshold: 15   Yellow threshold: 0

Name: aal5VccOverSizedSDUs   MIB: RFC-2515
OID: 1.3.6.1.2.1.37.1.12.1.5

Instantiated by: IfNumber.VccVpiIndex.VccVciIndex

Description:

The total number of packets that could not be reassembled from AAL5 cells because they exceeded the maximum size. This generally indicates a configuration problem.

Returns: counter

Preprocessing: rate

Suggested poll period: 7

Threshold comparison: >

Red threshold: 25   Orange threshold: 5   Yellow threshold: 0

Name: atmInterfaceDs3PlcpSEFSs   MIB: RFC-2515
OID: 1.3.6.1.2.1.37.1.3.1.1

Instantiated by: IfNumber

Description:

The number of Severely Errored Framing Seconds detected on this ATM-
based DS3 interface. SEFS are seconds containing 44 or more Pulse
Code Violations, Out Of Frame indication, or the receipt of AIS.

Returns: counter

Preprocessing: delta

Suggested poll period: 23

Threshold comparison: >

Red threshold: 0   Orange threshold: Yellow threshold:

Name: atmInterfaceDs3PlcpAlarmState   MIB: RFC-2515
OID: 1.3.6.1.2.1.37.1.3.1.2

Instantiated by: IfNumber

Description:

The alarm state of this ATM-based DS3 interface. A value of 3
indicates a near-end Loss Of Frame (LOF) and a value of 2 indicates
a far-end alarm.

Returns: integer

Preprocessing: none

Suggested poll period: 19

Threshold comparison: =

Red threshold: 3   Orange threshold: 2   Yellow threshold:

Name: atmInterfaceDs3PlcpUASs   MIB: RFC-2515
OID: 1.3.6.1.2.1.37.1.3.1.3

Instantiated by: IfNumber

Description:

The total number of unavailable seconds on this ATM-based DS3
interface. Unavailable seconds are the result of 10 or more
contiguous Severely Errored Seconds.

Returns: counter   Suggested poll period: 61
Preprocessing: delta   Threshold comparison: >

Red threshold: 0   Orange threshold: Yellow threshold:

Name: atmInterfaceOCDEvents   MIB: RFC-2515
OID: 1.3.6.1.2.1.37.1.4.1.1

Instantiated by: IfNumber

Description:

The total number of "out of cell delineation" events on this ATM-
based DS3 OR SONET TC interface. Each event indicates 7 or more
consecutive cells with header errors.

Returns: counter   Suggested poll period: 7
Preprocessing: rate   Threshold comparison: >

Red threshold: 5   Orange threshold: 0   Yellow threshold:

Name: atmInterfaceTCAlarmState   MIB: RFC-2515
OID: 1.3.6.1.2.1.37.1.4.1.2

Instantiated by: IfNumber

Description:

The "tc alarm state" of this ATM-based DS3 or SONET TC interface. A value of 2 indicates a loss of cell delineation failure.

Returns: integer

Preprocessing: none

Suggested poll period: 9

Threshold comparison: =

Red threshold: 2   Orange threshold: Yellow threshold:

Name: atmVplOperStatus

OID: 1.3.6.1.2.1.37.1.6.1.3

MIB: RFC-2515

Instantiated by: IfNumber.VplVpiIndex

Description:

The state of the interface that represents this virtual path link. A value of 2 indicates that the path is down, whereas 3 means the path is in an unknown state.

Returns: integer

Preprocessing: none

Suggested poll period: 7

Threshold comparison: =

Red threshold: 2   Orange threshold: 3   Yellow threshold:

Name: atmVplLastChange

OID: 1.3.6.1.2.1.37.1.6.1.4

MIB: RFC-2515

Instantiated by: IfNumber.VplVpiIndex

Description:

The length of time since this virtual path link last changed state.

Returns: timeticks

Preprocessing: none

Suggested poll period: 59

Threshold comparison: <

Red threshold: 1200   Orange threshold: Yellow threshold:

DS1 (T1/E1)

The dsx1LineIndex generally equals the interface index from the interfaces table.

Name: dsx1LineType   MIB: RFC-2495
OID: 1.3.6.1.2.1.10.18.6.1.5

Instantiated by: dsx1LineIndex

Description:

Indicates the current configuration of this circuit. The object is monitored for any deltas, which might indicate an unexpected telco change.

Returns: integer   Suggested poll period: 11
Preprocessing: delta   Threshold comparison: !

Red threshold: 0   Orange threshold: Yellow threshold:

Name: dsx1LineCoding   MIB: RFC-2495
OID: 1.3.6.1.2.1.10.18.6.1.6

Instantiated by: dsx1LineIndex

Description:

Indicates the current coding of this circuit. The object is monitored for any deltas, which might indicate an unexpected telco change.

Returns: integer   Suggested poll period: 11
Preprocessing: delta   Threshold comparison: !

Red threshold: 0   Orange threshold: Yellow threshold:

Name: dsx1LoopbackConfig   MIB: RFC-2495
OID: 1.3.6.1.2.1.10.18.6.1.9

Instantiated by: dsx1LineIndex

Description:

Indicates that this circuit is currently looped.

Returns: integer   Suggested poll period: 11
Preprocessing: none   Threshold comparison: >

Red threshold: 1   Orange threshold: Yellow threshold:

Name: dsx1LineStatus   MIB: RFC-2495
OID: 1.3.6.1.2.1.10.18.6.1.10

Instantiated by: dsx1LineIndex

Description:

A bitmask indicating line status. This object is monitored for the
error considered most severe at the moment. If red, the line is
looped or there is another line/status error. If orange, a near-end
loss of signal has been detected. If yellow, there is a near-end
loss of frame.

Returns: integer   Suggested poll period: 3
Preprocessing: none   Threshold comparison: >

Red threshold: 255   Orange threshold: 63   Yellow threshold: 31

Name: dsx1TransmitClockSource   MIB: RFC-2495
OID: 1.3.6.1.2.1.10.18.6.1.12

Instantiated by: dsx1LineIndex

Description:

This object indicates the source of the transmit clock for the CSU
(internal or line). It is monitored for any change, which can
result from telco or far-end CSU configuration errors.

Returns: integer   Suggested poll period: 9
Preprocessing: delta   Threshold comparison: !

Red threshold: 0   Orange threshold: Yellow threshold:

Name: dsx1CurrentESs   MIB: RFC-2495
OID: 1.3.6.1.2.1.10.18.7.1.2

Instantiated by: dsx1LineIndex

Description:

The total number of Errored Seconds observed on this circuit in the
current 15-minute sample interval. Errored seconds are generally
those in which CRC6 errors have been detected. Note that this value
will reset at the end of the interval.

Returns: gauge   Suggested poll period: 6
Preprocessing: delta   Threshold comparison: >

Red threshold: 3   Orange threshold: 2   Yellow threshold: 1

Name: dsx1CurrentSESs   MIB: RFC-2495
OID: 1.3.6.1.2.1.10.18.7.1.3

Instantiated by: dsx1LineIndex

Description:

The total number of Severely Errored Seconds observed on this circuit in the current 15-minute sample interval. Severely Errored seconds are generally those in which more than 320 CRC6 errors have been detected. Note that this value will reset at the end of the interval.

Returns: gauge   Suggested poll period: 6

Preprocessing: delta   Threshold comparison: >

Red threshold: 3   Orange threshold: 2   Yellow threshold: 1

Name: dsx1CurrentSEFSs   MIB: RFC-2495

OID: 1.3.6.1.2.1.10.18.7.1.4

Instantiated by: dsx1LineIndex

Description:

The total number of Severely Errored Framing Seconds observed on this circuit in the current 15-minute sample interval. Severely Errored Framing seconds are generally those in which more than 7 framing errors have been detected. Note that this value will reset at the end of the interval.

Returns: gauge   Suggested poll period: 6

Preprocessing: delta   Threshold comparison: >

Red threshold: 3   Orange threshold: 2   Yellow threshold: 1

Name: dsx1CurrentUASs   MIB: RFC-2495

OID: 1.3.6.1.2.1.10.18.7.1.5

Instantiated by: dsx1LineIndex

Description:

The total number of Unavailable Seconds observed on this circuit in the current 15-minute sample interval. Note that this value will reset at the end of the interval.

Returns: gauge

Suggested poll period: 6

Preprocessing: delta

Threshold comparison: >

Red threshold: 3   Orange threshold: 2   Yellow threshold: 0

Name: dsx1CurrentCSSs   MIB: RFC-2495
OID: 1.3.6.1.2.1.10.18.7.1.6

Instantiated by: dsx1LineIndex

Description:

The total number of Controlled Slip Seconds observed on this
circuit in the current 15-minute sample interval. Controlled slip
seconds are those in which frame slips have been detected, and may
indicate the presence of a malfunctioning telco DACS or MUX. Note
that this value will reset at the end of the interval.

Returns: gauge

Suggested poll period: 6

Preprocessing: delta

Threshold comparison: >

Red threshold: 3   Orange threshold: 2   Yellow threshold: 0

Name: dsx1CurrentPCVs   MIB: RFC-2495
OID: 1.3.6.1.2.1.10.18.7.1.7

Instantiated by: dsx1LineIndex

Description:

The total number of Path Coding Violations observed on this circuit
in the current 15-minute sample interval. Note that this value will
reset at the end of the interval.

Returns: gauge

Suggested poll period: 5

Preprocessing: delta

Threshold comparison: >

Red threshold: 15   Orange threshold: 10   Yellow threshold: 0

Name: dsx1CurrentLESs   MIB: RFC-2495
OID: 1.3.6.1.2.1.10.18.7.1.8

Instantiated by: dsx1LineIndex

Description:

The total number of Line Error Seconds observed on this circuit in
the current 15-minute sample interval. Note that this value will
reset at the end of the interval.

Returns: gauge   Suggested poll period: 6
Preprocessing: delta   Threshold comparison: >

Red threshold: 3   Orange threshold: 2   Yellow threshold: 1

Name: dsx1CurrentBESs   MIB: RFC-2495
OID: 1.3.6.1.2.1.10.18.7.1.9

Instantiated by: dsx1LineIndex

Description:

The total number of Bursty Errored Seconds observed on this circuit
in the current 15-minute sample interval. Bursty Errored seconds
are those in which between 1 and 320 CRC6 errors have been
detected. Note that this value will reset at the end of the
interval.

Returns: gauge   Suggested poll period: 6
Preprocessing: delta   Threshold comparison: >

Red threshold: 3   Orange threshold: 2   Yellow threshold: 1

Name: dsx1CurrentLCVs   MIB: RFC-2495
OID: 1.3.6.1.2.1.10.18.7.1.11

Instantiated by: dsx1LineIndex

Description:

The total number of Line Coding Violations observed on this circuit
in the current 15-minute sample interval. Line Coding Violations
are generally those in which CRC6 errors have been detected. Note
that this value will reset at the end of the interval.

Returns: gauge   Suggested poll period: 5
Preprocessing: delta   Threshold comparison: >

Red threshold: 15   Orange threshold: 10   Yellow threshold: 0

Name: dsx1FarEndCurrentESs   MIB: RFC-2495
OID: 1.3.6.1.2.1.10.18.10.1.4

Instantiated by: dsx1LineIndex

Description:

The total number of Errored Seconds observed on the remote end of
this circuit in the current 15-minute sample interval. Errored
seconds are generally those in which CRC6 errors have been
detected. Note that this value will reset at the end of the
interval.

Returns: gauge   Suggested poll period: 6
Preprocessing: delta   Threshold comparison: >

Red threshold: 3   Orange threshold: 2   Yellow threshold: 1

Name: dsx1FarEndCurrentSESs   MIB: RFC-2495
OID: 1.3.6.1.2.1.10.18.10.1.5

Instantiated by: dsx1LineIndex

Description:

The total number of Severely Errored Seconds observed on the far-end of this circuit in the current 15-minute sample interval. Severely Errored seconds are generally those in which over 320 CRC6 errors have been detected. Note that this value will reset at the end of the interval.

Returns: gauge   Suggested poll period: 6

Preprocessing: delta   Threshold comparison: >

Red threshold: 3   Orange threshold: 2   Yellow threshold: 1

Name: dsx1FarEndCurrentSEFSs   MIB: RFC-2495

OID: 1.3.6.1.2.1.10.18.10.1.6

Instantiated by: dsx1LineIndex

Description:

The total number of Severely Errored Framing Seconds observed on the remote end of this circuit in the current 15-minute sample interval. Severely Errored Framing seconds are generally those in which over 7 framing errors have been detected. Note that this value will reset at the end of the interval.

Returns: gauge   Suggested poll period: 6

Preprocessing: delta   Threshold comparison: >

Red threshold: 3   Orange threshold: 2   Yellow threshold: 1

Name: dsx1FarEndCurrentUASs   MIB: RFC-2495

OID: 1.3.6.1.2.1.10.18.10.1.7

Instantiated by: dsx1LineIndex

Description:

The total number of Unavailable Seconds observed on the far-end of this circuit in the current 15-minute sample interval. Note that this value will reset at the end of the interval.

Returns: gauge   Suggested poll period: 6

Preprocessing: delta   Threshold comparison: >

Red threshold: 3   Orange threshold: 2   Yellow threshold: 0

Name: dsx1FarEndCurrentCSSs   MIB: RFC-2495

OID: 1.3.6.1.2.1.10.18.10.1.8

Instantiated by: dsx1LineIndex

Description:

The total number of Controlled Slip Seconds observed on the remote end of this circuit in the current 15-minute sample interval. Controlled slip seconds are those in which frame slips have been detected, and may indicate the presence of a malfunctioning telco DACS or MUX. Note that this value will reset at the end of the interval.

Returns: gauge   Suggested poll period: 6

Preprocessing: delta   Threshold comparison: >

Red threshold: 3   Orange threshold: 2   Yellow threshold: 0

Name: dsx1FarEndCurrentPCVs   MIB: RFC-2495

OID: 1.3.6.1.2.1.10.18.10.1.10

Instantiated by: dsx1LineIndex

Description:

The total number of Path Coding Violations observed on the remote end of this circuit in the current 15-minute sample interval. Note that this value will reset at the end of the interval.

Returns: gauge

Preprocessing: delta

Suggested poll period: 5

Threshold comparison: >

Red threshold: 15   Orange threshold: 10   Yellow threshold: 0

Name: dsx1FarEndCurrentLESs   MIB: RFC-2495
OID: 1.3.6.1.2.1.10.18.10.1.9

Instantiated by: dsx1LineIndex

Description:

The total number of Line Error Seconds observed on the remote end of this circuit in the current 15-minute sample interval. Note that this value will reset at the end of the interval.

Returns: gauge

Preprocessing: delta

Suggested poll period: 6

Threshold comparison: >

Red threshold: 3   Orange threshold: 2   Yellow threshold: 1

Name: dsx1FarEndCurrentBESs   MIB: RFC-2495
OID: 1.3.6.1.2.1.10.18.10.1.11

Instantiated by: dsx1LineIndex

Description:

The total number of Bursty Errored Seconds observed on the remote end of this circuit in the current 15-minute sample interval. Bursty Errored seconds are those in which between 1 and 320 CRC6 errors have been detected. Note that this value will reset at the end of the interval.

Returns: gauge   Suggested poll period: 6
Preprocessing: delta   Threshold comparison: >

Red threshold: 3   Orange threshold: 2   Yellow threshold: 1

DS3 (T3/E3)

The dsx3LineIndex generally equals the interface index from the
interfaces table.

Name: dsx3LineStatus   MIB: RFC-2496
OID: 1.3.6.1.2.1.10.30.5.1.10

Instantiated by: dsx3LineIndex

Description:

Bitmask tested for most severe error at the time. Red indicates
that the line is looped, the CSU is receiving an unavailable
signal, or the carrier equipment is out of service. Orange
indicates a near-end loss of signal, whereas yellow means a near-
end loss of frame.

Returns: integer   Suggested poll period: 25
Preprocessing: none   Threshold comparison: >

Red threshold: 255   Orange threshold: 63   Yellow threshold: 31

Name: dsx3TransmitClockSource   MIB: RFC-2495
OID: 1.3.6.1.2.1.10.30.5.1.11

Instantiated by: dsx3LineIndex

Description:

This object indicates the source of the transmit clock for the CSU (internal or line). It is monitored for any change, which can result from telco or far-end CSU configuration errors.

Returns: integer   Suggested poll period: 11
Preprocessing: delta   Threshold comparison: !

Red threshold: 0   Orange threshold: Yellow threshold:

Name: dsx3CurrentPESs   MIB: RFC-2495
OID: 1.3.6.1.2.1.10.30.6.1.2

Instantiated by: dsx3LineIndex

Description:

Count of the total number of Pbit Errored Seconds in the current 15-minute sample interval. PESs are seconds that contain Pbit Coding Violations, Out Of Frame indications, or AIS ("Blue" alarm). Note that this value will reset at the end of the interval.

Returns: gauge   Suggested poll period: 6
Preprocessing: delta   Threshold comparison: >

Red threshold: 3   Orange threshold: 2   Yellow threshold: 1

Name: dsx3CurrentPSESs   MIB: RFC-2495
OID: 1.3.6.1.2.1.10.30.6.1.3

Instantiated by: dsx3LineIndex

Description:

Count of the total number of Pbit Severely Errored Seconds in the current 15-minute sample interval. PSESs are seconds that contain 44 or more Path Coding Violations, Out Of Frame errors, or AIS ("Blue" alarm) indications. Note that this value will reset at the end of the interval.

Returns: gauge

Preprocessing: delta

Suggested poll period: 27

Threshold comparison: >

Red threshold: 0   Orange threshold: Yellow threshold:

Name: dsx3CurrentSEFSs

OID: 1.3.6.1.2.1.10.30.6.1.4

MIB: RFC-2495

Instantiated by: dsx3LineIndex

Description:

Count of the total number of Severely Errored Framing Seconds in
the current 15-minute sample interval. SEFSs are seconds that
contain Out Of Frame indications or AIS ("Blue" alarm). Note that
this value will reset at the end of the interval.

Returns: gauge

Preprocessing: delta

Suggested poll period: 27

Threshold comparison: >

Red threshold: 0   Orange threshold: Yellow threshold:

Name: dsx3CurrentUASs

OID: 1.3.6.1.2.1.10.30.6.1.5

MIB: RFC-2495

Instantiated by: dsx3LineIndex

Description:

Count of the total number of Unavailable Seconds in the current 15-
minute sample interval. UASs are seconds following 10 or more
contiguous PSESs. Note that this value will reset at the end of the
interval.

Returns: gauge

Preprocessing: delta

Suggested poll period: 61

Threshold comparison: >

Red threshold: 0   Orange threshold: Yellow threshold:

Name: dsx3CurrentLCVs   MIB: RFC-2495
OID: 1.3.6.1.2.1.10.30.6.1.6

Instantiated by: dsx3LineIndex

Description:

Count of the total number of Line Coding Violations in the current
15-minute sample interval. LCVs are pulses of the same polarity as
the previous pulse without zero substitutions (excessive zeros and
related errors). Note that this value will reset at the end of the
interval.

Returns: gauge   Suggested poll period: 5
Preprocessing: delta   Threshold comparison: >

Red threshold: 10   Orange threshold: 5   Yellow threshold: 0

Name: dsx3CurrentPCVs   MIB: RFC-2495
OID: 1.3.6.1.2.1.10.30.6.1.7

Instantiated by: dsx3LineIndex

Description: Pbit Coding Violations

Count of the total number of Pbit Coding Violations in the current
15-minute sample interval. PCVs are Pbit parity errors on the M
frame. Note that this value will reset at the end of the interval.

Returns: gauge   Suggested poll period: 5
Preprocessing: delta   Threshold comparison: >

Red threshold: 10   Orange threshold: 5   Yellow threshold: 0

Name: dsx3CurrentLESs   MIB: RFC-2495
OID: 1.3.6.1.2.1.10.30.6.1.8

Instantiated by: dsx3LineIndex

Description:

Count of the total number of Line Errored Seconds in the current
15-minute sample interval. LESs are seconds that contain Coding
Violations or Loss Of Signal. Note that this value will reset at
the end of the interval.

Returns: gauge   Suggested poll period: 6
Preprocessing: delta   Threshold comparison: >

Red threshold: 0   Orange threshold: Yellow threshold:

Name: dsx3CurrentCCVs   MIB: RFC-2495
OID: 1.3.6.1.2.1.10.30.6.1.9

Instantiated by: dsx3LineIndex

Description:

Count of the total number of Cbit Coding Violations in the current
15-minute sample interval. CCVs are Cbit parity errors or other
Coding Violations (if using SYNTRAN). Note that this value will
reset at the end of the interval.

Returns: gauge   Suggested poll period: 5
Preprocessing: delta   Threshold comparison: >

Red threshold: 10   Orange threshold: 5   Yellow threshold: 0

Name: dsx3CurrentCESs   MIB: RFC-2495
OID: 1.3.6.1.2.1.10.30.6.1.10

Instantiated by: dsx3LineIndex

Description:

Count of the total number of Cbit Errored Seconds in the current
15-minute sample interval. CESs are seconds that contain CCVs, OOF,
or AIS. Note that this value will reset at the end of the interval.

Returns: gauge   Suggested poll period: 6
Preprocessing: delta   Threshold comparison: >

Red threshold: 0   Orange threshold: Yellow threshold:

Name: dsx3CurrentCSESs   MIB: RFC-2495
OID: 1.3.6.1.2.1.10.30.6.1.11

Instantiated by: dsx3LineIndex

Description:

Count of the total number of Cbit Severely Errored Seconds in the
current 15-minute sample interval. CSESs are seconds that contain
44 or more CCVs or any OOF or AIS indications. Note that this value
will reset at the end of the interval.

Returns: gauge   Suggested poll period: 6
Preprocessing: delta   Threshold comparison: >

Red threshold: 0   Orange threshold: Yellow threshold:

Name: dsx3FarEndCurrentUASs   MIB: RFC-2495
OID: 1.3.6.1.2.1.10.30.10.1.7

Instantiated by: dsx3LineIndex

Description:

Count of the total number of Unavailable Seconds observed on the
far end of this circuit in the current 15-minute sample interval.
UASs are seconds following 10 or more contiguous PSESs. Note that
this value will reset at the end of the interval.

Returns: gauge

Preprocessing: delta

Suggested poll period: 61

Threshold comparison: >

Red threshold: 0   Orange threshold: Yellow threshold:

Name: dsx3FarEndCurrentCCVs

OID: 1.3.6.1.2.1.10.30.10.1.6

MIB: RFC-2495

Instantiated by: dsx3LineIndex

Description:

Count of the total number of Cbit Coding Violations observed on the far end of this circuit in the current 15-minute sample interval. CCVs are Cbit parity errors or other Coding Violations (if using SYNTRAN). Note that this value will reset at the end of the interval.

Returns: gauge

Preprocessing: delta

Suggested poll period: 5

Threshold comparison: >

Red threshold: 10   Orange threshold: 5   Yellow threshold: 0

Name: dsx3FarEndCurrentCESs

OID: 1.3.6.1.2.1.10.30.10.1.4

MIB: RFC-2495

Instantiated by: dsx3LineIndex

Description:

Count of the total number of Cbit Errored Seconds observed on the far end of this circuit in the current 15-minute sample interval. CESs are seconds that contain CCVs, OOF, or AIS. Note that this value will reset at the end of the interval.

Returns: gauge

Preprocessing: delta

Suggested poll period: 6

Threshold comparison: >

Red threshold: 0   Orange threshold: Yellow threshold:

Name: dsx3FarEndCurrentCSESs   MIB: RFC-2495
OID: 1.3.6.1.2.1.10.30.10.1.5

Instantiated by: dsx3LineIndex

Description:

Count of the total number of Cbit Severely Errored Seconds observed on the far end of this circuit in the current 15-minute sample interval. CSESs are seconds that contain 44 or more CCVs, or any OOF or AIS indications. Note that this value will reset at the end of the interval.

Returns: gauge   Suggested poll period: 6
Preprocessing: delta   Threshold comparison: >

Red threshold: 0   Orange threshold: Yellow threshold:

Ethernet

Name: dot3StatsAlignmentErrors   MIB: RFC-1643
OID: 1.3.6.1.2.1.10.7.2.1.2

Instantiated by: ifNumber

Description:

The total number of frames received by this interface that failed to end on an 8-bit boundary. These are often caused by high levels of collisions, resulting in fragments. Collision rates, end-end propegation.delay, and the use of cutthrough switches are common causes of this error.

Returns: counter   Suggested poll period: 3
Preprocessing: rate   Threshold comparison: >

Red threshold: 100   Orange threshold: 50   Yellow threshold: 10

Name: dot3StatsFCSErrors   MIB: RFC-1643
OID: 1.3.6.1.2.1.10.7.2.1.3

Instantiated by: ifNumber

Description:

The total number of packets received by this interface that failed
the layer 2 checksum (CRC-16). Packet corruption can be caused by
noisy environments, bad hardware, and faulty cable.

Returns: counter   Suggested poll period: 5
Preprocessing: rate   Threshold comparison: >

Red threshold: 50   Orange threshold: 10   Yellow threshold: 1

Name: dot3StatsSingleCollisionFrames   MIB: RFC-1643
OID: 1.3.6.1.2.1.10.7.2.1.4

Instantiated by: ifNumber

Description:

The total number of frames successfully transmitted by this
interface that were deferred due to exactly one collision. This is
an early indication of congestion.

Returns: counter   Suggested poll period: 7
Preprocessing: rate   Threshold comparison: >

Red threshold: 100   Orange threshold: 80   Yellow threshold: 60

Name: dot3StatsMultipleCollisionFrames   MIB: RFC-1643
OID: 1.3.6.1.2.1.10.7.2.1.5

Instantiated by: ifNumber

Description:

The total number of frames successfully transmitted by this
interface that were deferred due to more than one collision. This
is an active indication of congestion.

Returns: counter   Suggested poll period: 7
Preprocessing: rate   Threshold comparison: >

Red threshold: 50   Orange threshold: 25   Yellow threshold: 5

Name: dot3StatsDeferredTransmissions   MIB: RFC-1643
OID: 1.3.6.1.2.1.10.7.2.1.7

Instantiated by: ifNumber

Description:

The total number of frames successfully transmitted by this
interface that were deferred without experiencing collisions. This
is an early indicator of congestion and suggests possible building
output queues.

Returns: counter   Suggested poll period: 10
Preprocessing: rate   Threshold comparison: >

Red threshold: 500   Orange threshold: 100   Yellow threshold: 10

Name: dot3StatsExcessiveCollisions   MIB: RFC-1643
OID: 1.3.6.1.2.1.10.7.2.1.9

Instantiated by: ifNumber

Description:

The total number of frames unsuccessfully transmitted by this
interface because they experienced 16 collisions and were
discarded. This is a dramatic indicator of congestion.

Returns: counter   Suggested poll period: 30
Preprocessing: rate   Threshold comparison: >

Red threshold: 10   Orange threshold: 5   Yellow threshold: 0

Name: dot3StatsInternalMacTransmitErrors MIB: RFC-1643
OID: 1.3.6.1.2.1.10.7.2.1.10

Instantiated by: ifNumber

Description:

The total number of frames unsuccessfully transmitted because of an
internal error in the MAC layer. This is often transmit underruns,
caused by the inability of the ethernet controller to replenish the
transmit FIFO.

Returns: counter   Suggested poll period: 7
Preprocessing: rate   Threshold comparison: >

Red threshold: 10   Orange threshold: 6   Yellow threshold: 1

Name: dot3StatsCarrierSenseErrors   MIB: RFC-1643
OID: 1.3.6.1.2.1.10.7.2.1.11

Instantiated by: ifNumber

Description:

The total number of frames unsuccessfully transmitted by this
interface because carrier sense was lost or never asserted during
transmission. This suggests an intermittent hardware or cable fault.

Returns: counter   Suggested poll period: 7
Preprocessing: rate   Threshold comparison: >

Red threshold: 10   Orange threshold: 5   Yellow threshold: 0

Name: dot3StatsFrameTooLongs   MIB: RFC-1643
OID: 1.3.6.1.2.1.10.7.2.1.13

Instantiated by: ifNumber

Description:

The total number of frames received by this interface that were
discarded because they exceeded the maximum receive packet size.

Returns: counter   Suggested poll period: 7
Preprocessing: rate   Threshold comparison: >

Red threshold: 10   Orange threshold: 6   Yellow threshold: 1

Name: dot3StatsInternalMacReceiveErrors MIB: RFC-1643
OID: 1.3.6.1.2.1.10.7.2.1.16

Instantiated by: ifNumber

Description:

The total number of frames unsuccessfully received because of an
internal error in the MAC layer. This is often receive overruns,
caused by the inability of the ethernet controller to empty the
receive FIFO.

Returns: counter   Suggested poll period: 7
Preprocessing: rate   Threshold comparison: >

Red threshold: 10   Orange threshold: 6   Yellow threshold: 1

Token Ring

Name: dot5RingStatus   MIB: RFC-1748
OID: 1.3.6.1.2.1.10.9.1.1.3

Instantiated by: ifNumber

Description:

A bitmask indicating ring status as seen by this interface. This object is monitored for the error considered most severe at the moment. If red, there is a hard error, signal loss, or the interface is not yet open. If orange, a beacon or soft error state has been detected. If yellow, there is an auto-remove error or wire fault.

Returns: integer   Suggested poll period: 2
Preprocessing: none   Threshold comparison: >

Red threshold: 16383   Orange threshold: 4095   Yellow threshold: 1023

Name: dot5RingState   MIB: RFC-1748
OID: 1.3.6.1.2.1.10.9.1.1.4

Instantiated by: ifNumber

Description:

The actual state of this interface. If red, there has been a ring failure. If orange, an open failure is reported. If yellow, the interface reports closed.

Returns: integer   Suggested poll period: 2
Preprocessing: none   Threshold comparison: =

Red threshold: 6   Orange threshold: 5   Yellow threshold: 2

Name: dot5RingOpenStatus   MIB: RFC-1748
OID: 1.3.6.1.2.1.10.9.1.1.5

Instantiated by: ifNumber

Description:

A state variable indicating the result of this interface's last
attempt to enter the ring. If red, the last attempt failed.

Returns: integer	Suggested poll period: 2
Preprocessing: none	Threshold comparison: <

Red threshold: 11   Orange threshold: Yellow threshold:

Name: dot5StatsLineErrors   MIB: RFC-1748
OID: 1.3.6.1.2.1.10.9.2.1.2

Instantiated by: ifNumber

Description:

The total number of times that a frame was copied or repeated with
the E bit set to 0, but an error was detected (either FCS or a
nondata bit between the start and end delimiters). This generally
indicates corruption between this station and the upstream
neighbor.

Returns: counter	Suggested poll period: 5
Preprocessing: rate	Threshold comparison: >

Red threshold: 50   Orange threshold: 10   Yellow threshold: 1

Name: dot5StatsBurstErrors   MIB: RFC-1748
OID: 1.3.6.1.2.1.10.9.2.1.3

Instantiated by: ifNumber

Description:

The total number of burst-5 errors seen by this interface. A burst-
5 error is declared when a station fails to see any clock
transitions for 5 consecutive half-bit times. This may indicate a
hardware failure or poorly seated cable.

Returns: counter   Suggested poll period: 4
Preprocessing: rate   Threshold comparison: >

Red threshold: 50   Orange threshold: 25   Yellow threshold: 5

Name: dot5StatsACErrors   MIB: RFC-1748
OID: 1.3.6.1.2.1.10.9.2.1.4

Instantiated by: ifNumber

Description:

The total number of times this station received an SMP frame with
the A and C bits set to zero immediately after an AMP or SMP frame
is received with the A and C bits set to zero (no intervening AMP
frame). This suggests a hardware failure in which an upstream
station is unable to correctly set the AC bits.

Returns: counter   Suggested poll period: 5
Preprocessing: rate   Threshold comparison: >

Red threshold: 10   Orange threshold: 5   Yellow threshold: 0

Name: dot5StatsAbortTransErrors   MIB: RFC-1748
OID: 1.3.6.1.2.1.10.9.2.1.5

Instantiated by: ifNumber

Description:

A count indicating the total number of times this station
transmitted an abort while sending a frame. This often indicates a
transmit FIFO underrun, likely due to buffer contention or CPU
overutilization on the card.

Returns: counter   Suggested poll period: 4
Preprocessing: rate   Threshold comparison: >

Red threshold: 25   Orange threshold: 15   Yellow threshold: 0

Name: dot5StatsInternalErrors   MIB: RFC-1748
OID: 1.3.6.1.2.1.10.9.2.1.6

Instantiated by: ifNumber

Description:

The total number of internal chipset errors reported by the MAC
layer of this station. This generally indicates a hardware failure.

Returns: counter   Suggested poll period: 5
Preprocessing: rate   Threshold comparison: >

Red threshold: 25   Orange threshold: 15   Yellow threshold: 0

Name: dot5StatsLostFrameErrors   MIB: RFC-1748
OID: 1.3.6.1.2.1.10.9.2.1.7

Instantiated by: ifNumber

Description:

The total number of times that this station failed to see the
trailer of a transmitted frame before its TRR timer expires. This
suggests that the frame was lost elsewhere on the ring prior to
being stripped.

Returns: counter   Suggested poll period: 4
Preprocessing: rate   Threshold comparison: >

Red threshold: 50   Orange threshold: 25   Yellow threshold: 5

Name: dot5StatsReceiveCongestions   MIB: RFC-1748
OID: 1.3.6.1.2.1.10.9.2.1.8

Instantiated by: ifNumber

Description:

The number of times that this interface dropped a frame addressed
to it because of a lack of buffers. Unless layer 2 traffic shaping
has been employed, this probably indicates a lack of resources
(buffers if the problem is seen in bursts, processing power or link
utilization if the counter constantly increments).

Returns: counter   Suggested poll period: 5
Preprocessing: rate   Threshold comparison: >

Red threshold: 50   Orange threshold: 25   Yellow threshold: 5

Name: dot5StatsFrameCopiedErrors   MIB: RFC-1748
OID: 1.3.6.1.2.1.10.9.2.1.9

Instantiated by: ifNumber

Description:

The number of times that this interface recognized a frame destined
to its particular address, but found the A bit set. This indicates
that the frame has already been received. Although possible that
this is the result of a failed strip, this is generally the result
of either noise or a duplicate MAC address.

Returns: counter   Suggested poll period: 4
Preprocessing: rate   Threshold comparison: >

Red threshold: 25   Orange threshold: 15   Yellow threshold: 0

Name: dot5StatsTokenErrors   MIB: RFC-1748
OID: 1.3.6.1.2.1.10.9.2.1.10

Instantiated by: ifNumber

Description:

The total number of times that this port, acting as the active monitor, detected a condition that required a new token to be transmitted. This is generally the result of a lost token.

Returns: counter   Suggested poll period: 3
Preprocessing: rate   Threshold comparison: >

Red threshold: 15   Orange threshold: 5   Yellow threshold: 0

Name: dot5StatsSoftErrors   MIB: RFC-1748
OID: 1.3.6.1.2.1.10.9.2.1.11

Instantiated by: ifNumber

Description:

The total number of recoverable errors detected by this port. These are often the result of frame corruption.

Returns: counter   Suggested poll period: 3
Preprocessing: rate   Threshold comparison: >

Red threshold: 50   Orange threshold: 25   Yellow threshold: 5

Name: dot5StatsHardErrors   MIB: RFC-1748
OID: 1.3.6.1.2.1.10.9.2.1.12

Instantiated by: ifNumber

Description:

The total number of temporarily fatal errors reported by this interface. Note that these are almost always due to the transmission or reception of beacon MAC frames.

Returns: counter   Suggested poll period: 4
Preprocessing: rate   Threshold Comparson: >

Red threshold: 50   Orange threshold: 25   Yellow threshold: 5

Name: dot5StatsSignalLoss   MIB: RFC-1748
OID: 1.3.6.1.2.1.10.9.2.1.13

Instantiated by: ifNumber

Description:

The total number of times that this station has detected a complete
loss of signal while inserted into the ring. This may be due to
intermittent cable connections or a hardware failure.

Returns: counter   Suggested poll period: 6
Preprocessing: delta   Threshold comparison: >

Red threshold: 10   Orange threshold: 5   Yellow threshold: 1

Name: dot5StatsTransmitBeacons   MIB: RFC-1748
OID: 1.3.6.1.2.1.10.9.2.1.14

Instantiated by: ifNumber

Description:

The total number of times that this port has transmitted a beacon
frame. This may indicate failing hardware.

Returns: counter   Suggested poll period: 3
Preprocessing: rate   Threshold comparison: >

Red threshold: 10   Orange threshold: 5   Yellow threshold: 1

Name: dot5StatsRecoverys   MIB: RFC-1748
OID: 1.3.6.1.2.1.10.9.2.1.15

Instantiated by: ifNumber

Description:

The number of times this station has observed ring purges. This is determined by counting the number of ring purge messages sent and received, and is an attempt to return to normal operating behavior.

Returns: counter   Suggested poll period: 4
Preprocessing: rate   Threshold comparison: >

Red threshold: 10   Orange threshold: 5   Yellow threshold: 2

Name: dot5StatsLobeWires   MIB: RFC-1748
OID: 1.3.6.1.2.1.10.9.2.1.16

Instantiated by: ifNumber

Description:

The number of times that this interface detected an open or short circuit (electrical failure). This will result in the interface being disabled.

Returns: counter   Suggested poll period: 5
Preprocessing: delta   Threshold comparison: >

Red threshold: 1   Orange threshold: 0   Yellow threshold:

Name: dot5StatsFreqErrors   MIB: RFC-1748
OID: 1.3.6.1.2.1.10.9.2.1.19

Instantiated by: ifNumber

Description:

The total number of times that this interface has detected a receive signal whose frequency fails to meet the 802.5 specification. This generally indicates a hardware failure between the port and its upstream neighbor, but can also result from poor cables and noise.

Returns: counter   Suggested poll period: 5
Preprocessing: rate   Threshold comparison: >

Red threshold: 5   Orange threshold: 0   Yellow threshold:

BGP

Name: bgpPeerState   MIB: RFC-1657
OID: 1.3.6.1.2.1.15.3.1.2

Instantiated by: peerAddress

Description:

A state variable, indicating the current status of the session with
this peer. If red, the session is not ESTABLISHED.

Returns: integer   Suggested poll period: 15
Preprocessing: none   Threshold comparison: !

Red threshold: 6   Orange threshold: Yellow threshold:

Name: bgpPeerInUpdates   MIB: RFC-1657
OID: 1.3.6.1.2.1.15.3.1.10

Instantiated by: peerAddress

Description:

The total number of BGP updates received from this peer. If high,
this peer may be destabilizing routing.

Returns: counter   Suggested poll period: 30
Preprocessing: rate   Threshold comparison: >

Red threshold: 75   Orange threshold: 50   Yellow threshold: 5

Name: bgpPeerOutUpdates   MIB: RFC-1657
OID: 1.3.6.1.2.1.15.3.1.11

Instantiated by: peerAddress

Description:

The total number of BGP updates received from this peer. If high,
this device may be destabilizing routing on the peer.

Returns: counter   Suggested poll period: 30
Preprocessing: rate   Threshold comparison: >

Red threshold: 75   Orange threshold: 50   Yellow threshold: 5

Name: bgpPeerFsmEstablishedTime   MIB: RFC-1657
OID: 1.3.6.1.2.1.15.3.1.16

Instantiated by: peerAddress

Description:

The total time since the referenced peering session last changed.
Note that we test for any state change.

Returns: gauge   Suggested poll period: 60
Preprocessing: none   Threshold comparison: <

Red threshold: 150   Orange threshold: Yellow threshold:

OSPF

Name: ospfExternLsaCount   MIB: RFC-1850
OID: 1.3.6.1.2.1.14.1.6

Instantiated by: 0

Description:

The total number of external (type 5) advertisements held in the link state database. Note that this is explicitly tested for a lack of any such entries.

Returns: gauge   Suggested poll period: 60
Preprocessing: none   Threshold comparison: =

Red threshold: 0   Orange threshold: Yellow threshold:

Name: ospfExternLsaCksumSum   MIB: RFC-1850
OID: 1.3.6.1.2.1.14.1.7

Instantiated by: 0

Description:

The sum of the checksum values computed across the external advertisements in the link state database. Changes in value indicate that the database has changed and suggest routing instability.

Returns: integer   Suggested poll period: 30
Preprocessing: delta   Threshold comparison: >

Red threshold: Orange threshold: Yellow threshold: 0

Name: ospfOriginateNewLsas   MIB: RFC-1850
OID: 1.3.6.1.2.1.14.1.9

Instantiated by: 0

Description:

The total number of unique Link State Announcements that this device has sent. This indicates routing updates that are being propagated by this device and suggest infrastructure instability.

Returns: counter   Suggested poll period: 60
Preprocessing: delta   Threshold comparison: >

Red threshold: 20   Orange threshold: 15   Yellow threshold: 5

Name: ospfRxNewLsas   MIB: RFC-1850
OID: 1.3.6.1.2.1.14.1.10

Instantiated by: 0

Description:

The total number of unique Link State Announcements that this
device has received. This indicates routing updates that are being
passed to this device and suggest infrastructure instability.

Returns: counter   Suggested poll period: 60
Preprocessing: delta   Threshold comparison: >

Red threshold: 40   Orange threshold: 30   Yellow threshold: 10

Name: ospfSpfRuns   MIB: RFC-1850
OID: 1.3.6.1.2.1.14.2.1.4

Instantiated by: ospfArea

Description:

The total number of times that the SPF algorithm has been run
against the link state database for the specified area. This is a
stronger indicator of changes to the route table than the
generation or reception of "new" LSAs.

Returns: counter   Suggested poll period: 15
Preprocessing: delta   Threshold comparison: >

Red threshold: 10   Orange threshold: 5   Yellow threshold: 0

Name: ospfAreaBdrRtrCount   MIB: RFC-1850
OID: 1.3.6.1.2.1.14.2.1.5

Instantiated by: ospfArea

Description:

The total number of border routers in the specified area, as
understood by this device. Zero border routers may indicate an
isolated area. Note that this is explicitly tested for a lack of
any such entries.

Returns: gauge   Suggested poll period: 45
Preprocessing: none   Threshold comparison: =

Red threshold: 0   Orange threshold: Yellow threshold:

Name: ospfAsBdrRtrCount   MIB: RFC-1850
OID: 1.3.6.1.2.1.14.2.1.6

Instantiated by: ospfArea

Description:

The total number of border routers in the specified AS, as
understood by this device. Zero border routers may indicate an
isolated AS. Note that this is explicitly tested for a lack of any
such entries.

Returns: gauge   Suggested poll period: 45
Preprocessing: none   Threshold comparison: =

Red threshold: 0   Orange threshold: Yellow threshold:

Name: ospfAreaLsaCksumSum   MIB: RFC-1850
OID: 1.3.6.1.2.1.14.2.1.8

Instantiated by: ospfArea

Description:

The sum of the checksum values computed across the area
advertisements in the link state database. Changes in value
indicate that the database has changed and suggest routing
instability.

Returns: integer   Suggested poll period: 30
Preprocessing: delta   Threshold comparison: !

Red threshold: Orange threshold: Yellow threshold: 0

Name: ospfIfState   MIB: RFC-1850
OID: 1.3.6.1.2.1.14.7.1.12

Instantiated by: ifIpAddr.addrlessIf

Description:

The state of the local OSPF interface. This is instantiated by the
interface's IP address and an addressless value, in case interfaces
on this device are not assigned individual IP addresses. Red
indicates a state of "down;" orange indicates a state of "looped."

Returns: integer   Suggested poll period: 7
Preprocessing: none   Threshold comparison: =

Red threshold: 1   Orange threshold: 2   Yellow threshold:

Name: ospfNbrState   MIB: RFC-1850
OID: 1.3.6.1.2.1.14.10.1.6

Instantiated by: nbrIpAddr.nbrAddrlessIf

Description:

The state of the OSPF neighbor's interface. This is instantiated by the interface's IP address and an addressless value, in case interfaces on that device are not assigned individual IP addresses. Red indicates a state of "down."

Returns: integer   Suggested poll period: 13
Preprocessing: none   Threshold comparison: =

Red threshold: 1   Orange threshold: Yellow threshold:

Name: ospfVirtIfState   MIB: RFC-1850
OID: 1.3.6.1.2.1.14.9.1.7

Instantiated by: virtIfAreaId.virtIfNeighbor

Description:

The state of the local OSPF virtual interface. This is instantiated by the interface's IP address and an addressless value, in case interfaces on this device are not assigned individual IP addresses. Red indicates a state of "down."

Returns: integer   Suggested poll period: 7
Preprocessing: none   Threshold comparison: =

Red threshold: 1   Orange threshold: Yellow threshold:

Name: ospfVirtNbrState   MIB: RFC-1850
OID: 1.3.6.1.2.1.14.11.1.5

Instantiated by: virtNbrAreaId.virtNbrNeighbor

Description:

The state of the OSPF neighbor's virtual interface. This is instantiated by the interface's IP address and an addressless value, in case interfaces on that device are not assigned individual IP addresses. Red indicates a state of "down."

Returns: integer   Suggested poll period: 13
Preprocessing: none   Threshold comparison: =

Red threshold: 1   Orange threshold: Yellow threshold:

DOCSIS Cable Modems

Name: docsIfDownChannelPower   MIB: RFC-2670
OID: 1.3.6.1.2.1.10.127.1.1.1.1.6

Instantiated by: ifNumber

Description:

The current downstream power, in dBmV, as received by this cable
modem or sent by the CMTS. Low power conditions can indicate
impedance, distance, or loading problems. This test should be run
at the CM.

Returns: integer   Suggested poll period: 11
Preprocessing: none   Threshold comparison: <

Red threshold: -75   Orange threshold: -70   Yellow threshold: -60

Name: docsIfSigQCorrecteds   MIB: RFC-2670
OID: 1.3.6.1.2.1.10.127.1.1.4.1.3

Instantiated by: ifNumber

Description:

The total number of corrupted codewords, received by this cable
modem, which were corrected. This indicates low levels of noise on
the downstream hfc plant. Note that this test is not run on a CMTS.

Returns: counter   Suggested poll period: 60
Preprocessing: delta   Threshold comparison: >

Red threshold: 50   Orange threshold: 30   Yellow threshold: 10

Name: docsIfSigQUncorrectables   MIB: RFC-2670
OID: 1.3.6.1.2.1.10.127.1.1.4.1.4

Instantiated by: ifNumber

Description:

The total number of corrupted codewords, received by this cable
modem, which were not correctable. This indicates moderate to high
levels of noise on the downstream hfc plant (depending on modulation
and burstiness of noise) for a CM and upstream for a CMTS.

Returns: counter   Suggested poll period: 60
Preprocessing: delta   Threshold comparison: >

Red threshold: 25   Orange threshold: 15   Yellow threshold: 5

Name: docsIfSigQSignalNoise   MIB: RFC-2670
OID: 1.3.6.1.2.1.10.127.1.1.4.1.5

Instantiated by: ifNumber

Description:

The current signal-to-noise ratio, in dB, as received by this cable
modem or CMTS. Low signal to noise can indicate problems with
power, loading, or corruption.

Returns: integer   Suggested poll period: 11
Preprocessing: none   Threshold comparison: <

Red threshold: 30   Orange threshold: 35   Yellow threshold: 40

Name: docsIfCmStatusValue   MIB: RFC-2670
OID: 1.3.6.1.2.1.10.127.1.2.2.1.1

Instantiated by: ifNumber

Description:

The current state of this cable modem's connectivity. Red indicates not ready (or other unknown state). Orange suggests that the modem is not synchronized, whereas yellow indicates that the upstream parameters have been acquired but ranging has not yet completed. Note that this test is not run on a CMTS.

Returns: integer   Suggested poll period: 9
Preprocessing: none   Threshold comparison: <

Red threshold: 3   Orange threshold: 5   Yellow threshold: 6

Name: docsIfCmStatusTxPower   MIB: RFC-2670
OID: 1.3.6.1.2.1.10.127.1.2.2.1.3

Instantiated by: ifNumber

Description:

The current transmit power level, in dBmV, for this modem's upstream interface. High power levels suggest that the modem is trying to compensate for plant problems, likely loading. Note that this test is not run on a CMTS.

Returns: integer   Suggested poll period: 9
Preprocessing: none   Threshold comparison: >

Red threshold: 580   Orange threshold: 565   Yellow threshold: 550

Name: docsIfCmStatusResets   MIB: RFC-2670
OID: 1.3.6.1.2.1.10.127.1.2.2.1.4

Instantiated by: ifNumber

Description:

The total number of times that this modem reset or initialized this interface. Common resets are often the result of block sync loss, and may indicate a loading or power problem. Note that this test is not run on a CMTS.

Returns: counter   Suggested poll period: 11
Preprocessing: delta   Threshold comparison: >

Red threshold: 5   Orange threshold: 3   Yellow threshold: 1

Name: docsIfCmStatusLostSyncs   MIB: RFC-2670
OID: 1.3.6.1.2.1.10.127.1.2.2.1.5

Instantiated by: ifNumber

Description:

The total number of times that this downstream interface has lost block sync. Inability to maintain sync suggests either a plant or hardware problem (correlate this object with power levels, microreflections, and in channel response to determine cause). Note that this test is not run on a CMTS.

Returns: counter   Suggested poll period: 11
Preprocessing: delta   Threshold comparison: >

Red threshold: 5   Orange threshold: 3   Yellow threshold: 1

Name: docsIfCmStatusInvalidMaps   MIB: RFC-2670
OID: 1.3.6.1.2.1.10.127.1.2.2.1.6

Instantiated by: ifNumber

Description:

The number of invalid MAP messages received by this downstream interface. MAP messages come from the CMTS and define the upstream transmission opportunities for the CM. Invalid MAP messages may indicate that the CMTS supports features the CM does not understand. Note that this test is not run on a CMTS.

Returns: counter   Suggested poll period: 11
Preprocessing: delta   Threshold comparison: >

Red threshold: 5   Orange threshold: 3   Yellow threshold: 1

Name: docsIfCmStatusInvalidUcds   MIB: RFC-2670
OID: 1.3.6.1.2.1.10.127.1.2.2.1.7

Instantiated by: ifNumber

Description:

The number of invalid UCD messages received by this downstream interface. The CMTS sends upstream channel descriptors (UCDs) to define the channel characteristics. Invalid UCD messages may indicate that the CMTS supports features the CM does not understand. Note that this test is not run on a CMTS.

Returns: counter   Suggested poll period: 11
Preprocessing: delta   Threshold comparison: >

Red threshold: 5   Orange threshold: 3   Yellow threshold: 1

Name: docsIfCmStatusInvalidRangingResp   MIB: RFC-2670
OID: 1.3.6.1.2.1.10.127.1.2.2.1.8

Instantiated by: ifNumber

Description:

The number of invalid ranging response messages received by this downstream interface. Note that this test is not run on a CMTS.

Returns: counter   Suggested poll period: 11
Preprocessing: delta   Threshold comparison: >

Red threshold: 5   Orange threshold: 3   Yellow threshold: 1

Name: docsIfCmStatusInvalidRegistrationResponses   MIB: RFC-2670
OID: 1.3.6.1.2.1.10.127.1.2.2.1.9

Instantiated by: ifNumber

Description:

The number of invalid registration messages received by this
downstream interface. Registration requests come from the CM to the
CMTS for service. Invalid registration response messages may
indicate that the CMTS supports features the CM does not
understand. Note that this test is not run on a CMTS.

Returns: counter	Suggested poll period: 11
Preprocessing: delta	Threshold comparison: >

Red threshold: 5   Orange threshold: 3   Yellow threshold: 1

Name: docsIfCmStatusT1Timeouts   MIB: RFC-2670
OID: 1.3.6.1.2.1.10.127.1.2.2.1.10

Instantiated by: ifNumber

Description:

The total number of times the t1 timer expired on this interface.
The t1 timer defines how long a CM should wait for an UCD message.
Timeouts here may indicate corruption and loss. Note that this test
is not run on a CMTS.

Returns: counter	Suggested poll period: 11
Preprocessing: delta	Threshold comparison: >

Red threshold: 5   Orange threshold: 3   Yellow threshold: 1

Name: docsIfCmStatusT2Timeouts   MIB: RFC-2670
OID: 1.3.6.1.2.1.10.127.1.2.2.1.11

Instantiated by: ifNumber

Description:

The total number of times the t2 timer expired on this interface.
The t2 timer defines how long a CM should wait for a broadcast
ranging request. Timeouts here may indicate corruption and loss.
Note that this test is not run on a CMTS.

Returns: counter   Suggested poll period: 11
Preprocessing: delta   Threshold comparison: >

Red threshold: 5   Orange threshold: 3   Yellow threshold: 1

Name: docsIfCmStatusT3Timeouts   MIB: RFC-2670
OID: 1.3.6.1.2.1.10.127.1.2.2.1.12

Instantiated by: ifNumber

Description:

The total number of times the t3 timer expired on this interface.
The t3 timer defines how long a CM should wait for a response from
its ranging request. Timeouts here may indicate corruption and
loss. Note that this test is not run on a CMTS.

Returns: counter   Suggested poll period: 11
Preprocessing: delta   Threshold comparison: >

Red threshold: 5   Orange threshold: 3   Yellow threshold: 1

Name: docsIfCmStatusT4Timeouts   MIB: RFC-2670
OID: 1.3.6.1.2.1.10.127.1.2.2.1.13

Instantiated by: ifNumber

Description:

The total number of times the t4 timer expired on this interface. The t4 timer defines how long a CM should wait for an unicast ranging opportunity. Timeouts here may indicate corruption and loss. Note that this test is not run on a CMTS.

Returns: counter   Suggested poll period: 11
Preprocessing: delta   Threshold comparison: >

Red threshold: 5   Orange threshold: 3   Yellow threshold: 1

Name: docsIfCmStatusRangingAborteds   MIB: RFC-2670
OID: 1.3.6.1.2.1.10.127.1.2.2.1.14

Instantiated by: ifNumber

Description:

The total number of times that the CMTS aborted the ranging process. This may indicate that a downstream CM failed to answer a ranging request from the CMTS.

Returns: counter   Suggested poll period: 11
Preprocessing: delta   Threshold comparison: >

Red threshold: 5   Orange threshold: 3   Yellow threshold: 1

Name: docsIfUpChanelFrequency   MIB: RFC-2670
OID: 1.3.6.1.2.1.10.127.1.1.2.1.2

Instantiated by: ifNumber

Description:

The current frequency of the upstream channel. Note that this is monitored for any change. Common changes indicate that the CMTS is having problems finding a channel with acceptable performance, suggesting a plant health or hardware problem. Note that this test is run on a CM or CMTS upstream channel interface only.

Returns: integer

Suggested poll period: 11

Preprocessing: delta

Threshold comparison: >

Red threshold: Orange threshold: Yellow threshold: 0

Name: docsIfUpChannelTimingOffset   **MIB:** RFC-2670
OID: 1.3.6.1.2.1.10.127.1.1.2.1.6

Instantiated by: ifNumber

Description:

The current round trip time measured by the CM, or maximum time seen by the CMTS, in units of 1/16 th of 6.25 microseconds. Excessive round trip time (loop delay) often causes increased collisions and data loss, as well as higher levels of plant instability.

Returns: unsigned32

Suggested poll period: 11

Preprocessing: none

Threshold comparison: >

Red threshold: 18   Orange threshold: 14   Yellow threshold: 10

Name: docsIfCmtsCmStatusRxPower   **MIB:** RFC-2670
OID: 1.3.6.1.2.1.10.127.1.3.3.1.6

Instantiated by: cmtsCmIndex

Description:

The current power level, in dBmV received from this CM at the CMTS. Note that this object is only monitored on the CMTS, and only for those modems whose performance is worthy of the polling traffic (the number of modems may preclude monitoring all if an inefficient polling platform is used).

Thresholds are computed using the following formulas:
if modulationType is QPSK, symbolBits= 2
if modulationType is 16QAM, symbolBits= 4

```
switch((ifSpeed * 8)/symbolBits ) {

  case 2560000:
        Pwr1= -30
        Pwr2= -25
        Pwr3= -20
break

  case 1280000:
        Pwr1= -60
        Pwr2= -50
        Pwr3= -40
break

  case 2560000:
        Pwr1= -30
        Pwr2= -25
        Pwr3= -20
break

  case 640000:
        Pwr1= -90
        Pwr2= -85
        Pwr3= -70
break

  case 320000:
        Pwr1= -120
        Pwr2= -110
        Pwr3= -100
break

  case 160000:
        Pwr1= -150
        Pwr2= -140
        Pwr3= -130
break
}
```

Returns: integer   Suggested poll period: 11

Preprocessing: none   Threshold comparison: <

Red threshold: Pwr1   Orange threshold: Pwr2   Yellow threshold: Pwr3

Name: docsIfCmtsCmStatusTimingOffset   MIB: RFC-2670
OID: 1.3.6.1.2.1.10.127.1.3.3.1.7

Instantiated by: cmtsCmIndex

Description:

The current round trip in units of 1/16 th of 6.25 microseconds.
Excessive round trip time (loop delay) often causes increased
collisions and data loss, as well as higher levels of plant
instability. Note that this object is only monitored on the CMTS,
and only for those modems whose performance is worthy of the
polling traffic (the number of modems may preclude monitoring all
if an inefficient polling platform is used).

Returns: unsigned32   Suggested poll period: 11
Preprocessing: delta   Threshold comparison: >

Red threshold: 18   Orange threshold: 14   Yellow threshold: 10

Name: docsIfCmtsCmStatusValue   MIB: RFC-2670
OID: 1.3.6.1.2.1.10.127.1.3.3.1.9

Instantiated by: cmtsCmIndex

Description:

The current state of this cable modem's connectivity. Red indicates
not ready (or other unknown state). Orange suggests that the modem is
not synchronized, whereas yellow indicates that the upstream
parameters have been acquired but ranging has not yet completed. Note
that this test is not run on a CMTS. Note that this object is only
monitored on the CMTS, and only for those modems whose performance is
worthy of the polling traffic (the number of modems may preclude
monitoring all if an inefficient polling platform is used).

Returns: integer   Suggested poll period: 11
Preprocessing: none   Threshold comparison: <

Red threshold: 3   Orange threshold: 5   Yellow threshold: 6

Name: docsIfCmtsCmStatusSignalNoise   MIB: RFC-2670
OID: 1.3.6.1.2.1.10.127.1.3.3.1.13

Instantiated by: cmtsCmIndex

Description:

The current signal-to-noise ratio, in dB, as received by CMTS on
the shared upstream link. Low signal-to-noise can indicate problems
with power, loading, or corruption. Note that this object is only
monitored on the CMTS, and only for those modems whose performance
is worthy of the polling traffic (the number of modems may preclude
monitoring all if an inefficient polling platform is used).

Returns: integer   Suggested poll period: 13
Preprocessing: none   Threshold comparison: <

Red threshold: 260   Orange threshold: 270   Yellow threshold: 280

Name: docsIfCmtsCmStatusCorrecteds   MIB: RFC-2670
OID: 1.3.6.1.2.1.10.127.1.3.3.1.11

Instantiated by: cmtsCmIndex

Description:

The total number of corrupted codewords, received from this cable
modem, which were corrected. This indicates low levels of noise on
the upsream hfc plant. Note that this object is only monitored on
the CMTS and only for those modems whose performance is worthy of
the polling traffic (the number of modems may preclude monitoring
all if an inefficient polling platform is used).

Returns: couter   Suggested poll period: 7
Preprocessing: delta   Threshold comparison: >

Red threshold: 10   Orange threshold: 5   Yellow threshold: 2

Name: docsIfCmtsCmStatusUncorrectables   MIB: RFC-2670
OID: 1.3.6.1.2.1.10.127.1.3.3.1.12

Instantiated by: cmtsCmIndex

Description:

The total number of corrupted codewords, received from this cable
modem, which were not correctable. This indicates low levels of
noise on the upstream hfc plant. Note that this object is only
monitored on the CMTS and only for those modems whose performance
is worthy of the polling traffic (the number of modems may preclude
monitoring all if an inefficient polling platform is used).

Returns: counter   Suggested poll period: 60
Preprocessing: delta   Threshold comparison: >

Red threshold: 25   Orange threshold: 15   Yellow threshold: 5

Name: docsIfDownChannelPower   MIB: RFC-2670
OID: 1.3.6.1.2.1.10.127.1.1.1.1.6

Instantiated by: ifNumber

Description:

The current downstream power, in dBmV, as received by this cable
modem or sent by the CMTS. High power levels suggest that the CMTS
is attempting to compensate for a plant problem, often related to
loading or termination. This test should be run at the CMTS.

Returns: integer   Suggested poll period: 11
Preprocessing: none   Threshold comparison: >

Red threshold: 61   Orange threshold: 60   Yellow threshold: 59

Name: docsIfCmtsStatusInvalidRangeReqs   MIB: RFC-2670
OID: 1.3.6.1.2.1.10.127.1.3.2.1.1

Instantiated by: ifNumber

Description:

The number of invalid ranging request messages received by this
upstream interface. The CM initiates a ranging request to the CMTS.
If the CMTS is unable to parse this message, it may indicate that
the CM software supports a message type that the CMTS does not.
Note that this test is not run on a CM.

Returns: counter   Suggested poll period: 7
Preprocessing: delta   Threshold comparison: >

Red threshold: 5   Orange threshold: 3   Yellow threshold: 1

Name: docsIfCmtsStatusInvalidRangingAborteds MIB: RFC-2670
OID: 1.3.6.1.2.1.10.127.1.3.2.1.2

Instantiated by: ifNumber

Description:

The number of ranging attempts on this interface that were aborted
by the CMTS. Note that this test is not run on a CM.

Returns: counter   Suggested poll period: 7
Preprocessing: delta   Threshold comparison: >

Red threshold: 5   Orange threshold: 3   Yellow threshold: 1

Name: docsIfCmStatusInvalidRegReqs   MIB: RFC-2670
OID: 1.3.6.1.2.1.10.127.1.3.2.1.3

Instantiated by: ifNumber

Description:

The total number of invalid registration request messages received on this upstream interface. Note that this test is not run on a CM.

Returns: counter   Suggested poll period: 7
Preprocessing: delta   Threshold comparison: >

Red threshold: 5   Orange threshold: 3   Yellow threshold: 1

Name: docsIfCmStatusFailedRegReqs   MIB: RFC-2670
OID: 1.3.6.1.2.1.10.127.1.3.2.1.4

Instantiated by: ifNumber

Description:

The total number of registration attempts on this upstream interface that failed. This is generally due to authentication failures, but requests for incorrect class of service can also be at fault. Note that this test is not run on a CM.

Returns: counter   Suggested poll period: 7
Preprocessing: delta   Threshold comparison: >

Red threshold: 5   Orange threshold: 3   Yellow threshold: 1

Name: docsIfCmStatusInvalidDataReqs   MIB: RFC-2670
OID: 1.3.6.1.2.1.10.127.1.3.2.1.5

Instantiated by: ifNumber

Description:

The total number of invalid data request messages received on this upstream interface. Data request messages from the CM to the CMTS ask for upstream transmission slots. This error may indicate that the CM software supports a message type that the CMTS does not. Note that this test is not run on a CM.

```
Returns: counter                  Suggested poll period: 7
Preprocessing: delta              Threshold comparison:  >


Red threshold: 5    Orange threshold: 3   Yellow threshold: 1
```

```
Name: docsIfCmtsStatusT5Timeouts      MIB: RFC-2670
OID: 1.3.6.1.2.1.10.127.1.3.2.1.6


Instantiated by: ifNumber


Description:


The total number of times the t5 timer expired on this upstream
interface. The t5 timer defines how long a CMTS should wait for an
upstream channel change. Timeouts here may indicate corruption and
loss. Note that this test is not run on a CM.


Returns: counter                  Suggested poll period: 7
Preprocessing: delta              Threshold comparison:  >


Red threshold: 5    Orange threshold: 3   Yellow threshold: 1
```

Cisco Routers (IOS)

Cisco replaced old environmental testpoints with new environmental tables. Unfortunately, they provided no enumerated object columns that specify what each row in the tables represent; only a displayString description (not suitable for parsing). As a result, we monitor the new tables for state variables only. Old testpoints, which clearly define each monitored entity, are still recommended for automated value thresholding.

```
Name: ccmHistoryRunningLastChanged      MIB: CiscoConfigMIB
OID: 1.3.6.1.4.1.9.9.43.1.1.1


Instantiated by: 0
```

Description:

The value of sysUpTime when the running configuration last changed. Note that this test looks for any change in value, indicating a new configuration.

Returns: timeticks	Suggested poll period: 10
Preprocessing: delta	Threshold comparison: >

Red threshold: Orange threshold: Yellow threshold: 0

Name: ccmHistoryRunningLastSaved   MIB: CiscoConfigMIB
OID: 1.3.6.1.4.1.9.9.43.1.1.2

Instantiated by: 0

Description:

The value of sysUpTime when the running configuration was last saved. Note that this test looks for any change in value, indicating a newly saved configuration.

Returns: timeticks	Suggested poll period: 10
Preprocessing: delta	Threshold comparison: >

Red threshold: Orange threshold: Yellow threshold: 0

Name: ccmHistoryStartupLastChanged   MIB: CiscoConfigMIB
OID: 1.3.6.1.4.1.9.9.43.1.1.3

Instantiated by: 0

Description:

The value of sysUpTime when the startup configuration last changed. This is the configuration that is loaded when the router does a cold boot. Note that this test looks for any change in value, indicating a new configuration.

Returns: timeticks   Suggested poll period: 10
Preprocessing: delta   Threshold comparison: >

Red threshold: Orange threshold: Yellow threshold: 0

Name: avgBusy1   MIB: OldCiscoSystemMIB
OID: 1.3.6.1.4.1.9.2.1.57

Instantiated by: 0

Description:

A one-minute exponentially decaying average of the CPU utilization.
If high, the box stability is threatened.

Returns: integer   Suggested poll period: 30
Preprocessing: none   Threshold comparison: >

Red threshold: 85   Orange threshold: 80   Yellow threshold: 70

Name: ciscoEnvMonVoltageState   MIB: CiscoEnvMonMIB
OID: 1.3.6.1.4.1.9.9.13.1.2.1.7

Instantiated by: CiscoEnvMonVoltageStatusIndex

Description:

An enumerated state variable indicating the current health of this
voltage test point.

Returns: integer   Suggested poll period: 60
Preprocessing: none   Threshold comparison: =

Red threshold: 4   Orange threshold: 3   Yellow threshold: 2

Name: ciscoEnvMonTemperatureState   MIB: CiscoEnvMonMIB
OID: 1.3.6.1.4.1.9.9.13.1.3.1.6

Instantiated by: CiscoEnvMonTemperatureStatusIndex

Description:

An enumerated state variable indicating the current health of this
temperature test point.

Returns: integer   Suggested poll period: 60
Preprocessing: none   Threshold comparison: =

Red threshold: 4   Orange threshold: 3   Yellow threshold: 2

Name: ciscoEnvMonFanState   MIB: CiscoEnvMonMIB
OID: 1.3.6.1.4.1.9.9.13.1.4.1.3

Instantiated by: CiscoEnvMonFanStatusIndex

Description:

An enumerated state variable indicating the current health of this
fan.

Returns: integer   Suggested poll period: 60
Preprocessing: none   Threshold comparison: =

Red threshold: 4   Orange threshold: 3   Yellow threshold: 2

Name: ciscoEnvMonSupplyState   MIB: CiscoEnvMonMIB
OID: 1.3.6.1.4.1.9.9.13.1.5.1.3

Instantiated by: CiscoEnvMonSuppplyStatusIndex

Description:

An enumerated state variable, indicating the current health of this
power supply.

Returns: integer   Suggested poll period: 60
Preprocessing: none   Threshold comparison: =

Red threshold: 4   Orange threshold: 3   Yellow threshold: 2

Name: envTestPt1Measure   MIB: OldCiscoEnvMonMIB
OID: 1.3.6.1.4.1.9.2.1.79

Instantiated by: 0

Description:

The temperature detected at the air intake, in degrees C. This may
indicate an enclosed chasis with insufficient airflow or overly
heated environment. High temperatures shorten hardware lifespans
and may cause devices to shut down. Note that this object is in a
deprecated branch, but uniquely identifies this parameter for
automated monitoring without displayString parsing.

Returns: integer   Suggested poll period: 60
Preprocessing: none   Threshold comparison: >

Red threshold: 53   Orange threshold: 50   Yellow threshold: 25

Name: envTestPt2Measure   MIB: OldCiscoEnvMonMIB
OID: 1.3.6.1.4.1.9.2.1.81

Instantiated by: 0

Description:

The temperature detected at the air outlet, in degrees C. This may
indicate an overly heated environment or insufficient airflow
through the device. High temperatures shorten hardware lifespans
and may cause devices to shut down. Note that this object is in a
deprecated branch, but uniquely identifies this parameter for
automated monitoring without displayString parsing.

Returns: integer

Preprocessing: none

Suggested poll period: 60

Threshold comparison: >

Red threshold: 55   Orange threshold: 53   Yellow threshold: 40

Name: envTestPt3Measure   MIB: OldCiscoEnvMonMIB
OID: 1.3.6.1.4.1.9.2.1.83

Instantiated by: 0

Description:

The voltage detected on the 5-volt power supply, in mV. This may
indicate an overly loaded system, or failing supply. Note that this
object is in a deprecated branch, but uniquely identifies this
parameter for automated monitoring without displayString parsing.

Returns: integer

Preprocessing: none

Suggested poll period: 60

Threshold comparison: <

Red threshold: 4500   Orange threshold: 4750   Yellow threshold:

Name: envTestPt4Measure   MIB: OldCiscoEnvMonMIB
OID: 1.3.6.1.4.1.9.2.1.85

Instantiated by: 0

Description:

The voltage detected on the 12-volt power supply, in mV. This may
indicate an overly loaded system, or failing supply. Note that this
object is in a deprecated branch, but uniquely identifies this
parameter for automated monitoring without displayString parsing.

Returns: integer

Preprocessing: none

Suggested poll period: 60

Threshold comparison: <

Red threshold: 10800   Orange threshold: 11400   Yellow threshold:

Name: bufferFail   MIB: OldCiscoMemoryMIB
OID: 1.3.6.1.4.1.9.2.1.46

Instantiated by: 0

Description:

The total number of times that buffer allocations from the system
free buffer pools failed, causing packets to be dropped. This does
not count packets dropped on an interface because of local card
buffer unavailability. This indicates that one or more pools may
require additional memory or a reallocation of resources.

Returns: integer   Suggested poll period: 20
Preprocessing: delta   Threshold comparison: >

Red threshold: 15   Orange threshold: 10   Yellow threshold: 1

Name: bufferNoMem   MIB: OldCiscoMemoryMIB
OID: 1.3.6.1.4.1.9.2.1.47

Instantiated by: 0

Description:

The total number of times that buffer creation failed due to a lack
of memory. Buffer creation is used to refill a system (not
interface) free pool in short supply. This suggests that buffer
tuning or additional memory may be required.

Returns: integer   Suggested poll period: 30
Preprocessing: delta   Threshold comparison: >

Red threshold: 35   Orange threshold: 25   Yellow threshold: 5

Name: bufferSmMiss   MIB: OldCiscoMemoryMIB
OID: 1.3.6.1.4.1.9.2.1.19

Instantiated by: 0

Description:

The total number of failed attempts to get system packet buffers
from the small buffer pool. This suggests a need to tune buffers.
Should that fail to resolve the issue, additional memory is
suggested.

Returns: integer   Suggested poll period: 30
Preprocessing: delta   Threshold comparison: >

Red threshold: 35   Orange threshold: 25   Yellow threshold: 5

Name: bufferMdMiss   MIB: OldCiscoMemoryMIB
OID: 1.3.6.1.4.1.9.2.1.27

Instantiated by: 0

Description:

The total number of failed attempts to get system packet buffers
from the medium buffer pool. This suggests a need to tune buffers.
Should that fail to resolve the issue, additional memory is
suggested.

Returns: integer   Suggested poll period: 30
Preprocessing: delta   Threshold comparison: >

Red threshold: 35   Orange threshold: 25   Yellow threshold: 5

Name: bufferBgMiss   MIB: OldCiscoMemoryMIB
OID: 1.3.6.1.4.1.9.2.1.35

Instantiated by: 0

Description:

The total number of failed attempts to get system packet buffers
from the big buffer pool. This suggests a need to tune buffers.
Should that fail to resolve the issue, additional memory is
suggested.

Returns: integer   Suggested poll period: 30
Preprocessing: delta   Threshold comparison: >

Red threshold: 35   Orange threshold: 25   Yellow threshold: 5

Name: bufferLgMiss   MIB: OldCiscoMemoryMIB
OID: 1.3.6.1.4.1.9.2.1.43

Instantiated by: 0

Description:

The total number of failed attempts to get system packet buffers
from the large buffer pool. This suggests a need to tune buffers.
Should that fail to resolve the issue, additional memory is
suggested.

Returns: integer   Suggested poll period: 30
Preprocessing: delta   Threshold comparison: >

Red threshold: 35   Orange threshold: 25   Yellow threshold: 5

Name: bufferHgMiss   MIB: OldCiscoMemoryMIB
OID: 1.3.6.1.4.1.9.2.1.67

Instantiated by: 0

Description:

The total number of failed attempts to get system packet buffers
from the huge buffer pool. This suggests a need to tune buffers.
Should that fail to resolve the issue, additional memory is
suggested.

Returns: integer

Suggested poll period: 30

Preprocessing: delta

Threshold comparison: >

Red threshold: 35   Orange threshold: 25   Yellow threshold: 5

Name: locIfotherInPkts

MIB: OldCiscoInterfacesMIB

OID: 1.3.6.1.4.1.9.2.2.1.1.38

Instantiated by: ifNumber

Description:

The total number of packets received by this interface that specify
a layer 3 protocol that this device does not support.

Returns: counter

Suggested poll period: 10

Preprocessing: rate

Threshold comparison: >

Red threshold: 10   Orange threshold: 5   Yellow threshold: 0

Name: locIfCarTrans

MIB: OldCiscoInterfacesMIB

OID: 1.3.6.1.4.1.9.2.2.1.1.21

Instantiated by: ifNumber

Description:

The total number of carrier transitions (up to down or down to up)
observed by this interface. Carrier transitions often indicate
unhealthy telco or interfaces, and should be treated as an early
warning of failure.

Returns: integer

Suggested poll period: 10

Preprocessing: delta

Threshold comparison: >

Red threshold: Orange threshold: Yellow threshold: 1

Name: locIfCollisions   MIB: OldCiscoInterfacesMIB
OID: 1.3.6.1.4.1.9.2.2.1.1.25

Instantiated by: ifNumber

Description:

The total number of collisions seen on this interface. Note that full-duplex interfaces will always have a value of 0.

Returns: integer   Suggested poll period: 13
Preprocessing: rate   Threshold comparison: >

Red threshold: 100   Orange threshold: 80   Yellow threshold: 60

Name: locIfInAbort   MIB: OldCiscoInterfacesMIB
OID: 1.3.6.1.4.1.9.2.2.1.1.16

Instantiated by: ifNumber

Description:

The total number of packets aborted by this interface during reception. Aborts are often the result of a clocking problem.

Returns: integer   Suggested poll period: 4
Preprocessing: rate   Threshold comparison: >

Red threshold: 30   Orange threshold: 10   Yellow threshold: 5

Name: locIfInCRC   MIB: OldCiscoInterfacesMIB
OID: 1.3.6.1.4.1.9.2.2.1.1.12

Instantiated by: ifNumber

Description:

The total number of packets received by this interface that were dropped because they failed a checksum verification. This often indicates either corruption or noise.

Returns: integer
Preprocessing: rate

Suggested poll period: 10
Threshold comparison: >

Red threshold: 10   Orange threshold: 5   Yellow threshold: 0

Name: locIfInFrame   MIB: OldCiscoInterfacesMIB
OID: 1.3.6.1.4.1.9.2.2.1.1.13

Instantiated by: ifNumber

Description:

The total number of packets received by this interface that were dropped during reception due to MAC layer framing errors. Framing errors are generally the result of corruption.

Returns: integer
Preprocessing: rate

Suggested poll period: 8
Threshold comparison: >

Red threshold: 10   Orange threshold: 5   Yellow threshold: 0

Name: locIfInGiants   MIB: OldCiscoInterfacesMIB
OID: 1.3.6.1.4.1.9.2.2.1.1.11

Instantiated by: ifNumber

Description:

The total number of packets received by this interface that were dropped because they exceeded the maximum packet size allowed by this media.

Returns: integer   Suggested poll period: 30
Preprocessing: delta   Threshold comparison: >

Red threshold: 10   Orange threshold: 5   Yellow threshold: 1

Name: locIfInIgnored   MIB: OldCiscoInterfacesMIB
OID: 1.3.6.1.4.1.9.2.2.1.1.15

Instantiated by: ifNumber

Description:

The total number of packets dropped by this interface during
reception due to a lack of receive buffers. This often indicates a
need for additional on-card memory or faster processing, but can
also be caused by moderate to high levels of noise.

Returns: integer   Suggested poll period: 13
Preprocessing: rate   Threshold comparison: >

Red threshold: 10   Orange threshold: 5   Yellow threshold: 0

Name: locIfInOverrun   MIB: OldCiscoInterfacesMIB
OID: 1.3.6.1.4.1.9.2.2.1.1.14

Instantiated by: ifNumber

Description:

The total number of times packets were dropped by this interface
because the MAC hardware was unable to write to packet memory and
the receive queue overflowed. This generally indicates an
overutilized interface, and may require a hardware upgrade or
shifting some traffic away from this card.

Returns: integer   Suggested poll period: 11
Preprocessing: rate   Threshold comparison: >

Red threshold: 20   Orange threshold: 10   Yellow threshold: 1

Name: locIfInputQueueDrops   MIB: OldCiscoInterfacesMIB
OID: 1.3.6.1.4.1.9.2.2.1.1.26

Instantiated by: ifNumber

Description:

The total number of packets that were dropped because the input
queue was full. This may suggest the need to optimize priority
queuing.

Returns: integer   Suggested poll period: 20
Preprocessing: rate   Threshold comparison: >

Red threshold: 10   Orange threshold: 5   Yellow threshold: 0

Name: locIfInRunts   MIB: OldCiscoInterfacesMIB
OID: 1.3.6.1.4.1.9.2.2.1.1.10

Instantiated by: ifNumber

Description:

The total number of packets received by this interface that were
dropped because they were smaller than the minimum packet size
required by this media.

Returns: integer   Suggested poll period: 30
Preprocessing: delta   Threshold comparison: >

Red threshold: 10   Orange threshold: 5   Yellow threshold: 1

Name: locIfLineProt   MIB: OldCiscoInterfacesMIB
OID: 1.3.6.1.4.1.9.2.2.1.1.2

Instantiated by: ifNumber

Description:

The current state of this interface, from the perspective of the
MAC layer protocol. This should only be tested on interfaces that
have ifAdminStatus set to "up".

Returns: integer	Suggested poll period: 3
Preprocessing: none	Threshold comparison: =

Red threshold: 2   Orange threshold: Yellow threshold:

Name: locIfOutputQueueDrops   MIB: OldCiscoInterfacesMIB
OID: 1.3.6.1.4.1.9.2.2.1.1.27

Instantiated by: ifNumber

Description:

The total number of packets that were dropped because the output
queue was full. This may suggest the need to optimize priority
queuing.

Returns: integer	Suggested poll period: 20
Preprocessing: rate	Threshold comparison: >

Red threshold: 10   Orange threshold: 5   Yellow threshold: 0

Name: locIfResets   MIB: OldCiscoInterfacesMIB
OID: 1.3.6.1.4.1.9.2.2.1.1.17

Instantiated by: ifNumber

Description:

The total number of times that this interface has been reset. Note
that misconfigured keepalives, only enabled at one end of the link,
can cause this to occur each 30 seconds.

Returns: integer   Suggested poll period: 90
Preprocessing: delta   Threshold comparison: >

Red threshold: Orange threshold: 2   Yellow threshold: 1

Name: locIfRestarts   MIB: OldCiscoInterfacesMIB
OID: 1.3.6.1.4.1.9.2.2.1.1.18

Instantiated by: ifNumber

Description:

The total number of times that this interface was reinitialized due
to errors. This may indicate high levels of other errors or may be
a hardware problem.

Returns: integer   Suggested poll period: 11
Preprocessing: delta   Threshold comparison: >

Red threshold: 1   Orange threshold: 0   Yellow threshold:

Name: locIfSlowInPkts   MIB: OldCiscoInterfacesMIB
OID: 1.3.6.1.4.1.9.2.2.1.1.30

Instantiated by: ifNumber

Description:

The total number of packets received by this interface that were
process switched. Process switching is generally reserved for
exceptions (e.g., broadcasts) and can consume significant resources
on smaller routers. If high levels exist and resources are being
depleted, common causes include non-unicast traffic, configuration
errors (backing store and route cache not enabled), and certain
protocols.

Returns: counter   Suggested poll period: 5
Preprocessing: rate   Threshold comparison: >

Red threshold: 100   Orange threshold: 50   Yellow threshold: 20

Name: locIfSlowOutPkts   MIB: OldCiscoInterfacesMIB
OID: 1.3.6.1.4.1.9.2.2.1.1.31

Instantiated by: ifNumber

Description:

The total number of packets sent by this interface that were
process switched. Process switching is generally reserved for
exceptions (e.g., broadcasts) and can consume significant resources
on smaller routers. If high levels exist and resources are being
depleted, common causes include non-unicast traffic, configuration
errors (backing store and route cache not enabled), and certain
protocols.

Returns: counter   Suggested poll period: 5
Preprocessing: rate   Threshold comparison: >

Red threshold: 100   Orange threshold: 50   Yellow threshold: 20

Cisco Remote Source Route Bridging Support

Name: rsrbRemotePeerState   MIB: ciscoRsrbMIB
OID: 1.3.6.1.4.1.9.9.29.1.2.1.1.5

Instantiated by: rsrbVirtRingIndex.rsrbRemotePeerIndex

Description:

The current state of the remote rsrb peer. Red indicates dead or
closed, whereas orange indicates a state other than connected.

Returns: integer   Suggested poll period: 3
Preprocessing: none   Threshold comparison: <

Red threshold: 3   Orange threshold: 9   Yellow threshold:

Name: rsrbRemotePeerDrops   MIB: ciscoRsrbMIB
OID: 1.3.6.1.4.1.9.9.29.1.2.1.1.12

Instantiated by: rsrbVirtRingIndex.rsrbRemotePeerIndex

Description:

The total number of packets received from the remote peer, but
locally dropped. Common reasons for this include limited resources
and protocol errors.

Returns: counter   Suggested poll period: 6
Preprocessing: rate   Threshold comparison: >

Red threshold: 15   Orange threshold: 10   Yellow threshold: 1

Name: rsrbRemotePeerExplorersRx   MIB: ciscoRsrbMIB
OID: 1.3.6.1.4.1.9.9.29.1.2.1.1.10

Instantiated by: rsrbVirtRingIndex.rsrbRemotePeerIndex

Description:

The total number of explorer packets received from this remote peer.
If excessive, this may indicate a protocol or configuration error.

Returns: counter   Suggested poll period: 6
Preprocessing: rate   Threshold comparison: >

Red threshold: 20   Orange threshold: 15   Yellow threshold: 1

Cisco VLAN Support

Name: vmVmpsChanges   MIB: ciscoVlanMembershipMIB
OID: 1.3.6.1.4.1.9.9.68.1.3.3

Instantiated by: 0

Description:

The total number of times that the Vlan Membership Policy Server
has been changed because it failed to respond to VQP requests.
Increasing counts here may be caused by high packet loss levels or
VMPS errors.

Returns: counter   Suggested poll period: 3
Preprocessing: delta   Threshold comparison: >

Red threshold: Orange threshold: Yellow threshold: 0

Name: vmVQPWrongDomain   MIB:
ciscoVlanMembershipMIB
OID: 1.3.6.1.4.1.9.9.68.1.3.6

Instantiated by: 0

Description:

The total number of times that this device has received a VQP
response from a VMPS that contains an unfamiliar management domain.
This likely is the result of a configuration error.

Returns: counter   Suggested poll period: 3
Preprocessing: delta   Threshold comparison: >

Red threshold: Orange threshold: Yellow threshold: 0

Name: vmVQPWrongVersion   MIB: ciscoVlanMembershipMIB
OID: 1.3.6.1.4.1.9.9.68.1.3.7

Instantiated by: 0

Description:

The total number of times that this device has received a VQP
response from a VMPS that contains an unfamiliar version. This
likely is the result of mismatched software.

Returns: counter   Suggested poll period: 3
Preprocessing: delta   Threshold comparison: >

Red threshold: Orange threshold: Yellow threshold: 0

Name: vmInsufficientResources   MIB: ciscoVlanMembershipMIB
OID: 1.3.6.1.4.1.9.9.68.1.3.8

Instantiated by: 0

Description:

The total number of times that this device has received a VQP
response from a VMPS, indicating that the VMPS does not have the
resources to verify membership assignment. This may indicate that
the VMPS hardware must be upgraded.

Returns: counter   Suggested poll period: 3
Preprocessing: delta   Threshold comparison: >

Red threshold: Orange threshold: 0   Yellow threshold:

Name: vtpConfigRevNumberErrors   MIB: ciscoVtpMIB
OID: 1.3.6.1.4.1.9.9.46.1.5.1.1.7

Instantiated by: managementDomainIndex

Description:

The total number of VTP advertisements received for this domain,
which had the same Configuration Revision Number as known to this
device and a digest value that differs from the locally known value.

Returns: Counter

Preprocessing: delta

Suggested poll period: 11

Threshold comparison: >

Red threshold: 4   Orange threshold: 2   Yellow threshold: 1

Name: vtpConfigDigestErrors   MIB: ciscoVtpMIB
OID: 1.3.6.1.4.1.9.9.46.1.5.1.1.8

Instantiated by: managementDomainIndex

Description:

The total number of VTP advertisements received for this domain,
which had a Configuration Revision Number greater than known to
this device and a digest value that differs from the value computed
locally using this advertisement's updates.

Returns: Counter

Preprocessing: delta

Suggested poll period: 11

Threshold comparison: >

Red threshold: 11   Orange threshold: 2   Yellow threshold: 1

Name: vtpVlanState   MIB: ciscoVtpMIB
OID: 1.3.6.1.4.1.9.9.46.1.3.1.1.2

Instantiated by: managementDomainIndex.vlanIndex

Description:

The current state of this VLAN. If red, this device cannot
participate in this VLAN because the VLAN's MTU exceeds either the
maximum MTU for the device or for at least one trunk port. This is
generally a configuration error.

Returns: Integer

Preprocessing: none

Suggested poll period: 9

Threshold comparison: >

Red threshold: 2   Orange threshold: Yellow threshold:

Cisco WSC Switch Support

Name: sysTraffic   MIB: ciscoStackMIB
OID: 1.3.6.1.4.1.9.5.1.1.8

Instantiated by: 0

Description:

The current backplane utilization of this switch, expressed as a
percentage of the total capacity. Sustained high levels indicate
the need to reduce data flows or upgrade the switch.

Returns: integer   Suggested poll period: 10
Preprocessing: none   Threshold comparison: >

Red threshold: 90   Orange threshold: 80   Yellow threshold: 70

Name: chassisPs1Status   MIB: ciscoStackMIB
OID: 1.3.6.1.4.1.9.5.1.2.4

Instantiated by: 0

Description:

The current state of power supply 1. Red indicates a major fault,
whereas orange indicates a minor one. Note that this should be
tested only if this entity exists.

Returns: integer   Suggested poll period: 13
Preprocessing: none   Threshold comparison: =

Red threshold: 4   Orange threshold: 3   Yellow threshold:

Name: chassisPs2Status   MIB: ciscoStackMIB
OID: 1.3.6.1.4.1.9.5.1.2.7

Instantiated by: 0

Description:

The current state of power supply 2. Red indicates a major fault, whereas orange indicates a minor one. Note that this should be tested only if this entity exists.

Returns: integer   Suggested poll period: 13
Preprocessing: none   Threshold comparison: =

Red threshold: 4   Orange threshold: 3   Yellow threshold:

Name: chassisFanStatus   MIB: ciscoStackMIB
OID: 1.3.6.1.4.1.9.5.1.2.9

Instantiated by: 0

Description:

The current state of the fan. Red indicates a major fault, orange indicates a minor one, and yellow indicates an "other" fault.

Returns: integer   Suggested poll period: 13
Preprocessing: none   Threshold comparison: =

Red threshold: 4   Orange threshold: 3   Yellow threshold: 1

Name: chassisMinorAlarm   MIB: ciscoStackMIB
OID: 1.3.6.1.4.1.9.5.1.2.11

Instantiated by: 0

Description:

The current health of this device. If orange, a "minor alarm" condition exists on this device.

Returns: integer   Suggested poll period: 13
Preprocessing: none   Threshold comparison: =

Red threshold: Orange threshold: 2   Yellow threshold:

Name: chassisMajorAlarm   MIB: ciscoStackMIB
OID: 1.3.6.1.4.1.9.5.1.2.12

Instantiated by: 0

Description:

The current health of this device. If red, a "major alarm"
condition exists on this device.

Returns: integer   Suggested poll period: 13
Preprocessing: none   Threshold comparison: =

Red threshold: 2   Orange threshold: Yellow threshold:

Name: chassisTempAlarm   MIB: ciscoStackMIB
OID: 1.3.6.1.4.1.9.5.1.2.13

Instantiated by: 0

Description:

If red, a "temperature alarm" condition exists on this device.

Returns: integer   Suggested poll period: 13
Preprocessing: none   Threshold comparison: =

Red threshold: 2   Orange threshold: Yellow threshold:

Name: moduleAction   MIB: ciscoStackMIB
OID: 1.3.6.1.4.1.9.5.1.3.1.1.12

Instantiated by: moduleSlot

Description:

The current state of this module. If red, this module has been disabled.

Returns: integer   Suggested poll period: 11
Preprocessing: none   Threshold comparison: =

Red threshold: 4   Orange threshold: Yellow threshold:

Name: moduleStatus   MIB: ciscoStackMIB
OID: 1.3.6.1.4.1.9.5.1.3.1.1.10

Instantiated by: moduleSlot

Description:

The current health of this module. If red, this module has declared a major fault. Orange indicates a minor fault, whereas yellow means the module is in an indeterminate state. ModuleTestResult should be consulted when this object is not "ok."

Returns: integer   Suggested poll period: 13
Preprocessing: none   Threshold comparison: =

Red threshold: 4   Orange threshold: 3   Yellow threshold: 1

Name: portOperStatus   MIB: ciscoStackMIB
OID: 1.3.6.1.4.1.9.5.1.4.1.1.6

Instantiated by: moduleSlot.modulePort

Description:

The current health of this port. If red, this port has declared a major fault. Orange indicates a minor fault, whereas yellow means the port is in an indeterminate state.

Returns: integer

Preprocessing: none

Suggested poll period: 13

Threshold comparison: =

Red threshold: 4   Orange threshold: 3   Yellow threshold: 1

Cisco uBR (Cable Modem) Support

Name: csmFlapListCurrentSize   MIB: ciscoUbrMIB
OID: 1.3.6.1.4.1.9.9.99991.1.1.2

Instantiated by: 0

Description:

The number of entries currently on the flap list. Large volumes of
changes suggest an unstable infrastructure.

Returns: gauge

Preprocessing: delta

Suggested poll period: 15

Threshold comparison: >

Red threshold: 20   Orange threshold: 15   Yellow threshold: 10

Name: cdxQosCtrlUpAdmissionRejects   MIB: ciscoUbrMIB
OID: 1.3.6.1.4.1.9.9.116.1.1.1.1.3

Instantiated by: ifNumber

Description:

The total number of CM registration requests that were rejected by
the CMTS because it could not reserve the minimum guaranteed
bandwidth for this QOS class. Frequent rejects suggest that this
upstream interface is oversubscribed.

Returns: counter

Preprocessing: delta

Suggested poll period: 15

Threshold comparison: >

Red threshold: 5   Orange threshold: 3   Yellow threshold: 0

Nortel Cable Modems

The following objects describe instrumentation for Nortel/LANCity cable modems, release 3.

Name: lcLcpTxFrequency　　　　　　　　MIB: LANCity3MIB
OID: 1.3.6.1.4.1.482.50.2.4.18

Instantiated by: 0

Description:

The current frequency of the upstream channel. Note that this is monitored for any change. Common changes indicate that the LCH is having problems finding a channel with acceptable performance, suggesting a plant health or hardware problem.

Returns: integer　　　　　　　　Suggested poll period: 35
Preprocessing: delta　　　　　　　Threshold comparison: !

Red threshold:　　　Orange threshold:　　　Yellow threshold: 0

Name: lcLcpRxFrequency　　　　　　　　MIB: LANCity3MIB
OID: 1.3.6.1.4.1.482.50.2.4.19

Instantiated by: 0

Description:

The current frequency of the downstream channel. Note that this is monitored for any change. Common changes indicate that the LCH is having problems finding a channel with acceptable performance, suggesting a plant health or hardware problem.

Returns: integer　　　　　　　　Suggested poll period: 35
Preprocessing: delta　　　　　　　Threshold comparison: !

Red threshold:　　　Orange threshold:　　　Yellow threshold: 0

Name: lcLcpTxEqMerit   MIB: LANCity3MIB
OID: 1.3.6.1.4.1.482.50.2.4.16

Instantiated by: 0

Description:

Equilization Merit is an indication of how hard the modem is
working to compensate for poor plant characteristics. It combines
the measurement of microreflections and in-channel frequency
response. Poor values suggest possible problems with line
termination, plant response, or power levels.

Returns: integer   Suggested poll period: 57
Preprocessing: none   Threshold comparison: <

Red threshold: 4   Orange threshold: 5   Yellow threshold: 6

Name: lcLcpTxPwrDbmvInt   MIB: LANCity3MIB
OID: 1.3.6.1.4.1.482.50.2.4.20

Instantiated by: 0

Description:

The current transmit power level, times 100. High transmit power
levels at the LCP indicate a plant-loading problem upstream.

Returns: integer   Suggested poll period: 11
Preprocessing: none   Threshold comparison: >

Red threshold: 5725   Orange threshold: 5700   Yellow threshold:
5675

Name: lcLcpAvgBSRxLevelDbmvInt   MIB: LANCity3MIB
OID: 1.3.6.1.4.1.482.50.2.4.21

Instantiated by: 0

Description:

The current receive power level, times 100. High receive power
levels at the LCP indicate a plant-loading problem downstream.

Returns: integer   Suggested poll period: 11
Preprocessing: none   Threshold comparison: <

Red threshold: 15   Orange threshold: 25   Yellow threshold: 50

Name: lcLcpBlockSyncState   MIB: LANCity3MIB
OID: 1.3.6.1.4.1.482.50.2.13.3

Instantiated by: 0

Description:

The current state of the block sync state machine. Red indicates
that the unilink is in the init state, orange indicates that it is
trying to establish sync, and yellow indicates that it is waiting
to establish sync.

Returns: integer   Suggested poll period: 5
Preprocessing: none   Threshold comparison: =

Red threshold: 1   Orange threshold: 2   Yellow threshold: 4

Name: lcLcpLostBlockSync   MIB: LANCity3MIB
OID: 1.3.6.1.4.1.482.50.2.13.6

Instantiated by: 0

Description:

The total number of times that this downstream interface has lost
block sync. Inability to maintain sync suggests either a plant or
hardware problem (correlate this object with power levels,

microreflections, and in-channel response to determine cause). Note
that this test is not run on an LCH.

Returns: counter   Suggested poll period: 13
Preprocessing: delta   Threshold comparison: >

Red threshold: 5   Orange threshold: 2   Yellow threshold: 0

Name: lcLcpLoopDelayBad   MIB: LANCity3MIB
OID: 1.3.6.1.4.1.482.50.2.13.10

Instantiated by: 0

Description:

The total number of times that the LCP was unable to compute loop
delay during a sample interval. Inability to compute loop delay may
indicate unilink stability problems.

Returns: counter   Suggested poll period: 39
Preprocessing: delta   Threshold comparison: !

Red threshold: Orange threshold: Yellow threshold: 0

Name: lcLcpLostPacerNotAllowed   MIB: LANCity3MIB
OID: 1.3.6.1.4.1.482.50.2.13.11

Instantiated by: 0

Description:

The total number of times this device lost pacer because it is not
permitted to be the pacer. Pacer loss results in a loss of
connectivity. Frequent pacer loss indicates either a configuration
error or plant health that is incapable of sustaining a connection.

Returns: counter   Suggested poll period: 41
Preprocessing: delta   Threshold comparison: !

Red threshold: Orange threshold: 1   Yellow threshold: 0

Name: lcLcpLostPacerOther   MIB: LANCity3MIB
OID: 1.3.6.1.4.1.482.50.2.13.12

Instantiated by: 0

Description:

The total number of times this device lost block sync while
attempting to become the pacer. Pacer loss results in a loss of
connectivity. Frequent pacer loss indicates either a configuration
error or plant health that is incapable of sustaining a connection.

Returns: counter   Suggested poll period: 41
Preprocessing: delta   Threshold comparison: !

Red threshold: Orange threshold: 0   Yellow threshold:

Name: lcLcpLostPacerNoActivity   MIB: LANCity3MIB
OID: 1.3.6.1.4.1.482.50.2.13.13.

Instantiated by: 0

Description:

The total number of times this device lost pacer because the
inactivity timer expired without any network activity. Pacer loss
results in a loss of connectivity. Frequent pacer loss indicates
either a configuration error or plant health that is incapable of
sustaining a connection.

Returns: counter   Suggested poll period: 41
Preprocessing: delta   Threshold comparison: !

Red threshold: Orange threshold: 1   Yellow threshold: 0

Name: lcLcpExcessivePacerAttempts   MIB: LANCity3MIB
OID: 1.3.6.1.4.1.482.50.2.13.14

Instantiated by: 0

Description:

The total number of times this device exceeded the maximum number
of attempts to become pacer without success. Pacer loss results in
a loss of connectivity. Frequent pacer loss indicates either a
configuration error or plant health that is incapable of sustaining
a connection.

Returns: counter   Suggested poll period: 31
Preprocessing: delta   Threshold comparison: !

Red threshold: 1   Orange threshold: 0   Yellow threshold:

Name: lcLcpTimeoutEstablishingSync   MIB: LANCity3MIB
OID: 1.3.6.1.4.1.482.50.2.13.15

Instantiated by: 0

Description:

The total number of times that this device failed to establish
block sync within the timeout parameters. Without block sync,
connectivity cannot be established.

Returns: counter   Suggested poll period: 90
Preprocessing: delta   Threshold comparison: !

Red threshold: 0   Orange threshold: Yellow threshold:

Name: lcLcpMcastRx   MIB: LANCity3MIB
OID: 1.3.6.1.4.1.482.50.2.15.7

Instantiated by: 0

Description:

The total number of multicast packets received on the ethernet
port. Multicast packets flood the bridging domain and should be
limited in volume.

Returns: counter   Suggested poll period: 15
Preprocessing: rate   Threshold comparison: >

Red threshold: 100   Orange threshold: 75   Yellow threshold: 25

Name: lcLcpBcastRx   MIB: LANCity3MIB
OID: 1.3.6.1.4.1.482.50.2.15.8

Instantiated by: 0

Description:

The total number of broadcast packets received on the ethernet
port. Broadcast packets flood the bridging domain and should be
limited in volume.

Returns: counter   Suggested poll period: 15
Preprocessing: rate   Threshold comparison: >

Red threshold: 100   Orange threshold: 75   Yellow threshold: 25

Name: lcLcpEthernetLocalLan   MIB: LANCity3MIB
OID: 1.3.6.1.4.1.482.50.2.17.1

Instantiated by: 0

Description:

The total number of packets dropped inbound on the ethernet
interface because the bridge forwarding table indicates that the
destination address is reached via the same interface. Very high
levels of this consume resources within the modem, suggest that a
significant network may be attached, and should be avoided.

Returns: counter   Suggested poll period: 30
Preprocessing: rate   Threshold comparison: >

Red threshold: 75   Orange threshold: 50   Yellow threshold: 20

Name: lcLcpAsicLocalLan   MIB: LANCity3MIB
OID: 1.3.6.1.4.1.482.50.2.17.2

Instantiated by: 0

Description:

The total number of packets dropped inbound on the unilink
interface because the bridge forwarding table indicates that the
destination address is reached via the same interface. Very high
levels of this consume resources within the modem, suggest that a
significant network may be attached, and should be avoided.

Returns: counter   Suggested poll period: 30
Preprocessing: rate   Threshold comparison: >

Red threshold: 50   Orange threshold: 40   Yellow threshold: 25

Name: lcLcpByteCntErr   MIB: LANCity3MIB
OID: 1.3.6.1.4.1.482.50.2.18.1

Instantiated by: 0

Description:

The total number of times the ethernet controller detected an error
in the length field of a packet it was transmitting. This often
indicates a hardware defect or software bug.

Returns: counter   Suggested poll period: 61
Preprocessing: delta   Threshold comparison: >

Red threshold: 5   Orange threshold: 3   Yellow threshold: 1

Name: lcLcpFifoUnderrun   MIB: LANCity3MIB
OID: 1.3.6.1.4.1.482.50.2.18.3

Instantiated by: 0

Description:

The total number of times that the ethernet controller had a FIFO
underrun during transmission. This often indicates buffer
contention or CPU overutilization on the card.

Returns: counter   Suggested poll period: 11
Preprocessing: delta   Threshold comparison: >

Red threshold: 10   Orange threshold: 6   Yellow threshold: 1

Name: lcLcpExcessDefs   MIB: LANCity3MIB
OID: 1.3.6.1.4.1.482.50.2.18.4

Instantiated by: 0

Description:

The total number of frames unsuccessfully transmitted by this
interface because they experienced 16 collisions and were
discarded. This is a dramatic indicator of congestion.

Returns: counter   Suggested poll period: 11
Preprocessing: rate   Threshold comparison: >

Red threshold: 10   Orange threshold: 5   Yellow threshold: 0

Name: lcLcpMissedPktErrs   MIB: LANCity3MIB
OID: 1.3.6.1.4.1.482.50.2.18.7

Instantiated by: 0

Description:

The total number of frames received by the ethernet controller, but
which were dropped due to local resource errors (FIFO overrun,
insufficient buffers, or a disabled receiver). This often indicates
an overutilized modem, which requires a hardware upgrade or reduced
traffic.

Returns: counter	Suggested poll period: 11
Preprocessing: rate	Threshold comparison: >

Red threshold: 10   Orange threshold: 6   Yellow threshold: 1

Name: lcLcpNoSysBuffs   MIB: LANCity3MIB
OID: 1.3.6.1.4.1.482.31.15.1

Instantiated by: 0

Description:

The total number of management packets that could not be
transmitted due to a lack of system buffers. This indicates a
significant potential for reduced management control. Additional
buffers should be added or the existing load reduced.

Returns: counter	Suggested poll period: 60
Preprocessing: delta	Threshold comparison: >

Red threshold: 5   Orange threshold: 1   Yellow threshold: 0

Name: lcLcpCatvMacRxErrors   MIB: LANCity3MIB
OID: 1.3.6.1.4.1.482.50.2.23.8

Instantiated by: 0

Description:

The total number of packets received on the unilink interface that contained errors. These are often checksum errors due to corruption.

Returns: counter   Suggested poll period: 21
Preprocessing: rate   Threshold comparison: >

Red threshold: 30   Orange threshold: 20   Yellow threshold: 1

Name: lcLcpCatvRetryPercentage   MIB: LANCity3MIB
OID: 1.3.6.1.4.1.482.50.2.23.10

Instantiated by: 0

Description:

The percentage of frames transmitted on the unilink that were retried. This is generally the result of unilink contention; high levels indicate excessive errors or congestion.

Returns: integer   Suggested poll period: 47
Preprocessing: none   Threshold comparison: >

Red threshold: 35   Orange threshold: 25   Yellow threshold: 15

Name: lcLcpEtherRetryPercentage   MIB: LANCity3MIB
OID: 1.3.6.1.4.1.482.50.2.23.11

Instantiated by: 0

Description:

The percentage of frames transmitted on the ethernet that were retried. This is generally the result of ethernet contention; high levels indicate excessive errors or congestion.

Returns: integer   Suggested poll period: 47
Preprocessing: none   Threshold comparison: >

Red threshold: 35   Orange threshold: 25   Yellow threshold: 15

Name: lcLcpMeasuredLoopDelay   MIB: LANCity3MIB
OID: 1.3.6.1.4.1.482.50.2.24.15

Instantiated by: 0

Description:

The current measured loop delay, in bytes. High values often result
in timing related errors and should be eliminated.

Returns: integer   Suggested poll period: 301
Preprocessing: none   Threshold comparison: >

Red threshold: 160   Orange threshold: 140   Yellow threshold: 100

The following objects describe instrumentation for Nortel/LANCity
DOCSIS cable modems.

Name: lccmtsCurrentTemp   MIB: LANCityMcnsMIB
OID: 1.3.6.1.4.1.482.60.2.2

Instantiated by: 0

Description:

The current temperature of this device, in degrees Celsius.
Thresholds here are based on the assumption that the
lccmtsHighTempThreshold >= 66. If not, the thresholds should be
adjusted accordingly.

Returns: integer   Suggested poll period: 19
Preprocessing: none   Threshold comparison: >

Red threshold: 64   Orange threshold: 60   Yellow threshold: 50

Name: lccmtsBOOTPRelayBadLengthDiscards MIB: LANCityMcnsMIB
OID: 1.3.6.1.4.1.482.60.5.8.3

Instantiated by: 0

Description:

The total number of outgoing BOOTP packets that were dropped due to
incorrectly calculated length fields. This often indicates a
hardware defect or software bug.

Returns: counter   Suggested poll period: 11
Preprocessing: rate   Threshold comparison: >

Red threshold: 10   Orange threshold: 6   Yellow threshold: 1

Name: lccmtsBOOTPRelayLocalOriginDiscards MIB: LANCityMcnsMIB
OID: 1.3.6.1.4.1.482.60.5.8.4

Instantiated by: 0

Description:

The total number of outgoing BOOTP packets that were dropped
because they originated in a CMTS. This should never happen and
suggests a configuration error or software defect.

Returns: counter   Suggested poll period: 11
Preprocessing: delta   Threshold comparison: >

Red threshold: 1   Orange threshold: 0   Yellow threshold:

Name: lccmtsBOOTPRelayExcessiveHopsDiscards MIB: LANCityMcnsMIB
OID: 1.3.6.1.4.1.482.60.5.8.5

Instantiated by: 0

Description:

The total number of BOOTP packets that were dropped because of an excessive hop count. This suggests an incorrectly configured topology.

Returns: counter   Suggested poll period: 11
Preprocessing: delta   Threshold comparison: >

Red threshold: 1   Orange threshold: 0   Yellow threshold:

Name:
lccmtsBOOTPRelayWrongGatewayAddrDiscards   MIB: LANCityMcnsMIB
OID: 1.3.6.1.4.1.482.60.5.8.8

Instantiated by: 0

Description:

The total number of BOOTP packets that were dropped because the server used a gateway address that did not belong to this device.

Returns: counter   Suggested poll period: 11
Preprocessing: rate   Threshold comparison: >

Red threshold: 5   Orange threshold: 1   Yellow threshold: 0

Name: lccmtsBOOTPRelayNoCopyBufDiscards MIB: LANCityMcnsMIB
OID: 1.3.6.1.4.1.482.60.5.8.9

Instantiated by: 0

Description:

The total number of BOOTP packets dropped because there was insufficient memory available to allocate a copy buffer. This suggests a need for either additional memory or fewer (booting) modems.

Returns: counter	Suggested poll period: 11
Preprocessing: rate	Threshold comparison: >

Red threshold: 10   Orange threshold: 5   Yellow threshold: 0

Name: lccmtsBOOTPRelayMiscSilentDiscards   MIB: LANCityMcnsMIB
OID: 1.3.6.1.4.1.482.60.5.8.10

Instantiated by: 0

Description:

The total number of outgoing BOOTP packets silently dropped for reasons not otherwise counted. This may indicate severe congestion or a device failure.

Returns: counter	Suggested poll period: 11
Preprocessing: rate	Threshold comparison: >

Red threshold: 10   Orange threshold: 5   Yellow threshold: 0

Name: lccmtsBOOTPRelayNoEpilBufDiscards   MIB: LANCityMcnsMIB
OID: 1.3.6.1.4.1.482.60.5.8.11

Instantiated by: 0

Description:

The total number of outgoing BOOTP packets dropped due to a lack of Epilogue UDP buffers.

Returns: counter	Suggested poll period: 11
Preprocessing: rate	Threshold comparison: >

Red threshold: 10   Orange threshold: 5   Yellow threshold: 0

Name: lccmtsBOOTPRelayClntDstPortDiscards   MIB: LANCityMcnsMIB
OID: 1.3.6.1.4.1.482.60.5.8.12

Instantiated by: 0

Description:

The total number of inbound packets dropped because the destination
port was for a BOOTP client.

Returns: counter   Suggested poll period: 11
Preprocessing: rate   Threshold comparison: >

Red threshold: 20   Orange threshold: 15   Yellow threshold: 10

Name: lccmtsBOOTPRelayWrongPortRqstDiscards   MIB: LANCityMcnsMIB
OID: 1.3.6.1.4.1.482.60.5.8.22

Instantiated by: 0

Description:

The total number of inbound BOOTP request packets dropped because
they did not originate on a CATV port. This suggests a
configuration or topology error.

Returns: counter   Suggested poll period: 11
Preprocessing: rate   Threshold comparison: >

Red threshold: 10   Orange threshold: 5   Yellow threshold: 1

Name: MIB: LANCityMcnsMIB
OID: 1.3.6.1.4.1.482.60.5.8.23

Instantiated by: 0

Description:

The total number of inbound BOOTP reply packets dropped because they did not originate on an ethernet port. This suggests a configuration or topology error.

Returns: counter	Suggested poll period: 11
Preprocessing: rate	Threshold comparison: >

Red threshold: 10   Orange threshold: 5   Yellow threshold: 1

Name: lcCmtsUpChannelPower   MIB: LANCityMcnsMIB
OID: 1.3.6.1.4.1.482.60.2.1.1.12

Instantiated by: ifNumber

Description:

The nominal receiver input power level, in tenths of dBmV, on this CMTS. This value may vary in response to a change in the channel's width. Frequent changes may indicate instability in the plant characteristics.

Returns: integer	Suggested poll period: 11
Preprocessing: delta	Threshold comparison: >

Red threshold: Orange threshold: 0   Yellow threshold:

Name: lcCmtsHealthUpTime   MIB: LANCityMcnsMIB
OID: 1.3.6.1.4.1.482.60.2.4.9.1.3

Instantiated by: ifNumber

Description:

The length of time that the current channel has held its configuration. Frequent changes may indicate instability in the plant characteristics.

Returns: timeticks   Suggested poll period: 9
Preprocessing: none   Threshold comparison: <

Red threshold: Orange threshold: Yellow threshold: 1800

Nortel Switches

The following objects describe instrumentation for Nortel/Accelar switches.

Name: rcSysBufferUtil   MIB: rapidCity
OID: 1.3.6.1.4.1.2272.1.1.13

Instantiated by: 0

Description:

Buffer utilization as a percentage of the total amount of buffer space in the system. A high value indicates congestion.

Returns: integer   Suggested poll period: 11
Preprocessing: none   Threshold comparison: >

Red threshold: 90   Orange threshold: 80   Yellow threshold: 70

Name: rcSysCpuUtil   MIB: rapidCity
OID: 1.3.6.1.4.1.2272.1.1.20

Instantiated by: 0

Description:

The current percentage of CPU utilization.

Returns: gauge   Suggested poll period: 3
Preprocessing: none   Threshold comparison: >

Red threshold: 90   Orange threshold: 80   Yellow threshold: 70

Name: rcSysSwitchFabricUtil   MIB: rapidCity
OID: 1.3.6.1.4.1.2272.1.1.21

Instantiated by: 0

Description:

The current percentage of Switching Fabric utilization.

Returns: gauge   Suggested poll period: 3
Preprocessing: none   Threshold comparison: >

Red threshold: 90   Orange threshold: 80   Yellow threshold: 70

Name: rcTblArFree   MIB: rapidCity
OID: 1.3.6.1.4.1.2272.1.7.8

Instantiated by: 0

Description:

The number of free entries that are available in the Address
Translation table. Thresholds should be computed as a percentage of
the table size.

Returns: integer   Suggested poll period: 11
Preprocessing: none   Threshold comparison: <

Red threshold: 2.5%   Orange threshold: 5%   Yellow threshold: 7%

Name: rcTblArNoSpace   MIB: rapidCity
OID: 1.3.6.1.4.1.2272.1.7.9

Instantiated by: 0

Description:

The total number of entries that could not be added to the Address Translation table due to lack of space.

Returns: integer   Suggested poll period: 31
Preprocessing: rate   Threshold comparison: >

Red threshold: 10   Orange threshold: 6   Yellow threshold: 1

Name: rcChasFanOperStatus   MIB: rapidCity
OID: 1.3.6.1.4.1.2272.1.4.7.1.1.2

Instantiated by: rcChasFanId

Description:

The current status of this fan. Red indicates that the fan is down; orange indicates that the state is unknown.

Returns: integer   Suggested poll period: 31
Preprocessing: none   Threshold comparison: =

Red threshold: 3   Orange threshold: 1   Yellow threshold:

Name: rcChasPowerSupplyOperStatus   MIB: rapidCity
OID: 1.3.6.1.4.1.2272.1.4.8.1.1.2

Instantiated by: rcChasPowerSupplyId

Description:

The current status of this power supply. Red indicates that the supply is down, Orange that the state is unknown.

Returns: integer   Suggested poll period: 31
Preprocessing: none   Threshold comparison: =

Red threshold: 4   Orange threshold: 1   Yellow threshold:

Name: rcStatFrameTooShorts   MIB: rapidCity
OID: 1.3.6.1.4.1.2272.1.12.1.1.2

Instantiated by: ifIndex

Description:

The total number of frames received on this port that were dropped
because they were too short.

Returns: counter   Suggested poll period: 7
Preprocessing: delta   Threshold comparison: >

Red threshold: 10   Orange threshold: 5   Yellow threshold:

Name: rcStatBridgeInMulticastFrames   MIB: rapidCity
OID: 1.3.6.1.4.1.2272.1.12.1.1.4

Instantiated by: ifIndex

Description:

The total number of multicast packets received by this interface.
Bridged multicast frames are flooded, so their levels should be
contained by minimizing broadcast domains.

Returns: counter   Suggested poll period: 15
Preprocessing: rate   Threshold comparison: >

Red threshold: 50   Orange threshold: 40   Yellow threshold: 20

Name: rcStatBridgeInBroadcastFrames   MIB: rapidCity
OID: 1.3.6.1.4.1.2272.1.12.1.1.5

Instantiated by: ifIndex

Description:

The total number of broadcast packets received by this interface.
Bridged broadcast frames are flooded, so their levels should be
contained by minimizing broadcast domains.

Returns: counter   Suggested poll period: 15
Preprocessing: rate   Threshold comparison: >

Red threshold: 50   Orange threshold: 40   Yellow threshold: 20

Name: rcStatBridgeInDiscards   MIB: rapidCity
OID: 1.3.6.1.4.1.2272.1.12.1.1.6

Instantiated by: ifIndex

Description:

The total number of frames discarded by this bridge.

Returns: counter   Suggested poll period: 29
Preprocessing: rate   Threshold comparison: >

Red threshold: 20   Orange threshold: 10   Yellow threshold: 1

Name: rcStatBridgeOutMulticastFrames   MIB: rapidCity
OID: 1.3.6.1.4.1.2272.1.12.1.1.8

Instantiated by: ifIndex

Description:
The total number of multicast packets sent by this interface.
Bridged multicast frames are flooded, so their levels should be
contained by minimizing broadcast domains.

Returns: counter   Suggested poll period: 15
Preprocessing: rate   Threshold comparison: >

Red threshold: 50   Orange threshold: 40   Yellow threshold: 20

Name: rcStatBridgeOutBroadcastFrames   MIB: rapidCity
OID: 1.3.6.1.4.1.2272.1.12.1.1.9

Instantiated by: ifIndex

Description:

The total number of broadcast packets sent by this interface.
Bridged broadcast frames are flooded, so their levels should be
contained by minimizing broadcast domains.

Returns: counter   Suggested poll period: 15
Preprocessing: rate   Threshold comparison: >

Red threshold: 50   Orange threshold: 40   Yellow threshold: 20

Name: rcStatStgForwardTransitions   MIB: rapidCity
OID: 1.3.6.1.4.1.2272.1.12.1.1.15

Instantiated by: ifIndex

Description:

The number of times this port has transitioned from learning to the
forwarding state. This should be monitored on all ports that are
expected to always be enabled (connected to routers or servers).

Returns: counter   Suggested poll period: 30
Preprocessing: delta   Threshold comparison: !

Red threshold: Orange threshold: 0   Yellow threshold:

Name: rcStatStgInConfigBpdus   MIB: rapidCity
OID: 1.3.6.1.4.1.2272.1.12.1.1.16

Instantiated by: ifIndex

Description:

The number of Config BPDUs received by this port.

Returns: counter   Suggested poll period: 13
Preprocessing: rate   Threshold comparison: >

Red threshold: 10   Orange threshold: 5   Yellow threshold:

Name: rcStatStgInTcnBpdus   MIB: rapidCity
OID: 1.3.6.1.4.1.2272.1.12.1.1.17

Instantiated by: ifIndex

Description:

The total number of topology updates received by this port.
Occasional updates are normal, but higher levels suggest flapping
interfaces and an unstable infrastructure.

Returns: counter   Suggested poll period: 6
Preprocessing: rate   Threshold comparison: >

Red threshold: 5   Orange threshold: 0   Yellow threshold:

Name: rcStatStgInBadBpdus   MIB: rapidCity
OID: 1.3.6.1.4.1.2272.1.12.1.1.18

Instantiated by: ifIndex

Description:

The total number of invalid BPDUs received by this port. This may
indicate a defective interface or software error.

Returns: counter   Suggested poll period: 13
Preprocessing: rate   Threshold comparison: >

Red threshold: 10   Orange threshold: 0   Yellow threshold:

Name: rcStatStgOutTcnBpdus   MIB: rapidCity
OID: 1.3.6.1.4.1.2272.1.12.1.1.20

Instantiated by: ifIndex

Description:

The total number of topology updates sent by this port. Occasional
updates are normal, but higher levels suggest flapping interfaces
and an unstable infrastructure.

Returns: counter   Suggested poll period: 6
Preprocessing: rate   Threshold comparison: >

Red threshold: 5   Orange threshold: 0   Yellow threshold:

Name: rcStatGigLinkFailures   MIB: rapidCity
OID: 1.3.6.1.4.1.2272.1.12.2.1.2

Instantiated by: ifIndex

Description:

The total number of link failures observed by this interface. Link
failures may indicate faulty ports or cable. Note that this is
monitored only on gigabit interfaces.

Returns: counter   Suggested poll period: 7
Preprocessing: delta   Threshold comparison: >

Red threshold: 2   Orange threshold: 0   Yellow threshold:

Name: rcStatGigPacketErrors   MIB: rapidCity
OID: 1.3.6.1.4.1.2272.1.12.2.1.3

Instantiated by: ifIndex

Description:

The total number of packet errors observed by this interface.
Packet errors are generally corruption, and may indicate bad cable.
Note that this is monitored only on gigabit interfaces.

Returns: counter   Suggested poll period: 7
Preprocessing: rate   Threshold comparison: >

Red threshold: 20   Orange threshold: 15   Yellow threshold: 5

Name: rcStatGigCarrierErrors   MIB: rapidCity
OID: 1.3.6.1.4.1.2272.1.12.2.1.4

Instantiated by: ifIndex

Description:

The total number of carrier failures observed by this interface.
Carrier failures may indicate faulty (remote) ports or cable. Note
that this is monitored only on gigabit interfaces.

Returns: counter   Suggested poll period: 7
Preprocessing: delta   Threshold comparison: >

Red threshold: 2   Orange threshold: 0   Yellow threshold:

Name: rcStatGigLinkInactiveErrors   MIB: rapidCity
OID: 1.3.6.1.4.1.2272.1.12.2.1.5

Instantiated by: ifIndex

Description:

The total number of inactivity errors observed by this interface.
These may indicate faulty ports. Note that this is monitored only
on gigabit interfaces.

```
Returns: counter               Suggested poll period: 7
Preprocessing: delta           Threshold comparison:  >


Red threshold: 2   Orange threshold: 0   Yellow threshold:
```

The following objects describe instrumentation for Nortel/
Centillion switches.

```
Name: chassisFanFailStatus          MIB: Centillion
OID: 1.3.6.1.4.1.930.2.1.1.5


Instantiated by: 0


Description:


The current fan status for this box. If red, one or both of the
fans have failed.

Returns: integer               Suggested poll period: 60
Preprocessing: none            Threshold comparison:  =


Red threshold: 0   Orange threshold:    Yellow threshold:
```

```
Name: chassisPs1FailStatus          MIB: Centillion
OID: 1.3.6.1.4.1.930.2.1.1.3


Instantiated by: 0


Description:


The current status of power supply 1. If red, the supply has
failed.

Returns: integer               Suggested poll period: 60
Preprocessing: none            Threshold comparison:  =


Red threshold: 0   Orange threshold:    Yellow threshold:
```

Name: chassisPs2FailStatus   MIB: Centillion
OID: 1.3.6.1.4.1.930.2.1.1.4

Instantiated by: 0

Description:

The current status of power supply 2. If red, the supply has
failed.

Returns: integer   Suggested poll period: 60
Preprocessing: none   Threshold comparison: =

Red threshold: 0   Orange threshold: Yellow threshold:

Name: slotModuleStatus   MIB: Centillion
OID: 1.3.6.1.4.1.930.2.1.1.9.1.6

Instantiated by: xxxmodule

Description:

The current status of the card in this slot. If red, the card has
failed.

Returns: integer   Suggested poll period: 13
Preprocessing: none   Threshold comparison: =

Red threshold: 2   Orange threshold: Yellow threshold:

Nortel Routers

Name: wfTxDropCtrNoGrant   MIB: wellfleetBbMIB
OID: 1.3.6.1.4.1.18.3.3.2.5.4.1.3

Instantiated by: wfBackboneSlot

Description:

The total number of packets that were dropped because the backplane bus was not granted for transmission. The SRM is not granting access to the PPX. The SRM should be tested for failure. If ok and the router contains only SRM-L, the addition of an SRM-F may help.

Returns: counter   Suggested poll period: 5
Preprocessing: rate   Threshold comparison: >

Red threshold: 10   Orange threshold: 6   Yellow threshold: 1

Name: wfTxDropCtrFlowCtrl   MIB: wellfleetBbMIB
OID: 1.3.6.1.4.1.18.3.3.2.5.4.1.4

Instantiated by: wfBackboneSlot

Description:

The total number of packets that were dropped because backplane flow control prevented their transmission. This may indicate overutilization of the destination card or a tendency of this slot to monopolize the bus.

Returns: counter   Suggested poll period: 5
Preprocessing: rate   Threshold comparison: >

Red threshold: 10   Orange threshold: 6   Yellow threshold: 1

Name: wfTxDied   MIB: wellfleetBbMIB
OID: 1.3.6.1.4.1.18.3.3.2.5.4.1.5

Instantiated by: wfBackboneSlot

Description:

The total number of times that the backplane transmit state machine has been terminated on this adapter. This may indicate a packet clocking failure on the part of the FRE blade.

Returns: counter

Suggested poll period: 5

Preprocessing: delta

Threshold comparison: >

Red threshold: 10   Orange threshold: 5   Yellow threshold: 0

Name: wfTxDramDied

MIB: wellfleetBbMIB

OID: 1.3.6.1.4.1.18.3.3.2.5.4.1.6

Instantiated by: wfBackboneSlot

Description:

The total number of times that the backplane dram transmit state machine has been terminated on this adapter. This is likely the result of a hardware failure on this blade.

Returns: counter

Suggested poll period: 5

Preprocessing: delta

Threshold comparison: >

Red threshold: 10   Orange threshold: 5   Yellow threshold: 0

Name: wfTxIdleErrors

MIB: wellfleetBbMIB

OID: 1.3.6.1.4.1.18.3.3.2.5.4.1.7

Instantiated by: wfBackboneSlot

Description:

The total number of times both backplane transmit pipeline state machines were active simultaneously. This is likely the result of a hardware failure on this blade.

Returns: counter

Suggested poll period: 5

Preprocessing: delta

Threshold comparison: >

Red threshold: 10   Orange threshold: 5   Yellow threshold: 0

Name: wfTxNoSomErrors   MIB: wellfleetBbMIB
OID: 1.3.6.1.4.1.18.3.3.2.5.4.1.8

Instantiated by: wfBackboneSlot

Description:

The total number of times the backplane transmit state machine left
the idle state without a start of message delimiter. This is likely
the result of a hardware failure on this blade.

Returns: counter   Suggested poll period: 5
Preprocessing: delta   Threshold comparison: >

Red threshold: 10   Orange threshold: 5   Yellow threshold: 0

Name: wfTxPktSomErrors   MIB: wellfleetBbMIB
OID: 1.3.6.1.4.1.18.3.3.2.5.4.1.9

Instantiated by: wfBackboneSlot

Description:

The total number of times the backplane transmit packet state
machine left the idle state without a start of message delimiter.
This is likely the result of a hardware failure on this blade.

Returns: counter   Suggested poll period: 5
Preprocessing: delta   Threshold comparison: >

Red threshold: 10   Orange threshold: 5   Yellow threshold: 0

Name: wfTxDropEomErrors   MIB: wellfleetBbMIB
OID: 1.3.6.1.4.1.18.3.3.2.5.4.1.10

Instantiated by: wfBackboneSlot

Description:

The total number of times the backplane transmitter detected a dropped end of message. This is likely the result of a hardware failure on this blade.

Returns: counter   Suggested poll period: 5
Preprocessing: delta   Threshold comparison: >

Red threshold: 10   Orange threshold: 5   Yellow threshold: 0

Name: wfTxOverflowErrors   MIB: wellfleetBbMIB
OID: 1.3.6.1.4.1.18.3.3.2.5.4.1.11

Instantiated by: wfBackboneSlot

Description:

The total number of times the backplane transmitter detected an overflow. This may indicate congestion or resource limitations on this card.

Returns: counter   Suggested poll period: 11
Preprocessing: rate   Threshold comparison: >

Red threshold: 20   Orange threshold: 10   Yellow threshold: 1

Name: wfTxSofErrors   MIB: wellfleetBbMIB
OID: 1.3.6.1.4.1.18.3.3.2.5.4.1.12

Instantiated by: wfBackboneSlot

Description:

The total number of times the backplane transmitter detected a start offset error. This is likely the result of a hardware failure on this blade.

Returns: counter   Suggested poll period: 5

Preprocessing: delta   Threshold comparison: >

Red threshold: 10   Orange threshold: 5   Yellow threshold: 0

Name: wfTxDataptrErrors   MIB: wellfleetBbMIB

OID: 1.3.6.1.4.1.18.3.3.2.5.4.1.13

Instantiated by: wfBackboneSlot

Description:

The total number of times the backplane transmitter detected that
an increment of the data pointer caused the address to overflow.
This is likely the result of a hardware failure on this blade.

Returns: counter   Suggested poll period: 5

Preprocessing: delta   Threshold comparison: >

Red threshold: 10   Orange threshold: 5   Yellow threshold: 0

Name: wfTxEndptrErrors   MIB: wellfleetBbMIB

OID: 1.3.6.1.4.1.18.3.3.2.5.4.1.14

Instantiated by: wfBackboneSlot

Description:

The total number of times the backplane transmitter detected that
an end data pointer would cause the address to overflow (start
pointer plus offset). This is likely the result of a hardware
failure on this blade.

Returns: counter   Suggested poll period: 5

Preprocessing: delta   Threshold comparison: >

Red threshold: 10   Orange threshold: 5   Yellow threshold: 0

Name: wfRxPktNumErrors   MIB: wellfleetBbMIB
OID: 1.3.6.1.4.1.18.3.3.2.5.4.1.24

Instantiated by: wfBackboneSlot

Description:

The total number of times the backplane receiver detected a packet
number error. This is likely the result of a hardware failure on
this blade.

Returns: counter   Suggested poll period: 5
Preprocessing: delta   Threshold comparison: >

Red threshold: 10   Orange threshold: 5   Yellow threshold: 0

Name: wfRxAddrOvrErrors   MIB: wellfleetBbMIB
OID: 1.3.6.1.4.1.18.3.3.2.5.4.1.25

Instantiated by: wfBackboneSlot

Description:

The total number of times the backplane receiver detected an
address overrun. This is likely the result of a hardware failure on
this blade.

Returns: counter   Suggested poll period: 5
Preprocessing: delta   Threshold comparison: >

Red threshold: 10   Orange threshold: 5   Yellow threshold: 0

Name: wfRxSomErrors   MIB: wellfleetBbMIB
OID: 1.3.6.1.4.1.18.3.3.2.5.4.1.26

Instantiated by: wfBackboneSlot

Description:

The total number of times the backplane receiver state machine
detected a start of message error. This is likely the result of a
hardware failure on this blade.

Returns: counter   Suggested poll period: 5
Preprocessing: delta   Threshold comparison: >

Red threshold: 10   Orange threshold: 5   Yellow threshold: 0

Name: wfRxDied   MIB: wellfleetBbMIB
OID: 1.3.6.1.4.1.18.3.3.2.5.4.1.27

Instantiated by: wfBackboneSlot

Description:

The total number of times the backplane receive state machine died.
This is likely the result of a hardware failure on this blade.

Returns: counter   Suggested poll period: 5
Preprocessing: delta   Threshold comparison: >

Red threshold: 10   Orange threshold: 5   Yellow threshold: 0

Name: wfRxUnloadErrors   MIB: wellfleetBbMIB
OID: 1.3.6.1.4.1.18.3.3.2.5.4.1.28

Instantiated by: wfBackboneSlot

Description:

The total number of times the backplane receiver attempted to
unload an empty FIFO. This is likely the result of a software bug
or hardware failure on this blade.

Returns: counter   Suggested poll period: 5
Preprocessing: delta   Threshold comparison: >

Red threshold: 10   Orange threshold: 5   Yellow threshold: 0

Name: wfRxDropCtr   MIB: wellfleetBbMIB
OID: 1.3.6.1.4.1.18.3.3.2.5.4.1.29

Instantiated by: wfBackboneSlot

Description:

The total number of packets the backplane receiver dropped. This is
likely the result of congestion or resource limitations on this blade.

Returns: counter   Suggested poll period: 5
Preprocessing: rate   Threshold comparison: >

Red threshold: 10   Orange threshold: 6   Yellow threshold: 1

Name: wfRxSofErrors   MIB: wellfleetBbMIB
OID: 1.3.6.1.4.1.18.3.3.2.5.4.1.30

Instantiated by: wfBackboneSlot

Description:

The total number of times the backplane receiver detected start
offset error. This is likely the result of a hardware failure on
this or the sending blade.

Returns: counter   Suggested poll period: 5
Preprocessing: delta   Threshold comparison: >

Red threshold: 10   Orange threshold: 5   Yellow threshold: 0

Name: wfRxCrcErrors   MIB: wellfleetBbMIB
OID: 1.3.6.1.4.1.18.3.3.2.5.4.1.31

Instantiated by: wfBackboneSlot

Description:

The total number of times the backplane receiver detected a crc
error. This is likely the result of a hardware failure on this
blade, the sending blade, or the backplane itself.

Returns: counter   Suggested poll period: 5
Preprocessing: delta   Threshold comparison: >

Red threshold: 10   Orange threshold: 5   Yellow threshold: 1

Name: wfRxOvrErrors   MIB: wellfleetBbMIB
OID: 1.3.6.1.4.1.18.3.3.2.5.4.1.32

Instantiated by: wfBackboneSlot

Description:

The total number of times the backplane receiver detected a FIFO
overrun. This is likely the result of resource utilization or
congestion on this blade.

Returns: counter   Suggested poll period: 7
Preprocessing: rate   Threshold comparison: >

Red threshold: 10   Orange threshold: 6   Yellow threshold: 1

Name: wfBCNPwrSupply1   MIB: wellfleetHardwareMIB
OID: 1.3.6.1.4.1.18.3.1.1.4

Instantiated by: 0

Description:

The current status of power supply 1. Red indicates that the supply has failed. Orange indicates not present. Note that this is only monitored on a BCN.

Returns: integer	Suggested poll period: 19
Preprocessing: none	Threshold comparison: =

Red threshold: 2   Orange threshold: 3   Yellow threshold:

Name: wfBCNPwrSupply2   MIB: wellfleetHardwareMIB
OID: 1.3.6.1.4.1.18.3.1.1.5

Instantiated by: 0

Description:

The current status of power supply 2. Red indicates that the supply has failed. Orange indicates not present. Note that this is only monitored on a BCN.

Returns: integer	Suggested poll period: 19
Preprocessing: none	Threshold comparison: =

Red threshold: 2   Orange threshold: 3   Yellow threshold:

Name: wfBCNPwrSupply3   MIB: wellfleetHardwareMIB
OID: 1.3.6.1.4.1.18.3.1.1.6

Instantiated by: 0

Description:

The current status of power supply 3. Red indicates that the supply has failed. Orange indicates not present. Note that this is only monitored on a BCN.

Returns: integer

Preprocessing: none

Suggested poll period: 19

Threshold comparison: =

Red threshold: 2   Orange threshold: 3   Yellow threshold:

Name: wfBCNPwrSupply4   MIB: wellfleetHardwareMIB
OID: 1.3.6.1.4.1.18.3.1.1.7

Instantiated by: 0

Description:

The current status of power supply 4. Red indicates that the supply has failed. Orange indicates not present. Note that this is only monitored on a BCN.

Returns: integer

Preprocessing: none

Suggested poll period: 19

Threshold comparison: =

Red threshold: 2   Orange threshold: 3   Yellow threshold:

Name: wfBCNFanStatus   MIB: wellfleetHardwareMIB
OID: 1.3.6.1.4.1.18.3.1.1.8

Instantiated by: 0

Description:

The current status of the fan tray. Red indicates that it has failed. Orange indicates not present. Note that this is only monitored on a BCN.

Returns: integer

Preprocessing: none

Suggested poll period: 19

Threshold comparison: =

Red threshold: 2   Orange threshold: 3   Yellow threshold:

Name: wfBCNTemperature   MIB: wellfleetHardwareMIB
OID: 1.3.6.1.4.1.18.3.1.1.9

Instantiated by: 0

Description:

The current status of the temperature sensor. Red indicates
caution. Orange indicates not present. Note that this is only
monitored on a BCN.

Returns: integer   Suggested poll period: 19
Preprocessing: none   Threshold comparison: =

Red threshold: 2   Orange threshold: 3   Yellow threshold:

Name: wfRASNPwrSupply1   MIB: wellfleetHardwareMIB
OID: 1.3.6.1.4.1.18.3.1.2.1.41

Instantiated by: wfHwSlot

Description:

The current status of power supply 1. Red indicates that the supply
has failed. Orange indicates not present. Note that this is only
monitored on an ASN.

Returns: integer   Suggested poll period: 19
Preprocessing: none   Threshold comparison: =

Red threshold: 2   Orange threshold: 3   Yellow threshold:

Name: wfRASNPwrSupply2   MIB: wellfleetHardwareMIB
OID: 1.3.6.1.4.1.18.3.1.2.1.42

Instantiated by: wfHwSlot

Description:

The current status of power supply 2. Red indicates that the supply
has failed. Orange indicates not present. Note that this is only
monitored on an ASN.

Returns: integer   Suggested poll period: 19
Preprocessing: none   Threshold comparison: =

Red threshold: 2   Orange threshold: 3   Yellow threshold:

Name: wfKernelMemorySegsFree   MIB: wellfleetGameStatsMIB
OID: 1.3.6.1.4.1.18.3.3.2.5.1.1.5

Instantiated by: wfKernelSlot

Description:

The total number of unallocated memory segments in the kernel.
Thresholds should be computed as a percentage of the total segment
count.

Returns: integer   Suggested poll period: 7
Preprocessing: none   Threshold comparison: <

Red threshold: 5%   Orange threshold: 10%   Yellow threshold: 25%

Name: wfKernelAliasBuffsDropped   MIB: wellfleetGameStatsMIB
OID: 1.3.6.1.4.1.18.3.3.2.5.1.1.53

Instantiated by: wfKernelSlot

Description:

The total number of alias buffers dropped because of a lack of copy
buffers.

Returns: integer

Preprocessing: rate

Suggested poll period: 11

Threshold comparison: >

Red threshold: 10   Orange threshold: 5   Yellow threshold: 1

Name: wfKernelBallocFail

OID: 1.3.6.1.4.1.18.3.3.2.5.1.1.54

MIB: wellfleetGameStatsMIB

Instantiated by: wfKernelSlot

Description:

The total number of times a buffer couldn't be allocated via g_balloc because the free buffer pool was empty.

Returns: integer

Preprocessing: delta

Suggested poll period: 7

Threshold comparison: >

Red threshold: 10   Orange threshold: 6   Yellow threshold: 1

Name: wfKernelReplenEmpty

OID: 1.3.6.1.4.1.18.3.3.2.5.1.1.55

MIB: wellfleetGameStatsMIB

Instantiated by: wfKernelSlot

Description:

The number of times the buffer pool was emptied via q_bneplen.

Returns: integer

Preprocessing: delta

Suggested poll period: 7

Threshold comparison: >

Red threshold: 10   Orange threshold: 6   Yellow threshold: 1

Name: wfKernelAliasNoMembers

OID: 1.3.6.1.4.1.18.3.3.2.5.1.1.57

MIB: wellfleetGameStatsMIB

Instantiated by: wfKernelSlot

Description:

The number of alias buffers dropped because of no members or
GID_GAME is the only member.

Returns: integer   Suggested poll period: 11
Preprocessing: delta   Threshold comparison: >

Red threshold: 10   Orange threshold: 5   Yellow threshold: 1

Name: wfKernelMemoryFree   MIB: wellfleetGameStatsMIB
OID: 1.3.6.1.4.1.18.3.3.2.5.1.1.3

Instantiated by: wfKernelSlot

Description:

The total number of unallocated memory in the kernel, in bytes.
Thresholds should be computed as a percentage of the total memory.

Returns: integer   Suggested poll period: 7
Preprocessing: none   Threshold comparison: <

Red threshold: 5%   Orange threshold: 10%   Yellow threshold: 25%

Name: wfKernelBuffersFree   MIB: wellfleetGameStatsMIB
OID: 1.3.6.1.4.1.18.3.3.2.5.1.1.8

Instantiated by: wfKernelSlot

Description:

The total number of unallocated memory packet buffers in the
kernel's free pool. Thresholds should be computed as a percentage
of the total packet buffers.

Returns: integer   Suggested poll period: 11
Preprocessing: none   Threshold comparison: <

Red threshold: 5%   Orange threshold: 10%   Yellow threshold: 25%

Name: wfResourceTotalCpuUsed   MIB: wellFleetResourceMIB
OID: 1.3.6.1.4.1.18.3.3.2.5.7.1.2

Instantiated by: wfResourceTotalSlot

Description:

The total amount of time, in hundredths of a second, that the CPU
has run code from any entity. Note that by making this a rate, we
get the percent utilization between successive polls.

Returns: integer   Suggested poll period: 31
Preprocessing: rate   Threshold comparison: >

Red threshold: 90   Orange threshold: 85   Yellow threshold: 75

Name: wfResourceTotalMemoryUsed   MIB: wellFleetResourceMIB
OID: 1.3.6.1.4.1.18.3.3.2.5.7.1.5

Instantiated by: wfResourceTotalSlot

Description:

The current amount of local memory (used for protocols, processes,
tables, etc.) by all entities on this card. Thresholds should be
computed as a percentage of the total local memory.

Returns: gauge   Suggested poll period: 27
Preprocessing: none   Threshold comparison: >

Red threshold: 90%   Orange threshold: 85%   Yellow threshold: 75%

Name: wfResourceTotalBuffersUsed   MIB: wellFleetResourceMIB
OID: 1.3.6.1.4.1.18.3.3.2.5.7.1.8

Instantiated by: wfResourceTotalSlot

Description:

The current amount of global memory (used for packet buffers) by
all entities on this card. Thresholds should be computed as a
percentage of the total global memory.

Returns: gauge   Suggested poll period: 21
Preprocessing: none   Threshold comparison: >

Red threshold: 90%   Orange threshold: 85%   Yellow threshold: 75%

The following objects are rows in the wfResourceUseTable, which is
indexed by entity number and slot number. For convenience, we have
extended the OID by appending the entity number and listed only the
slot number as an instance.

Name: wfResourceUsedCpuKernel   MIB: wellfleetResourceMIB
OID: 1.3.6.1.4.1.18.3.3.2.5.6.1.4.1

Instantiated by: wfResourceUseSlot

Description:

The total amount of time, in hundredths of a second, that the CPU
has run kernel code. Note that by making this a rate, we get the
percent utilization between successive polls.

Returns: integer   Suggested poll period: 31
Preprocessing: rate   Threshold comparison: >

Red threshold: 70   Orange threshold: 60   Yellow threshold: 50

Name: wfResourceUsedCpuQenet   MIB: wellfleetResourceMIB
OID: 1.3.6.1.4.1.18.3.3.2.5.6.1.4.3

Instantiated by: wfResourceUseSlot

Description:

The total amount of time, in hundredths of a second, that the CPU
has run quad ethernet code. Note that by making this a rate, we get
the percent utilization between successive polls.

Returns: integer   Suggested poll period: 33
Preprocessing: rate   Threshold comparison: >

Red threshold: 70   Orange threshold: 60   Yellow threshold: 50

Name: wfResourceUsedCpuIlacc   MIB: wellfleetResourceMIB
OID: 1.3.6.1.4.1.18.3.3.2.5.6.1.4.13

Instantiated by: wfResourceUseSlot

Description:

The total amount of time, in hundredths of a second, that the CPU
has run Ilacc chip code. Note that by making this a rate, we get
the percent utilization between successive polls.

Returns: integer   Suggested poll period: 31
Preprocessing: rate   Threshold comparison: >

Red threshold: 70   Orange threshold: 60   Yellow threshold: 50

Name: wfResourceUsedCpuIP   MIB: wellfleetResourceMIB
OID: 1.3.6.1.4.1.18.3.3.2.5.6.1.4.21

Instantiated by: wfResourceUseSlot

Description:

The total amount of time, in hundredths of a second, that the CPU
has run IP code. Note that by making this a rate, we get the
percent utilization between successive polls.

Returns: integer   Suggested poll period: 31
Preprocessing: rate   Threshold comparison: >

Red threshold: 70   Orange threshold: 60   Yellow threshold: 50

Name: wfResourceUsedCpuIPX   MIB: wellfleetResourceMIB
OID: 1.3.6.1.4.1.18.3.3.2.5.6.1.4.26

Instantiated by: wfResourceUseSlot

Description:

The total amount of time, in hundredths of a second, that the CPU
has run IPX code. Note that by making this a rate, we get the
percent utilization between successive polls.

Returns: integer   Suggested poll period: 33
Preprocessing: rate   Threshold comparison: >

Red threshold: 70   Orange threshold: 60   Yellow threshold: 50

Name: wfResourceUsedCpuFr   MIB: wellfleetResourceMIB
OID: 1.3.6.1.4.1.18.3.3.2.5.6.1.4.29

Instantiated by: wfResourceUseSlot

Description:

The total amount of time, in hundredths of a second, that the CPU
has run frame relay code. Note that by making this a rate, we get
the percent utilization between successive polls.

Returns: integer

Preprocessing: rate

Suggested poll period: 31

Threshold comparison: >

Red threshold: 70   Orange threshold: 60   Yellow threshold: 50

Name: wfResourceUsedCpuDlsw   MIB: wellfleetResourceMIB
OID: 1.3.6.1.4.1.18.3.3.2.5.6.1.4.32

Instantiated by: wfResourceUseSlot

Description:

The total amount of time, in hundredths of a second, that the CPU
has run dlsw code. Note that by making this a rate, we get the
percent utilization between successive polls.

Returns: integer

Preprocessing: rate

Suggested poll period: 33

Threshold comparison: >

Red threshold: 70   Orange threshold: 60   Yellow threshold: 50

Name: wfResourceUsedCpuArp   MIB: wellfleetResourceMIB
OID: 1.3.6.1.4.1.18.3.3.2.5.6.1.4.33

Instantiated by: wfResourceUseSlot

Description:

The total amount of time, in hundredths of a second, that the CPU
has run ARP code. Note that by making this a rate, we get the
percent utilization between successive polls.

Returns: integer

Preprocessing: rate

Suggested poll period: 31

Threshold comparison: >

Red threshold: 70   Orange threshold: 60   Yellow threshold: 50

Name: wfResourceUsedCpuSnmp   MIB: wellfleetResourceMIB
OID: 1.3.6.1.4.1.18.3.3.2.5.6.1.4.35

Instantiated by: wfResourceUseSlot

Description:

The total amount of time, in hundredths of a second, that the CPU
has run SNMP code. Note that by making this a rate, we get the
percent utilization between successive polls.

Returns: integer   Suggested poll period: 33
Preprocessing: rate   Threshold comparison: >

Red threshold: 70   Orange threshold: 60   Yellow threshold: 50

Name: wfResourceUsedCpuTcp   MIB: wellfleetResourceMIB
OID: 1.3.6.1.4.1.18.3.3.2.5.6.1.4.37

Instantiated by: wfResourceUseSlot

Description:

The total amount of time, in hundredths of a second, that the CPU
has run TCP code. Note that by making this a rate, we get the
percent utilization between successive polls.

Returns: integer   Suggested poll period: 31
Preprocessing: rate   Threshold comparison: >

Red threshold: 70   Orange threshold: 60   Yellow threshold: 50

Name: wfResourceUsedCpuBgp   MIB: wellfleetResourceMIB
OID: 1.3.6.1.4.1.18.3.3.2.5.6.1.4.38

Instantiated by: wfResourceUseSlot

Description:

The total amount of time, in hundredths of a second, that the CPU has run BGP code. Note that by making this a rate, we get the percent utilization between successive polls.

Returns: integer   Suggested poll period: 31
Preprocessing: rate   Threshold comparison: >

Red threshold: 70   Orange threshold: 60   Yellow threshold: 50

Name: wfResourceUsedCpuOspf   MIB: wellfleetResourceMIB
OID: 1.3.6.1.4.1.18.3.3.2.5.6.1.4.40

Instantiated by: wfResourceUseSlot

Description:

The total amount of time, in hundredths of a second, that the CPU has run OSPF code. Note that by making this a rate, we get the percent utilization between successive polls.

Returns: integer   Suggested poll period: 31
Preprocessing: rate   Threshold comparison: >

Red threshold: 70   Orange threshold: 60   Yellow threshold: 50

Name: wfResourceUsedCpuPcap   MIB: wellfleetResourceMIB
OID: 1.3.6.1.4.1.18.3.3.2.5.6.1.4.45

Instantiated by: wfResourceUseSlot

Description:

The total amount of time, in hundredths of a second, that the CPU has run packet capture code. Note that by making this a rate, we get the percent utilization between successive polls.

Returns: integer   Suggested poll period: 33

Preprocessing: rate   Threshold comparison: >

Red threshold: 70   Orange threshold: 60   Yellow threshold: 50

Name: wfResourceUsedCpuMunich   MIB: wellfleetResourceMIB

OID: 1.3.6.1.4.1.18.3.3.2.5.6.1.4.47

Instantiated by: wfResourceUseSlot

Description:

The total amount of time, in hundredths of a second, that the CPU has run (T1/E1) Munich chip code. Note that by making this a rate, we get the percent utilization between successive polls.

Returns: integer   Suggested poll period: 31

Preprocessing: rate   Threshold comparison: >

Red threshold: 70   Orange threshold: 60   Yellow threshold: 50

Name: wfResourceUsedCpuQuicsync   MIB: wellfleetResourceMIB

OID: 1.3.6.1.4.1.18.3.3.2.5.6.1.4.48

Instantiated by: wfResourceUseSlot

Description:

The total amount of time, in hundredths of a second, that the CPU has run quicsync chip code. Note that by making this a rate, we get the percent utilization between successive polls.

Returns: integer   Suggested poll period: 33

Preprocessing: rate   Threshold comparison: >

Red threshold: 70   Orange threshold: 60   Yellow threshold: 50

Name: wfResourceUsedCpuAsnmod   MIB: wellfleetResourceMIB
OID: 1.3.6.1.4.1.18.3.3.2.5.6.1.4.50

Instantiated by: wfResourceUseSlot

Description:

The total amount of time, in hundredths of a second, that the CPU
has run asnmod code. Note that by making this a rate, we get the
percent utilization between successive polls.

Returns: integer   Suggested poll period: 31
Preprocessing: rate   Threshold comparison: >

Red threshold: 70   Orange threshold: 60   Yellow threshold: 50

Name: wfResourceUsedCpuDebug   MIB: wellfleetResourceMIB
OID: 1.3.6.1.4.1.18.3.3.2.5.6.1.4.54

Instantiated by: wfResourceUseSlot

Description:

The total amount of time, in hundredths of a second, that the CPU
has run debug code. Note that by making this a rate, we get the
percent utilization between successive polls.

Returns: integer   Suggested poll period: 33
Preprocessing: rate   Threshold comparison: >

Red threshold: 70   Orange threshold: 60   Yellow threshold: 50

Name: wfResourceUsedCpuPing   MIB: wellfleetResourceMIB
OID: 1.3.6.1.4.1.18.3.3.2.5.6.1.4.69

Instantiated by: wfResourceUseSlot

Description:

The total amount of time, in hundredths of a second, that the CPU
has run ping code. Note that by making this a rate, we get the
percent utilization between successive polls.

Returns: integer   Suggested poll period: 33
Preprocessing: rate   Threshold comparison: >

Red threshold: 70   Orange threshold: 60   Yellow threshold: 50

Name: wfResourceUsedCpuSyslog   MIB: wellfleetResourceMIB
OID: 1.3.6.1.4.1.18.3.3.2.5.6.1.4.78

Instantiated by: wfResourceUseSlot

Description:

The total amount of time, in hundredths of a second, that the CPU
has run syslog code. Note that by making this a rate, we get the
percent utilization between successive polls.

Returns: integer   Suggested poll period: 33
Preprocessing: rate   Threshold comparison: >

Red threshold: 70   Orange threshold: 60   Yellow threshold: 50

Name: wfResourceUsedCpuNsc100m   MIB: wellfleetResourceMIB
OID: 1.3.6.1.4.1.18.3.3.2.5.6.1.4.84

Instantiated by: wfResourceUseSlot

Description:

The total amount of time, in hundredths of a second, that the CPU
has run National Semiconductor DP83810 chip code. Note that by
making this a rate, we get the percent utilization between
successive polls.

Returns: integer   Suggested poll period: 31
Preprocessing: rate   Threshold comparison: >

Red threshold: 70   Orange threshold: 60   Yellow threshold: 50

Name: wfResourceUsedCpuATMSig   MIB: wellfleetResourceMIB
OID: 1.3.6.1.4.1.18.3.3.2.5.6.1.4.93

Instantiated by: wfResourceUseSlot

Description:

The total amount of time, in hundredths of a second, that the CPU has run ATM signaling code. Note that by making this a rate, we get the percent utilization between successive polls.

Returns: integer   Suggested poll period: 31
Preprocessing: rate   Threshold comparison: >

Red threshold: 70   Orange threshold: 60   Yellow threshold: 50

Name: wfResourceUsedCpuNat   MIB: wellfleetResourceMIB
OID: 1.3.6.1.4.1.18.3.3.2.5.6.1.4.119

Instantiated by: wfResourceUseSlot

Description:

The total amount of time, in hundredths of a second, that the CPU has run NAT code. Note that by making this a rate, we get the percent utilization between successive polls.

Returns: integer   Suggested poll period: 31
Preprocessing: rate   Threshold comparison: >

Red threshold: 70   Orange threshold: 60   Yellow threshold: 50

Name: wfResourceUseMemoryKernel   MIB: wellfleetResourceMIB
OID: 1.3.6.1.4.1.18.3.3.2.5.6.1.5.1

Instantiated by: wfResourceUseSlot

Description:

The amount of local memory, in bytes, currently consumed by the
kernel. Thresholds should be computed as a percentage of the total
memory.

Returns: gauge   Suggested poll period: 27
Preprocessing: none   Threshold comparison: >

Red threshold: 65%   Orange threshold: 55%   Yellow threshold: 45%

Name: wfResourceUseMemoryQenet   MIB: wellfleetResourceMIB
OID: 1.3.6.1.4.1.18.3.3.2.5.6.1.5.3

Instantiated by: wfResourceUseSlot

Description:

The amount of local memory, in bytes, currently consumed by the
quad ethernet. Thresholds should be computed as a percentage of the
total memory.

Returns: gauge   Suggested poll period: 29
Preprocessing: none   Threshold comparison: >

Red threshold: 65%   Orange threshold: 55%   Yellow threshold: 45%

Name: wfResourceUseMemoryIlacc   MIB: wellfleetResourceMIB
OID: 1.3.6.1.4.1.18.3.3.2.5.6.1.5.13

Instantiated by: wfResourceUseSlot

Description:

The amount of local memory, in bytes, currently consumed by the ilacc chip driver. Thresholds should be computed as a percentage of the total memory.

Returns: gauge   Suggested poll period: 29
Preprocessing: none   Threshold comparison: >

Red threshold: 65%   Orange threshold: 55%   Yellow threshold: 45%

Name: wfResourceUseMemoryIp   MIB: wellfleetResourceMIB
OID: 1.3.6.1.4.1.18.3.3.2.5.6.1.5.21

Instantiated by: wfResourceUseSlot

Description:

The amount of local memory, in bytes, currently consumed by IP. Thresholds should be computed as a percentage of the total memory.

Returns: gauge   Suggested poll period: 27
Preprocessing: none   Threshold comparison: >

Red threshold: 65%   Orange threshold: 55%   Yellow threshold: 45%

Name: wfResourceUseMemoryIpx   MIB: wellfleetResourceMIB
OID: 1.3.6.1.4.1.18.3.3.2.5.6.1.5.26

Instantiated by: wfResourceUseSlot

Description:

The amount of local memory, in bytes, currently consumed by IPX. Thresholds should be computed as a percentage of the total memory.

Returns: gauge   Suggested poll period: 29
Preprocessing: none   Threshold comparison: >

Red threshold: 65%   Orange threshold: 55%   Yellow threshold: 45%

Name: wfResourceUseMemoryFr   MIB: wellfleetResourceMIB
OID: 1.3.6.1.4.1.18.3.3.2.5.6.1.5.29

Instantiated by: wfResourceUseSlot

Description:

The amount of local memory, in bytes, currently consumed by frame
relay. Thresholds should be computed as a percentage of the total
memory.

Returns: gauge   Suggested poll period: 27
Preprocessing: none   Threshold comparison: >

Red threshold: 65%   Orange threshold: 55%   Yellow threshold: 45%

Name: wfResourceUseMemoryDlsw   MIB: wellfleetResourceMIB
OID: 1.3.6.1.4.1.18.3.3.2.5.6.1.5.32

Instantiated by: wfResourceUseSlot

Description:

The amount of local memory, in bytes, currently consumed by dlsw.
Thresholds should be computed as a percentage of the total memory.

Returns: gauge   Suggested poll period: 29
Preprocessing: none   Threshold comparison: >

Red threshold: 65%   Orange threshold: 55%   Yellow threshold: 45%

Name: wfResourceUseMemoryArp   MIB: wellfleetResourceMIB
OID: 1.3.6.1.4.1.18.3.3.2.5.6.1.5.33

Instantiated by: wfResourceUseSlot

Description:

The amount of local memory, in bytes, currently consumed by ARP.
Thresholds should be computed as a percentage of the total memory.

Returns: gauge   Suggested poll period: 27
Preprocessing: none   Threshold comparison: >

Red threshold: 65%   Orange threshold: 55%   Yellow threshold: 45%

Name: wfResourceUseMemorySnmp   MIB: wellfleetResourceMIB
OID: 1.3.6.1.4.1.18.3.3.2.5.6.1.5.35

Instantiated by: wfResourceUseSlot

Description:

The amount of local memory, in bytes, currently consumed by SNMP.
Thresholds should be computed as a percentage of the total memory.

Returns: gauge   Suggested poll period: 29
Preprocessing: none   Threshold comparison: >

Red threshold: 65%   Orange threshold: 55%   Yellow threshold: 45%

Name: wfResourceUseMemoryTcp   MIB: wellfleetResourceMIB
OID: 1.3.6.1.4.1.18.3.3.2.5.6.1.5.37

Instantiated by: wfResourceUseSlot

Description:

The amount of local memory, in bytes, currently consumed by TCP.
Thresholds should be computed as a percentage of the total memory.

Returns: gauge   Suggested poll period: 27
Preprocessing: none   Threshold comparison: >

Red threshold: 65%   Orange threshold: 55%   Yellow threshold: 45%

Name: wfResourceUseMemoryBgp   MIB: wellfleetResourceMIB
OID: 1.3.6.1.4.1.18.3.3.2.5.6.1.5.38

Instantiated by: wfResourceUseSlot

Description:

The amount of local memory, in bytes, currently consumed by BGP.
Thresholds should be computed as a percentage of the total memory.

Returns: gauge   Suggested poll period: 27
Preprocessing: none   Threshold comparison: >

Red threshold: 65%   Orange threshold: 55%   Yellow threshold: 45%

Name: wfResourceUseMemoryOspf   MIB: wellfleetResourceMIB
OID: 1.3.6.1.4.1.18.3.3.2.5.6.1.5.40

Instantiated by: wfResourceUseSlot

Description:

The amount of local memory, in bytes, currently consumed by OSPF.
Thresholds should be computed as a percentage of the total memory.

Returns: gauge   Suggested poll period: 27
Preprocessing: none   Threshold comparison: >

Red threshold: 65%   Orange threshold: 55%   Yellow threshold: 45%

Name: wfResourceUseMemoryPcap   MIB: wellfleetResourceMIB
OID: 1.3.6.1.4.1.18.3.3.2.5.6.1.5.45

Instantiated by: wfResourceUseSlot

Description:

The amount of local memory, in bytes, currently consumed by packet
capture. Thresholds should be computed as a percentage of the total
memory.

Returns: gauge   Suggested poll period: 29
Preprocessing: none   Threshold comparison: >

Red threshold: 65%   Orange threshold: 55%   Yellow threshold: 45%

Name: wfResourceUseMemoryMunich   MIB: wellfleetResourceMIB
OID: 1.3.6.1.4.1.18.3.3.2.5.6.1.5.47

Instantiated by: wfResourceUseSlot

Description:

The amount of local memory, in bytes, currently consumed by the
(t1/e1) Munich chip driver. Thresholds should be computed as a
percentage of the total memory.

Returns: gauge   Suggested poll period: 27
Preprocessing: none   Threshold comparison: >

Red threshold: 65%   Orange threshold: 55%   Yellow threshold: 45%

Name: wfResourceUseMemoryQuicsync   MIB: wellfleetResourceMIB
OID: 1.3.6.1.4.1.18.3.3.2.5.6.1.5.48

Instantiated by: wfResourceUseSlot

Description:

The amount of local memory, in bytes, currently consumed by the
quicsync chip driver. Thresholds should be computed as a percentage
of the total memory.

Returns: gauge   Suggested poll period: 29
Preprocessing: none   Threshold comparison: >

Red threshold: 65%   Orange threshold: 55%   Yellow threshold: 45%

Name: wfResourceUseMemoryAsnmod   MIB: wellfleetResourceMIB
OID: 1.3.6.1.4.1.18.3.3.2.5.6.1.5.50

Instantiated by: wfResourceUseSlot

Description:

The amount of local memory, in bytes, currently consumed by the
asnmod code. Thresholds should be computed as a percentage of the
total memory.

Returns: gauge   Suggested poll period: 27
Preprocessing: none   Threshold comparison: >

Red threshold: 65%   Orange threshold: 55%   Yellow threshold: 45%

Name: wfResourceUseMemoryDebug   MIB: wellfleetResourceMIB
OID: 1.3.6.1.4.1.18.3.3.2.5.6.1.5.54

Instantiated by: wfResourceUseSlot

Description:

The amount of local memory, in bytes, currently consumed by the
debug code. Thresholds should be computed as a percentage of the
total memory.

Returns: gauge   Suggested poll period: 29
Preprocessing: none   Threshold comparison: >

Red threshold: 65%   Orange threshold: 55%   Yellow threshold: 45%

Name: wfResourceUseMemoryPing   MIB: wellfleetResourceMIB
OID: 1.3.6.1.4.1.18.3.3.2.5.6.1.5.69

Instantiated by: wfResourceUseSlot

Description:

The amount of local memory, in bytes, currently consumed by the
ping code. Thresholds should be computed as a percentage of the
total memory.

Returns: gauge   Suggested poll period: 29
Preprocessing: none   Threshold comparison: >

Red threshold: 65%   Orange threshold: 55%   Yellow threshold: 45%

Name: wfResourceUseMemorySyslog   MIB: wellfleetResourceMIB
OID: 1.3.6.1.4.1.18.3.3.2.5.6.1.5.78

Instantiated by: wfResourceUseSlot

Description:

The amount of local memory, in bytes, currently consumed by the
syslog code. Thresholds should be computed as a percentage of the
total memory.

Returns: gauge   Suggested poll period: 29
Preprocessing: none   Threshold comparison: >

Red threshold: 65%   Orange threshold: 55%   Yellow threshold: 45%

Name: wfResourceUseMemoryNsc100m   MIB: wellfleetResourceMIB
OID: 1.3.6.1.4.1.18.3.3.2.5.6.1.5.84

Instantiated by: wfResourceUseSlot

Description:

The amount of local memory, in bytes, currently consumed by the
National Semiconductor DP83810 chip driver. Thresholds should be
computed as a percentage of the total memory.

Returns: gauge   Suggested poll period: 29
Preprocessing: none   Threshold comparison: >

Red threshold: 65%   Orange threshold: 55%   Yellow threshold: 45%

Name: wfResourceUseMemoryATMSig   MIB: wellfleetResourceMIB
OID: 1.3.6.1.4.1.18.3.3.2.5.6.1.5.93

Instantiated by: wfResourceUseSlot

Description:

The amount of local memory, in bytes, currently consumed by ATM
signaling. Thresholds should be computed as a percentage of the
total memory.

Returns: gauge   Suggested poll period: 27
Preprocessing: none   Threshold comparison: >

Red threshold: 65%   Orange threshold: 55%   Yellow threshold: 45%

Name: wfResourceUseMemoryNat   MIB: wellfleetResourceMIB
OID: 1.3.6.1.4.1.18.3.3.2.5.6.1.5.119

Instantiated by: wfResourceUseSlot

Description:

The amount of local memory, in bytes, currently consumed by NAT.
Thresholds should be computed as a percentage of the total memory.

Returns: gauge   Suggested poll period: 27
Preprocessing: none   Threshold comparison: >

Red threshold: 65%   Orange threshold: 55%   Yellow threshold: 45%

Name: wfResourceUseBuffersKernel   MIB: wellfleetResourceMIB
OID: 1.3.6.1.4.1.18.3.3.2.5.6.1.6.1

Instantiated by: wfResourceUseSlot

Description:

The amount of global memory, in bytes, currently consumed by the
kernel. Thresholds should be computed as a percentage of the total
buffers.

Returns: gauge   Suggested poll period: 21
Preprocessing: none   Threshold comparison: >

Red threshold: 65%   Orange threshold: 55%   Yellow threshold: 45%

Name: wfResourceUseBuffersQenet   MIB: wellfleetResourceMIB
OID: 1.3.6.1.4.1.18.3.3.2.5.6.1.6.3

Instantiated by: wfResourceUseSlot

Description:

The amount of global memory, in bytes, currently consumed by the
quad ethernet driver. Thresholds should be computed as a percentage
of the total buffers.

Returns: gauge   Suggested poll period: 23
Preprocessing: none   Threshold comparison: >

Red threshold: 65%   Orange threshold: 55%   Yellow threshold: 45%

Name: wfResourceUseBuffersIlacc   MIB: wellfleetResourceMIB
OID: 1.3.6.1.4.1.18.3.3.2.5.6.1.6.13

Instantiated by: wfResourceUseSlot

Description:

The amount of global memory, in bytes, currently consumed by the
Ilacc chip driver. Thresholds should be computed as a percentage of
the total buffers.

Returns: gauge   Suggested poll period: 23
Preprocessing: none   Threshold comparison: >

Red threshold: 65%   Orange threshold: 55%   Yellow threshold: 45%

Name: wfResourceUseBuffersIP   MIB: wellfleetResourceMIB
OID: 1.3.6.1.4.1.18.3.3.2.5.6.1.6.21

Instantiated by: wfResourceUseSlot

Description:

The amount of global memory, in bytes, currently consumed by IP.
Thresholds should be computed as a percentage of the total buffers.

Returns: gauge   Suggested poll period: 21
Preprocessing: none   Threshold comparison: >

Red threshold: 65%   Orange threshold: 55%   Yellow threshold: 45%

Name: wfResourceUseBuffersIpx   MIB: wellfleetResourceMIB
OID: 1.3.6.1.4.1.18.3.3.2.5.6.1.6.26

Instantiated by: wfResourceUseSlot

Description:

The amount of global memory, in bytes, currently consumed by IPX.
Thresholds should be computed as a percentage of the total buffers.

Returns: gauge   Suggested poll period: 23
Preprocessing: none   Threshold comparison: >

Red threshold: 65%   Orange threshold: 55%   Yellow threshold: 45%

Name: wfResourceUseBuffersFr   MIB: wellfleetResourceMIB
OID: 1.3.6.1.4.1.18.3.3.2.5.6.1.6.29

Instantiated by: wfResourceUseSlot

Description:

The amount of global memory, in bytes, currently consumed by frame
relay. Thresholds should be computed as a percentage of the total
buffers.

Returns: gauge   Suggested poll period: 21
Preprocessing: none   Threshold comparison: >

Red threshold: 65%   Orange threshold: 55%   Yellow threshold: 45%

Name: wfResourceUseBuffersDlsw   MIB: wellfleetResourceMIB
OID: 1.3.6.1.4.1.18.3.3.2.5.6.1.6.32

Instantiated by: wfResourceUseSlot

Description:

The amount of global memory, in bytes, currently consumed by dlsw.
Thresholds should be computed as a percentage of the total buffers.

Returns: gauge   Suggested poll period: 23
Preprocessing: none   Threshold comparison: >

Red threshold: 65%   Orange threshold: 55%   Yellow threshold: 45%

Name: wfResourceUseBuffersArp   MIB: wellfleetResourceMIB
OID: 1.3.6.1.4.1.18.3.3.2.5.6.1.6.33

Instantiated by: wfResourceUseSlot

Description:

The amount of global memory, in bytes, currently consumed by ARP.
Thresholds should be computed as a percentage of the total buffers.

Returns: gauge   Suggested poll period: 21
Preprocessing: none   Threshold comparison: >

Red threshold: 65%   Orange threshold: 55%   Yellow threshold: 45%

Name: wfResourceUseBuffersSnmp   MIB: wellfleetResourceMIB
OID: 1.3.6.1.4.1.18.3.3.2.5.6.1.6.35

Instantiated by: wfResourceUseSlot

Description:

The amount of global memory, in bytes, currently consumed by SNMP.
Thresholds should be computed as a percentage of the total buffers.

Returns: gauge   Suggested poll period: 23
Preprocessing: none   Threshold comparison: >

Red threshold: 65%   Orange threshold: 55%   Yellow threshold: 45%

Name: wfResourceUseBuffersTcp   MIB: wellfleetResourceMIB
OID: 1.3.6.1.4.1.18.3.3.2.5.6.1.6.37

Instantiated by: wfResourceUseSlot

Description:

The amount of global memory, in bytes, currently consumed by TCP.
Thresholds should be computed as a percentage of the total buffers.

Returns: gauge   Suggested poll period: 21
Preprocessing: none   Threshold comparison: >

Red threshold: 65%   Orange threshold: 55%   Yellow threshold: 45%

Name: wfResourceUseBuffersBgp   MIB: wellfleetResourceMIB
OID: 1.3.6.1.4.1.18.3.3.2.5.6.1.6.38

Instantiated by: wfResourceUseSlot

Description:

The amount of global memory, in bytes, currently consumed by BGP.
Thresholds should be computed as a percentage of the total buffers.

Returns: gauge   Suggested poll period: 21
Preprocessing: none   Threshold comparison: >

Red threshold: 65%   Orange threshold: 55%   Yellow threshold: 45%

Name: wfResourceUseBuffersOspf   MIB: wellfleetResourceMIB
OID: 1.3.6.1.4.1.18.3.3.2.5.6.1.6.40

Instantiated by: wfResourceUseSlot

Description:

The amount of global memory, in bytes, currently consumed by OSPF.
Thresholds should be computed as a percentage of the total buffers.

Returns: gauge   Suggested poll period: 21
Preprocessing: none   Threshold comparison: >

Red threshold: 65%   Orange threshold: 55%   Yellow threshold: 45%

Name: wfResourceUseBuffersPcap   MIB: wellfleetResourceMIB
OID: 1.3.6.1.4.1.18.3.3.2.5.6.1.6.45

Instantiated by: wfResourceUseSlot

Description:

The amount of global memory, in bytes, currently consumed by packet
capture. Thresholds should be computed as a percentage of the total
buffers.

Returns: gauge   Suggested poll period: 23
Preprocessing: none   Threshold comparison: >

Red threshold: 65%   Orange threshold: 55%   Yellow threshold: 45%

Name: wfResourceUseBuffersMunich   MIB: wellfleetResourceMIB
OID: 1.3.6.1.4.1.18.3.3.2.5.6.1.6.47

Instantiated by: wfResourceUseSlot

Description:

The amount of global memory, in bytes, currently consumed by the
(t1/e1) Munich chip driver. Thresholds should be computed as a
percentage of the total buffers.

Returns: gauge   Suggested poll period: 21
Preprocessing: none   Threshold comparison: >

Red threshold: 65%   Orange threshold: 55%   Yellow threshold: 45%

Name: wfResourceUseBuffersQuicsync   MIB: wellfleetResourceMIB
OID: 1.3.6.1.4.1.18.3.3.2.5.6.1.6.48

Instantiated by: wfResourceUseSlot

Description:

The amount of global memory, in bytes, currently consumed by the
quicsync chip code. Thresholds should be computed as a percentage
of the total buffers.

Returns: gauge   Suggested poll period: 23
Preprocessing: none   Threshold comparison: >

Red threshold: 65%   Orange threshold: 55%   Yellow threshold: 45%

Name: wfResourceUseBuffersAsnmod   MIB: wellfleetResourceMIB
OID: 1.3.6.1.4.1.18.3.3.2.5.6.1.6.50

Instantiated by: wfResourceUseSlot

Description:

The amount of global memory, in bytes, currently consumed by
Asnmod. Thresholds should be computed as a percentage of the total
buffers.

Returns: gauge   Suggested poll period: 21
Preprocessing: none   Threshold comparison: >

Red threshold: 65%   Orange threshold: 55%   Yellow threshold: 45%

Name: wfResourceUseBuffersDebug   MIB: wellfleetResourceMIB
OID: 1.3.6.1.4.1.18.3.3.2.5.6.1.6.54

Instantiated by: wfResourceUseSlot

Description:

The amount of global memory, in bytes, currently consumed by the
debug code. Thresholds should be computed as a percentage of the
total buffers.

Returns: gauge   Suggested poll period: 23
Preprocessing: none   Threshold comparison: >

Red threshold: 65%   Orange threshold: 55%   Yellow threshold: 45%

Name: wfResourceUseBuffersPing   MIB: wellfleetResourceMIB
OID: 1.3.6.1.4.1.18.3.3.2.5.6.1.6.69

Instantiated by: wfResourceUseSlot

Description:

The amount of global memory, in bytes, currently consumed by ping.
Thresholds should be computed as a percentage of the total buffers.

Returns: gauge   Suggested poll period: 23
Preprocessing: none   Threshold comparison: >

Red threshold: 65%   Orange threshold: 55%   Yellow threshold: 45%

Name: wfResourceUseBuffersSyslog   MIB: wellfleetResourceMIB
OID: 1.3.6.1.4.1.18.3.3.2.5.6.1.6.78

Instantiated by: wfResourceUseSlot

Description:

The amount of global memory, in bytes, currently consumed by syslog. Thresholds should be computed as a percentage of the total buffers.

Returns: gauge   Suggested poll period: 23
Preprocessing: none   Threshold comparison: >

Red threshold: 65%   Orange threshold: 55%   Yellow threshold: 45%

Name: wfResourceUseBuffersNsc100m   MIB: wellfleetResourceMIB
OID: 1.3.6.1.4.1.18.3.3.2.5.6.1.6.84

Instantiated by: wfResourceUseSlot

Description:

The amount of global memory, in bytes, currently consumed by the National Semiconductor DP83810 code. Thresholds should be computed as a percentage of the total buffers.

Returns: gauge   Suggested poll period: 23
Preprocessing: none   Threshold comparison: >

Red threshold: 65%   Orange threshold: 55%   Yellow threshold: 45%

Name: wfResourceUseBuffersATMSig   MIB: wellfleetResourceMIB
OID: 1.3.6.1.4.1.18.3.3.2.5.6.1.6.93

Instantiated by: wfResourceUseSlot

Description:

The amount of global memory, in bytes, currently consumed by ATM signaling. Thresholds should be computed as a percentage of the total buffers.

Returns: gauge   Suggested poll period: 21
Preprocessing: none   Threshold comparison: >

Red threshold: 65%   Orange threshold: 55%   Yellow threshold: 45%

Name: wfResourceUseBuffersNat   MIB: wellfleetResourceMIB
OID: 1.3.6.1.4.1.18.3.3.2.5.6.1.6.119

Instantiated by: wfResourceUseSlot

Description:

The amount of global memory, in bytes, currently consumed by NAT.
Thresholds should be computed as a percentage of the total buffers.

Returns: gauge   Suggested poll period: 23
Preprocessing: none   Threshold comparison: >

Red threshold: 65%   Orange threshold: 55%   Yellow threshold: 45%

The following objects describe instrumentation for Nortel/Bay ethernet interfaces. Bay routers do not support many of the standard MIBs, though they duplicate many standard objects in private space.

Name: wfCSMACDState   MIB: wellfleetCsmacdMIB
OID: 1.3.6.1.4.1.18.3.4.1.1.3

Instantiated by: wfCSMACDSlot.wfCSMACDConnector

Description:

The current state of the ethernet port. If red, the line driver is
down.

Returns: integer   Suggested poll period: 7
Preprocessing: none   Threshold comparison: =

Red threshold: 2   Orange threshold: Yellow threshold:

Name: wfCSMACDDeferredTx   MIB: wellfleetCsmacdMIB
OID: 1.3.6.1.4.1.18.3.4.1.1.15

Instantiated by: wfCSMACDSlot.wfCSMACDConnector

Description:

The total number of frames successfully transmitted by this
interface that were deferred without experiencing collisions. This
is an early indicator of congestion and suggests possible building
output queues.

Returns: counter   Suggested poll period: 10
Preprocessing: rate   Threshold comparison: >

Red threshold: 500   Orange threshold: 100   Yellow threshold: 10

Name: wfCSMACDLateCollnTx   MIB: wellfleetCsmacdMIB
OID: 1.3.6.1.4.1.18.3.4.1.1.16

Instantiated by: wfCSMACDSlot.wfCSMACDConnector

Description:

The total number of collisions seen by this ethernet port that
occurred after the preamble. This suggests that the propagation
delay of the ethernet (including bridges and switches) may exceed
the ethernet spec. If cutthrough switches are in use, store and
forward may help.

Returns: counter   Suggested poll period: 7
Preprocessing: rate   Threshold comparison: >

Red threshold: 50   Orange threshold: 25   Yellow threshold: 5

Name: wfCSMACDExcessvCollnTx   MIB: wellfleetCsmacdMIB
OID: 1.3.6.1.4.1.18.3.4.1.1.17

Instantiated by: wfCSMACDSlot.wfCSMACDConnector

Description:

The total number of frames unsuccessfully transmitted by this
interface because they experienced 16 collisions and were
discarded. This is a dramatic indicator of congestion.

Returns: counter   Suggested poll period: 30
Preprocessing: rate   Threshold comparison: >

Red threshold: 10   Orange threshold: 5   Yellow threshold: 1

Name: wfCSMACDBufErrorTx   MIB: wellfleetCsmacdMIB
OID: 1.3.6.1.4.1.18.3.4.1.1.19

Instantiated by: wfCSMACDSlot.wfCSMACDConnector

Description:

The total number of internal buffer errors detected during
transmission on this port.

Returns: counter   Suggested poll period: 13
Preprocessing: rate   Threshold comparison: >

Red threshold: 20   Orange threshold: 15   Yellow threshold: 5

Name: wfCSMACDLcarTx   MIB: wellfleetCsmacdMIB
OID: 1.3.6.1.4.1.18.3.4.1.1.20

Instantiated by: wfCSMACDSlot.wfCSMACDConnector

Description:

The total number of times that carrier was lost on this interface.

Returns: counter

Suggested poll period: 10

Preprocessing: delta

Threshold comparison: >

Red threshold: Orange threshold: Yellow threshold: 1

Name: wfCSMACDUfloTx

MIB: wellfleetCsmacdMIB

OID: 1.3.6.1.4.1.18.3.4.1.1.21

Instantiated by: wfCSMACDSlot.wfCSMACDConnector

Description:

The total number of times packets were dropped by this interface because the MAC hardware was unable to fetch from packet memory and the transmit queue underflowed. This generally indicates an overutilized interface and may require a hardware upgrade or shifting some traffic away from this card.

Returns: counter

Suggested poll period: 11

Preprocessing: rate

Threshold comparison: >

Red threshold: 20   Orange threshold: 10   Yellow threshold: 1

Name: wfCSMACDFcsErrorRx

MIB: wellfleetCsmacdMIB

OID: 1.3.6.1.4.1.18.3.4.1.1.22

Instantiated by: wfCSMACDSlot.wfCSMACDConnector

Description:

The total number of packets received by this interface that failed the layer 2 checksum (CRC-16). Packet corruption can be caused by noisy environments, bad hardware, and faulty cable.

Returns: counter

Suggested poll period: 5

Preprocessing: rate

Threshold comparison: >

Red threshold: 50   Orange threshold: 10   Yellow threshold: 0

Name: wfCSMACDAlignErrorRx   MIB: wellfleetCsmacdMIB
OID: 1.3.6.1.4.1.18.3.4.1.1.23

Instantiated by: wfCSMACDSlot.wfCSMACDConnector

Description:

The total number of frames received by this interface that failed
to end on an 8-bit boundary. These are often caused by high levels
of collisions, resulting in fragments. Collision rates, end-end
propegation delay, and the use of cutthrough switches are common
causes of this error.

Returns: counter   Suggested poll period: 3
Preprocessing: rate   Threshold comparison: >

Red threshold: 100   Orange threshold: 50   Yellow threshold: 10

Name: wfCSMACDLackRescErrorRx   MIB: wellfleetCsmacdMIB
OID: 1.3.6.1.4.1.18.3.4.1.1.24

Instantiated by: wfCSMACDSlot.wfCSMACDConnector

Description:

Counts the number of packets that were dropped inbound on this
interface due to a lack of local buffers. This generally indicates
a local resource problem on the hardware, but can also be the
result of filters.

Returns: counter   Suggested poll period: 7
Preprocessing: rate   Threshold comparison: >

Red threshold: 20   Orange threshold: 10   Yellow threshold: 1

Name: wfCSMACDTooLongErrorRx   MIB: wellfleetCsmacdMIB
OID: 1.3.6.1.4.1.18.3.4.1.1.25

Instantiated by: wfCSMACDSlot.wfCSMACDConnector

Description:

The total number of frames received by this interface that were
discarded because they exceeded the maximum receive packet size.

Returns: counter   Suggested poll period: 7
Preprocessing: rate   Threshold comparison: >

Red threshold: 10   Orange threshold: 6   Yellow threshold: 1

Name: wfCSMACDOfloRx   MIB: wellfleetCsmacdMIB
OID: 1.3.6.1.4.1.18.3.4.1.1.26

Instantiated by: wfCSMACDSlot.wfCSMACDConnector

Description:

The total number of times packets were dropped by this interface
because the MAC hardware was unable to write to packet memory and
the receive queue overflowed. This generally indicates an
overutilized interface, and may require a hardware upgrade or
shifting some traffic away from this card.

Returns: counter   Suggested poll period: 11
Preprocessing: rate   Threshold comparison: >

Red threshold: 20   Orange threshold: 10   Yellow threshold: 1

Name: wfCSMACDMerr   MIB: wellfleetCsmacdMIB
OID: 1.3.6.1.4.1.18.3.4.1.1.27

Instantiated by: wfCSMACDSlot.wfCSMACDConnector

Description:

The total number of local memory errors detected by this interface.
This may be caused by either a software bug or hardware defect.

Returns: counter   Suggested poll period: 7
Preprocessing: rate   Threshold comparison: >

Red threshold: 10   Orange threshold: 6   Yellow threshold: 0

Name: wfCSMACDTxClipFrames   MIB: wellfleetCsmacdMIB
OID: 1.3.6.1.4.1.18.3.4.1.1.32

Instantiated by: wfCSMACDSlot.wfCSMACDConnector

Description:

The total number of frames truncated during transmission due to
congestion.

Returns: counter   Suggested poll period: 11
Preprocessing: rate   Threshold comparison: >

Red threshold: 20   Orange threshold: 15   Yellow threshold: 5

Name: wfCSMACDRxReplenMisses   MIB: wellfleetCsmacdMIB
OID: 1.3.6.1.4.1.18.3.4.1.1.33

Instantiated by: wfCSMACDSlot.wfCSMACDConnector

Description:

The total number of times the chipset driver failed to get a packet
buffer to replenish the available receive ring. This indicates
either insufficient processing power or excessive congestion on
this card.

Returns: counter   Suggested poll period: 13
Preprocessing: rate   Threshold comparison: >

Red threshold: 20   Orange threshold: 10   Yellow threshold: 1

Name: wfCSMACDSingleCollisionFrames   MIB: wellfleetCsmacdMIB
OID: 1.3.6.1.4.1.18.3.4.1.1.49

Instantiated by: wfCSMACDSlot.wfCSMACDConnector

Description:

The total number of frames successfully transmitted by this
interface that were deferred due to exactly one collision. This is
an early indication of congestion.

Returns: counter   Suggested poll period: 7
Preprocessing: rate   Threshold comparison: >

Red threshold: 100   Orange threshold: 80   Yellow threshold: 60

Name: wfCSMACDMultipleCollisionFrames   MIB: wellfleetCsmacdMIB
OID: 1.3.6.1.4.1.18.3.4.1.1.50

Instantiated by: wfCSMACDSlot.wfCSMACDConnector

Description:

The total number of frames successfully transmitted by this
interface that were deferred due to exactly one collision. This is
an active indication of congestion.

Returns: counter   Suggested poll period: 7
Preprocessing: rate   Threshold comparison: >

Red threshold: 50   Orange threshold: 25   Yellow threshold: 5

Name: wfCSMACDInternalMacTxErrors   MIB: wellfleetCsmacdMIB
OID: 1.3.6.1.4.1.18.3.4.1.1.51

Instantiated by: wfCSMACDSlot.wfCSMACDConnector

Description:

The total number of frames unsuccessfully transmitted because of an
internal error in the MAC layer. This is often transmit underruns,
caused by the inability of the ethernet controller to replenish the
transmit FIFO.

Returns: counter   Suggested poll period: 7
Preprocessing: rate   Threshold comparison: >

Red threshold: 10   Orange threshold: 6   Yellow threshold: 1

Name: wfCSMACDInternalMacRxErrors   MIB: wellfleetCsmacdMIB
OID: 1.3.6.1.4.1.18.3.4.1.1.55

Instantiated by: wfCSMACDSlot.wfCSMACDConnector

Description:

The total number of frames unsuccessfully received because of an
internal error in the MAC layer. This is often receiver overruns,
caused by the inability of the ethernet controller to flush the
receive FIFO.

Returns: counter   Suggested poll period: 7
Preprocessing: rate   Threshold comparison: >

Red threshold: 10   Orange threshold: 6   Yellow threshold: 1

Name: wfCSMACDRxFlushes   MIB: wellfleetCsmacdMIB
OID: 1.3.6.1.4.1.18.3.4.1.1.57

```
Instantiated by: wfCSMACDSlot.wfCSMACDConnector
```

Description:

The total number of times that the hardware had to reset itself by flushing the receive FIFO. This is generally the result of FIFO overflows or truncated receive packets.

Returns: counter   Suggested poll period: 7
Preprocessing: delta   Threshold comparison: >

Red threshold: 5   Orange threshold: 3   Yellow threshold: 1

Name: wfCSMACDTxDeadlocks   MIB: wellfleetCsmacdMIB
OID: 1.3.6.1.4.1.18.3.4.1.1.58

Instantiated by: wfCSMACDSlot.wfCSMACDConnector

Description:

The total number of times that the software had to correct a hardware deadlock. This is unexpected and suggests either a software bug or hardware failure.

Returns: counter   Suggested poll period: 5
Preprocessing: delta   Threshold comparison: >

Red threshold: 10   Orange threshold: 5   Yellow threshold: 0

Nortel Routing Protocols

The following objects describe instrumentation for Nortel/Bay BGP. Bay routers do not support many of the standard MIBs, although they duplicate many standard objects in private space.

Name: wfBgpPeerConnState   MIB: wellfleetBgpMIB
OID: 1.3.6.1.4.1.18.3.5.3.2.5.1.2.1.19

```
Instantiated by: wfBgpPeerLocalAddr.wfBgpPeerRemoteAddr
```

Description:

A state variable, indicating the current status of the session with this peer. If red, the session is not ESTABLISHED.

```
Returns: integer                    Suggested poll period: 15
Preprocessing: none                 Threshold comparison:  !
```

```
Red threshold: 6   Orange threshold:     Yellow threshold:
```

```
Name: wfBgpPeerInUpdates              MIB: wellfleetBgpMIB
OID: 1.3.6.1.4.1.18.3.5.3.2.5.1.2.1.21
```

```
Instantiated by: wfBgpPeerLocalAddr.wfBgpPeerRemoteAddr
```

Description:

The total number of BGP updates received from this remote peer. If high, this peer may be destabilizing routing.

```
Returns: counter                    Suggested poll period: 30
Preprocessing: rate                 Threshold comparison:  >
```

```
Red threshold: 75   Orange threshold: 50   Yellow threshold: 5
```

```
Name: wfBgpPeerOutUpdates             MIB: wellfleetBgpMIB
OID: 1.3.6.1.4.1.18.3.5.3.2.5.1.2.1.22
```

```
Instantiated by: wfBgpPeerLocalAddr.wfBgpPeerRemoteAddr
```

Description:

The total number of BGP updates sent to this remote peer. If high, this local box may be destabilizing routing.

```
Returns: counter                Suggested poll period: 30
Preprocessing: rate             Threshold comparison:  >


Red threshold: 75   Orange threshold: 50   Yellow threshold: 5
```

```
Name: wfBgpPeerFsmEstablishedTime       MIB: wellfleetBgpMIB
OID: 1.3.6.1.4.1.18.3.5.3.2.5.1.2.1.28


Instantiated by: wfBgpPeerLocalAddr.wfBgpPeerRemoteAddr


Description:


The total time since the referenced peering session last changed.
Note that we test for any state change.


Returns: gauge                  Suggested poll period: 60
Preprocessing: none             Threshold comparison:  <


Red threshold: 150   Orange threshold:    Yellow threshold:
```

The following objects describe instrumentation for Nortel/Bay OSPF. Bay routers do not support many of the standard MIBs, although they duplicate many standard objects in private space.

```
Name: wfOspfSpfCnt                      MIB: wellfleetOspfMIB
OID: 1.3.6.1.4.1.18.3.5.3.2.3.2.1.9


Instantiated by: wfOspfAreaId


Description:


The total number of times that the SPF algorithm has been run
against the link state database for the specified area. This is a
stronger indicator of changes to the route table than the
generation or reception of "new" LSAs.


Returns: counter                Suggested poll period: 15
Preprocessing: delta            Threshold comparison:  >


Red threshold: 10   Orange threshold: 5   Yellow threshold: 0
```

Name: wfOspfIfState   MIB: wellfleetOspfMIB
OID: 1.3.6.1.4.1.18.3.5.3.2.3.5.1.3

Instantiated by: wfOspfIfIpAddr.wfOspfAddrlessIf

Description:

The state of the local OSPF interface. This is instantiated by the
interface's IP address and an addressless value, in case interfaces
on this device are not assigned individual IP addresses. Red
indicates a state of "down"; orange indicates a state of "looped."

Returns: integer   Suggested poll period: 7
Preprocessing: none   Threshold comparison: =

Red threshold: 1   Orange threshold: 2   Yellow threshold:

Name: wfOspfIfTxLinkStateUpds   MIB: wellfleetOspfMIB
OID: 1.3.6.1.4.1.18.3.5.3.2.3.5.1.21

Instantiated by: wfOspfIfIpAddr.wfOspfAddrlessIf

Description:

The total number of unique Link State updates that this interface
has sent. This indicates routing updates that are being propagated
by the referenced interface, and suggest infrastructure
instability.

Returns: counter   Suggested poll period: 60
Preprocessing: delta   Threshold comparison: >

Red threshold: 20   Orange threshold: 15   Yellow threshold: 5

Name: wfOspfIfRxLinkStateUpds   MIB: wellfleetOspfMIB
OID: 1.3.6.1.4.1.18.3.5.3.2.3.5.1.26

Instantiated by: wfOspfIfIpAddr.wfOspfAddrlessIf

Description:

The total number of unique Link State Announcements that this
device has received. This indicates routing updates that are being
passed to this interface and suggest infrastructure instability.

Returns: counter   Suggested poll period: 30
Preprocessing: delta   Threshold comparison: >

Red threshold: 40   Orange threshold: 30   Yellow threshold: 10

Name: wfOspfVirtIfState   MIB: wellfleetOspfMIB
OID: 1.3.6.1.4.1.18.3.5.3.2.3.6.1.3

Instantiated by: wfVirtIfAreaId.wfVirtIfNbr

Description:

The state of the OSPF virtual interface. Red indicates a state of
"down."

Returns: integer   Suggested poll period: 7
Preprocessing: none   Threshold comparison: =

Red threshold: 1   Orange threshold: Yellow threshold:

Name: wfOspfVirtIfTxLinkStateUpds   MIB: wellfleetOspfMIB
OID: 1.3.6.1.4.1.18.3.5.3.2.3.6.1.14

Instantiated by: wfVirtIfAreaId.wfVirtIfNbr

Description:

The total number of unique Link State Announcements that this
virtual interface has sent. This indicates routing updates that are
being passed to this interface and suggests infrastructure
instability.

Returns: counter   Suggested poll period: 30
Preprocessing: delta   Threshold comparison: >

Red threshold: 20   Orange threshold: 15   Yellow threshold: 5

Name: wfOspfNbrState   MIB: wellfleetOspfMIB
OID: 1.3.6.1.4.1.18.3.5.3.2.3.7.1.3

Instantiated by: wfOspfNbrIpAddr.wfOspfNbrAddrLessIndex

Description:

The state of the OSPF neighbor's interface. This is instantiated by
the interface's IP address and an addressless value, in case
interfaces on that device are not assigned individual IP addresses.
Red indicates a state of "down."

Returns: integer   Suggested poll period: 13
Preprocessing: none   Threshold comparison: =

Red threshold: 1   Orange threshold: Yellow threshold:

Name: wfOspfVirtNbrState   MIB: wellfleetOspfMIB
OID: 1.3.6.1.4.1.18.3.5.3.2.3.8.1.5

Instantiated by: wfOspfVirtNbrAreaId.wfOspfVirtNbrRtrId

Description:

The state of the local OSPF virtual interface. Red indicates a
state of "down."

Returns: integer   Suggested poll period: 13
Preprocessing: none   Threshold comparison: =

Red threshold: 1   Orange threshold: Yellow threshold:

Motorola Cable Routers

Name: xmtrTransmitLevel   MIB: CableRouterMIB
OID: 1.3.6.1.4.1.161.7.10.1.2.3.1.5

Instantiated by: ifNumber

Description:

The current transmitter power level, in dBmV. High power levels
suggest that the router is trying to compensate for plant problems,
likely downstream loading.

Returns: integer   Suggested poll period: 31
Preprocessing: none   Threshold comparison: >

Red threshold: 52   Orange threshold: 50   Yellow threshold:

Name: xmtrChannel   MIB: CableRouterMIB
OID: 1.3.6.1.4.1.161.7.10.1.2.3.1.6

Instantiated by: ifNumber

Description:

The current number of the transmitter's downstream channel, which
maps to a frequency. Note that this is monitored for any change.
Common changes indicate that the router is having problems finding
a channel with acceptable performance, suggesting a plant health or
hardware problem.

Returns: integer   Suggested poll period: 11
Preprocessing: delta   Threshold comparison: >

Red threshold: Orange threshold: Yellow threshold: 0

Name: xmtrErrorsXmtd   MIB: CableRouterMIB
OID: 1.3.6.1.4.1.161.7.10.1.2.3.1.9

Instantiated by: ifNumber

Description:

The total number of frames (data and control) transmitted by this
downstream interface that were received by a modem with errors.

Returns: counter   Suggested poll period: 60
Preprocessing: rate   Threshold comparison: >

Red threshold: 25   Orange threshold: 15   Yellow threshold: 5

Name: xmtrFreeBuffs   MIB: CableRouterMIB
OID: 1.3.6.1.4.1.161.7.10.1.2.3.1.16

Instantiated by: ifNumber

Description:

The current number of free data buffers available to transmit
frames. Thresholds provided are a percentage of the total number of
transmit buffers for this interface.

Returns: gauge   Suggested poll period: 7
Preprocessing: none   Threshold comparison: <

Red threshold: 20%   Orange threshold: 25%   Yellow threshold: 35%

Name: xmtrBuffOverruns   MIB: CableRouterMIB
OID: 1.3.6.1.4.1.161.7.10.1.2.3.1.17

Instantiated by: ifNumber

Description:

The total number of data frames dropped because of a lack of
available buffers.

Returns: counter   Suggested poll period: 7
Preprocessing: rate   Threshold comparison: >

Red threshold: 10   Orange threshold: 7   Yellow threshold: 1

Name: niOperStatus   MIB: CableRouterMIB
OID: 1.3.6.1.4.1.161.7.10.1.2.5.1.10

Instantiated by: ifNumber

Description:

The current operational state of this interface. Red indicates the
interface is down; orange indicates that it is congested.

Returns: integer   Suggested poll period: 3
Preprocessing: none   Threshold comparison: =

Red threshold: 2   Orange threshold: 4   Yellow threshold:

Name: rcvrCurrChan   MIB: CableRouterMIB
OID: 1.3.6.1.4.1.161.7.10.1.2.4.1.6

Instantiated by: ifNumber

Description:

The current number of the receiver's downstream channel, which maps
to a frequency. Note that this is monitored for any change. Common
changes indicate that the modem is having problems finding a
channel with acceptable performance, suggesting a plant health or
hardware problem.

Returns: integer   Suggested poll period: 11
Preprocessing: delta   Threshold comparison: >

Red threshold: Orange threshold: Yellow threshold: 0

Name: rcvrErrorsRecvd   MIB: CableRouterMIB
OID: 1.3.6.1.4.1.161.7.10.1.2.4.1.8

Instantiated by: ifNumber

Description:

The total number of frames (data and control) received by this
upstream interface that contained errors.

Returns: counter   Suggested poll period: 13
Preprocessing: rate   Threshold comparison: >

Red threshold: 10   Orange threshold: 5   Yellow threshold: 3

Name: rcvrNaksRecvd   MIB: CableRouterMIB
OID: 1.3.6.1.4.1.161.7.10.1.2.4.1.13

Instantiated by: ifNumber

Description:

The total number of NACKs received in response to a poll from this
interface. This may be the result of a configuration mismatch
between the modems and the router, or an error with one of the
modems.

Returns: counter   Suggested poll period: 40
Preprocessing: rate   Threshold comparison: >

Red threshold: 5   Orange threshold:3   Yellow threshold: 1

Name: rcvrModeTransitions   MIB: CableRouterMIB
OID: 1.3.6.1.4.1.161.7.10.1.2.4.1.19

Instantiated by: ifNumber

Description:

The total number of transitions between modulation encoding methods
(QPSK and 16-QAM). Changes in encoding generally indicate
configuration errors or severe connectivity problems.

Returns: counter   Suggested poll period: 14
Preprocessing: delta   Threshold comparison: >

Red threshold: 3   Orange threshold: 2   Yellow threshold: 0

Name: rcvrFreeBuffs   MIB: CableRouterMIB
OID: 1.3.6.1.4.1.161.7.10.1.2.4.1.23

Instantiated by: ifNumber

The current number of free data buffers available to receive
frames. Thresholds provided are a percentage of the total number of
receive buffers for this interface.

Returns: gauge   Suggested poll period: 7
Preprocessing: none   Threshold comparison: <

Red threshold: 10%   Orange threshold: 15%   Yellow threshold: 25%

Name: rcvrBuffOverruns   MIB: CableRouterMIB
OID: 1.3.6.1.4.1.161.7.10.1.2.4.1.24

Instantiated by: ifNumber

Description:

The total number of times that packets were received by this
upstream interface, but were discarded due to a lack of receive
buffers.

Returns: counter   Suggested poll period: 11
Preprocessing: rate   Threshold comparison: >

Red threshold: 20   Orange threshold: 15   Yellow threshold: 3

Name: modemCurrentState   MIB: CableRouterMIB
OID: 1.3.6.1.4.1.161.7.10.1.4.1.1.9

Instantiated by: modemIndex

Description:

The current state of this modem. Red indicates that the modem has
been deregistered, orange indicates that the modem is
deregistering, and yellow indicates that software is currently
downloading into the modem.

Returns: integer   Suggested poll period: 7
Preprocessing: none   Threshold comparison: =

Red threshold: 1   Orange threshold: 5   Yellow threshold: 3

Name: modemDeregReason   MIB: CableRouterMIB
OID: 1.3.6.1.4.1.161.7.10.1.4.1.1.10

Instantiated by: modemIndex

Description:

The reason that the referenced modem was last deregistered. Note
that a value of 18 indicates no reason and may optionally be
ignored.

Returns: integer   Suggested poll period: 7
Preprocessing: none   Threshold comparison: >

Red threshold: 1   Orange threshold: Yellow threshold:

Name: modemReceiveLevel   MIB: CableRouterMIB
OID: 1.3.6.1.4.1.161.7.10.1.4.4.1.5

Instantiated by: modemIndex

Description:

The current received power level at the modem, in dBmV. Low power
conditions can indicate impedance, distance, or loading problems,
probably downstream.

Returns: integer   Suggested poll period: 31
Preprocessing: none   Threshold comparison: <

Red threshold: 46   Orange threshold: 48   Yellow threshold:

Name: modemTransmitLevel   MIB: CableRouterMIB
OID: 1.3.6.1.4.1.161.7.10.1.4.4.1.6

Instantiated by: modemIndex

Description:

The current transmit power level at the modem, in dBmV. High power
levels suggest that the modem is trying to compensate for plant
problems, probably loading upstream.

Returns: integer   Suggested poll period: 31
Preprocessing: none   Threshold comparison: >

Red threshold: 52   Orange threshold: 50   Yellow threshold:

Name: modemFramesRcvdInError   MIB: CableRouterMIB
OID: 1.3.6.1.4.1.161.7.10.1.4.4.1.11

Instantiated by: modemIndex

Description:

The total number of frames (data and control) received by this
modem that contained errors.

Returns: counter   Suggested poll period: 13
Preprocessing: rate   Threshold comparison: >

Red threshold: 15   Orange threshold: 10   Yellow threshold: 5

Name: modemFramesXmtdInError   MIB: CableRouterMIB
OID: 1.3.6.1.4.1.161.7.10.1.4.4.1.12

Instantiated by: modemIndex

Description:

The total number of frames (data and control) sent by this modem
that contained errors when received by the head end router.

Returns: counter   Suggested poll period: 13
Preprocessing: rate   Threshold comparison: >

Red threshold: 15   Orange threshold: 10   Yellow threshold: 5

Name: modemLanStatus   MIB: CableRouterMIB
OID: 1.3.6.1.4.1.1617.10.1.4.4.1.13

Instantiated by: modemIndex

Description:

The current state of the ethernet interface on the referenced cable modem. Red indicates down and orange indicates that the interface is undergoing diagnostic tests.

Returns: integer   Suggested poll period: 11
Preprocessing: none   Threshold comparison: =

Red threshold: 2   Orange threshold: 3   Yellow threshold:

Name: modemCurrSND   MIB: CableRouterMIB
OID: 1.3.6.1.4.1.161.7.10.1.4.4.1.20

Instantiated by: modemIndex

Description:

The currently computed value of signal to noise plus distortion (SND) received by the cable router from the referenced modem. If the value is less than or equal to zero, this object indicates a state indicating why SND is not available.

Returns: integer   Suggested poll period: 11
Preprocessing: none   Threshold comparison: <

Red threshold: 260   Orange threshold: 270   Yellow threshold: 280

Name: modemDownRxOverruns   MIB: CableRouterMIB
OID: 1.3.6.1.4.1.161.7.10.1.4.4.1.21

Instantiated by: modemIndex

Description:

The total number of times that packets were received by the referenced modem's downstream interface, but were discarded due to a lack of receive buffers.

Returns: counter

Preprocessing: rate

Suggested poll period: 11

Threshold comparison: >

Red threshold: 10   Orange threshold: 7   Yellow threshold: 3

Name: modemEthernetXmtdFrameErrors   MIB: CableRouterMIB
OID: 1.3.6.1.4.1.161.7.10.1.4.20.1.2

Instantiated by: modemIndex

Description:

The total number of frames sent by the reference modem's ethernet
interface that were found to contain errors during transmission.
Errors include FIFO underruns, size mismatches, and excessive
collisions.

Returns: counter

Preprocessing: rate

Suggested poll period: 11

Threshold comparison: >

Red threshold: 10   Orange threshold: 6   Yellow threshold: 2

Name: modemEthernetRcvdFrameErrors   MIB: CableRouterMIB
OID: 1.3.6.1.4.1.161.7.10.1.4.20.1.3

Instantiated by: modemIndex

Description:

The total number of frames received by the reference modem's
ethernet interface that were found to contain errors. Errors
include CRC and alignment errors.

Returns: counter

Preprocessing: rate

Suggested poll period: 11

Threshold comparison: >

Red threshold: 10   Orange threshold: 6   Yellow threshold: 2

Name: modemEthernetRxOverruns   MIB: CableRouterMIB
OID: 1.3.6.1.4.1.161.7.10.1.4.20.1.7

Instantiated by: modemIndex

Description:

The total number of frames received by the reference modem's
ethernet interface that were dropped due to a lack of receive
buffers.

Returns: counter   Suggested poll period: 11
Preprocessing: rate   Threshold comparison: >

Red threshold: 10   Orange threshold: 7   Yellow threshold: 3

Name: dialModemStatsUpdateStatus   MIB: CableRouterMIB
OID: 1.3.6.1.4.1.161.7.10.1.8.4.1.3

Instantiated by: modemIndex

Description:

The current state of the dial profile stored in the referenced
modem. Orange indicates that the profile, once proved to be good,
now fails and the modem is using its generic profile. The modem
will not attempt registration until fixed. Yellow is similar,
except that the modem has never connected with the current profile,
so it has not yet been demonstrated to be valid.

Returns: integer   Suggested poll period: 13
Preprocessing: none   Threshold comparison: =

Red threshold: Orange threshold: 3   Yellow threshold: 5

Name: atmStatsFRSigState   MIB: CableRouterMIB
OID: 1.3.6.1.4.1.161.7.10.1.9.3.1.9

Instantiated by: ifNumber

Description:

The current state of the ATM Remote Line Defect Indicator. If red, the circuit has failed.

Returns: integer   Suggested poll period: 11
Preprocessing: none   Threshold comparison: =

Red threshold: 1   Orange threshold: Yellow threshold:

Name: atmStatsLOSSigState   MIB: CableRouterMIB
OID: 1.3.6.1.4.1.161.7.10.1.9.3.1.10

Instantiated by: ifNumber

Description:

The current state of the Loss of Signal detection circuit. If red, the interface has observed approximately 20 microseconds of an all-zeros pattern.

Returns: integer   Suggested poll period: 11
Preprocessing: none   Threshold comparison: =

Red threshold: 1   Orange threshold: Yellow threshold:

Name: atmStatsLOFSigState   MIB: CableRouterMIB
OID: 1.3.6.1.4.1.161.7.10.1.9.3.1.11

Instantiated by: ifNumber

Description:

The current state of the Loss of Frame detection circuit. If red, the interface has observed approximately 3 milliseconds of Severely Errored Frame or Out Of Frame errors.

Returns: integer   Suggested poll period: 11
Preprocessing: none   Threshold comparison: =

Red threshold: 1   Orange threshold: Yellow threshold:

Name: atmStatsOOFSigState   MIB: CableRouterMIB
OID: 1.3.6.1.4.1.161.7.10.1.9.3.1.12

Instantiated by: ifNumber

Description:

The current state of the Loss of Signal detection circuit. If red, the
interface has observed four contiguous errored frame alignment words.

Returns: integer   Suggested poll period: 11
Preprocessing: none   Threshold comparison: =

Red threshold: 1   Orange threshold: Yellow threshold:

Name: atmStatsAISSigState   MIB: CableRouterMIB
OID: 1.3.6.1.4.1.161.7.10.1.9.3.1.13

Instantiated by: ifNumber

Description:

The current state of the Loss of Signal detection circuit. If red,
the interface has observed a "blue" alarm, indicating an upstream
failure in the circuit.

Returns: integer   Suggested poll period: 11
Preprocessing: none   Threshold comparison: =

Red threshold: 1   Orange threshold: Yellow threshold:

Name: atmStatsCellsFlushed   MIB: CableRouterMIB
OID: 1.3.6.1.4.1.161.7.10.1.9.3.1.14

Instantiated by: ifNumber

Description:

The total number of cells dropped by the Segmentation and
Reassembly (SAR) logic due to a lack of free buffers during
reassembly. This strongly indicates the need for additional memory
or a reduction in traffic levels.

Returns: counter   Suggested poll period: 11
Preprocessing: none   Threshold comparison: =

Red threshold: 25   Orange threshold: 15   Yellow threshold: 0

Name: atmStatsPacketTimeouts   MIB: CableRouterMIB
OID: 1.3.6.1.4.1.161.7.10.1.9.3.1.15

Instantiated by: ifNumber

Description:

The total number of packets that could not be reassembled from AAL5
cells due to timeouts. This tends to indicate packet loss along the
circuit.

Returns: counter   Suggested poll period: 7
Preprocessing: rate   Threshold comparison: >

Red threshold: 25   Orange threshold: 15   Yellow threshold: 0

Name: atmStatsPacketCRCErrors   MIB: CableRouterMIB
OID: 1.3.6.1.4.1.161.7.10.1.9.3.1.16

Instantiated by: ifNumber

Description:

The total number of packets found to contain CRC errors after being reassembled from ATM cells.

Returns: counter   Suggested poll period: 7
Preprocessing: rate   Threshold comparison: >

Red threshold: 30   Orange threshold: 20   Yellow threshold: 0

Name: atmStatsBufferOverFlows   MIB: CableRouterMIB
OID: 1.3.6.1.4.1.161.7.10.1.9.3.1.17

Instantiated by: ifNumber

Description:

The total number of packets that could not be reassembled from AAL5 cells because they exceeded the maximum size. This generally indicates a configuration problem.

Returns: counter   Suggested poll period: 7
Preprocessing: rate   Threshold comparison: >

Red threshold: 25   Orange threshold: 5   Yellow threshold: 0

Name: atmStatsPcktsExpCong   MIB: CableRouterMIB
OID: 1.3.6.1.4.1.161.7.10.1.9.3.1.18

Instantiated by: ifNumber

Description:

The total number of received AAL5 frames that indicate they experienced congestion in transit.

Returns: counter

Preprocessing: none

Suggested poll period: 11

Threshold comparison: >

Red threshold: 50   Orange threshold: 25   Yellow threshold: 0

Name: atmStatsCellsInvaidVP   MIB: CableRouterMIB
OID: 1.3.6.1.4.1.161.7.10.1.9.3.1.20

Instantiated by: ifNumber

Description:

The total number of cells that have been received by this interface
on invalid virtual paths. This suggests a configuration error.

Returns: counter

Preprocessing: delta

Suggested poll period: 17

Threshold comparison: >

Red threshold: 10   Orange threshold: 5   Yellow threshold: 0

Name: atmStatsCellsInvaidVC   MIB: CableRouterMIB
OID: 1.3.6.1.4.1.161.7.10.1.9.3.1.19

Instantiated by: ifNumber

Description:

The total number of cells that have been received by this interface
on invalid virtual circuits. This suggests a configuration error.

Returns: counter

Preprocessing: delta

Suggested poll period: 17

Threshold comparison: >

Red threshold: 10   Orange threshold: 5   Yellow threshold: 0

Name: atmStatsRxPacketsDropped   MIB: CableRouterMIB
OID: 1.3.6.1.4.1.161.7.10.1.9.3.1.22

Instantiated by: ifNumber

Description:

The total number of received AAL5 frames that were dropped because
of insufficient buffers on this interface.

Returns: counter   Suggested poll period: 7
Preprocessing: rate   Threshold comparison: >

Red threshold: 10   Orange threshold: 5   Yellow threshold: 0

Name: atmStatsTxPacketsDropped   MIB: CableRouterMIB
OID: 1.3.6.1.4.1.161.7.10.1.9.3.1.23

Instantiated by: ifNumber

Description:

The total number of AAL5 frames to transmit that were dropped
because of insufficient buffers on this interface.

Returns: counter   Suggested poll period: 7
Preprocessing: rate   Threshold comparison: >

Red threshold: 10   Orange threshold: 5   Yellow threshold: 0

Name: atmStatsCellsDropped   MIB: CableRouterMIB
OID: 1.3.6.1.4.1.161.7.10.1.9.3.1.25

Instantiated by: ifNumber

Description:

The total number of atm cells received by this interface that were dropped due to header checksum errors. This often indicates corruption on the atm circuit.

Returns: counter   Suggested poll period: 7
Preprocessing: rate   Threshold comparison: >

Red threshold: 5   Orange threshold: 3   Yellow threshold: 0

Name: atmStatsFreeQEmptied   MIB: CableRouterMIB
OID: 1.3.6.1.4.1.161.7.10.1.9.3.1.27

Instantiated by: ifNumber

Description:

The total number of times that this interface attempted to fetch a receive buffer and failed. This will result in one or more dropped packets.

Returns: counter   Suggested poll period: 5
Preprocessing: rate   Threshold comparison: >

Red threshold: 5   Orange threshold: 2   Yellow threshold: 0

GLOSSARY

access control list A type of packet filter, applied to Cisco routers.

access device A network element that sits at the edge of the cloud, closest to the end user or server. Access devices typically connect into distribution devices.

Access layer The complete set of access devices.

active management A network management discipline in which automated, corrective steps are taken as soon as a problem is diagnosed.

agent An SNMP entity that responds to queries.

application service provider *See* ASP.

ARP *Address Resolution Protocol* Typically used to map between MAC and IP addresses.

ASN.1 *Abstract Syntax Notation 1* An ISO standard for encoding arbitrary, formatted data.

ASP *Application Service Provider* An entity that sells access to shared, hosted applications.

ATM *Asynchronous Transfer Mode* An ISO standard protocol for the transmission of data formatted into small cells. ATM is generally used to provision point-to-point virtual circuits.

atomically At the same exact moment. For example, in SNMP, atomically setting all fields in a PDU requires that all objects be updated together.

autodiscovery A network management technique in which one attempts to learn the existence of elements and their interconnections (topology).

BadValue An SNMP error indicating that the provided value was outside of the supported range.

baseline A network management technique in which one attempts to learn the typical behavior of one or more network elements and normalize thresholds.

BER *Basic Encoding Rules* Governs the implementation of ASN.1.

BGP *Border Gateway Protocol* An IETF standard for exchanging routing information.

branch   A term in graph theory indicating an edge in a tree. These edges are lines that connect vertices.

CA   *Computer Associates International*, Inc.   A large software vendor.

child   A term in graph theory indicating a vertex, or node, that is contained under another vertex (the parent). In a tree structure, a parent may have multiple children, but a child may have only one parent.

CMIP   *Common Management Information Protocol*   An ISO standard protocol for managing networks.

CMOT   *CMIP Over TCP*   An IETF protocol defining the use of CMIP using TCP as its underlying transport.

construct   A term used in ASN.1 to denote an object.

constructed objects   A term used in ASN.1 to denote complex objects, generally those that contain other objects.

core device   A network element that sits in the center of the cloud and typically connects into a distribution device.

Core layer   A complete set of core devices.

Counter   An ASN.1 type, as defined by the SMI. Counters are 32- or 64-bit unsigned numbers that monotonically increase and that wrap when they hit their maximum value.

CPU   A *Central Processing Unit* or main computer chip.

CRC   *Cyclic Redundancy Code*   Similar to a checksum and is used to detect corrupted data messages.

discards   Used in MIBs to denote packets dropped even though they contained no errors. This action is often the result of filters or resource constraints.

DisplayString   An ASN.1 type, as defined by the SMI. A DisplayString is a textual convention format of an OCTET STRING that is printable as ASCII text.

distribution device   A network element that sits between the edge of the cloud and the core, aggregating access devices.

Distribution layer   The complete set of distribution devices.

diverse routing   Having multiple physical paths between two points.

DNS   *Domain Name System*   A protocol for converting between IP addresses and names.

domain   A collection of elements, generally grouped by topology or function.

Dotted Decimal Notation   A method for expressing strings of numbers, in base 10, using decimal points as delimiters.

drops   The combination of discards and errors.

Echo requests   A type of ICMP message that solicits a response message. Most commonly used by the ping program.

ecosystem   A collection of programs, each designed to perform a specific task, which interoperate to solve a greater problem.

edge   A term in graph theory that indicates the line connecting two vertices.

EGP   *External Gateway Protocol*   A protocol used to exchange routing information with other administrative domains.

element   A single device.

enterprise   A MIB term for an independent organization or company, generally responsible for producing its own MIB subtree.

errors   Messages that are dropped due to problems with their integrity or format.

EPA   *Environmental Protection Agency.*

fault analysis   The act of analyzing collected data to find the existence, location, and cause of failures.

fault detection   The act of analyzing data to find the existence of failures.

fault prediction   The act of analyzing data to perform fault analysis prior to typical fault detection.

flow   A related stream of messages that make up a single conversation; also called a *session*.

forwarding table   A table indicating the next step or path to take in order to reach a specific destination address.

frame relay   A protocol for the transmission of data formatted into variable size messages. Frame relay is generally used to provision point-to-point virtual circuits

gauge   An ASN.1 type, as defined by the SMI. Gauges are 32- or 64-bit unsigned numbers that monotonically increase and decrease and that stick when they hit their limits. They are encoded as unsigned integer.

GenError   An SNMP error indicating that the request was unable to be fulfilled due to an internal problem, such as resource limitations.

GUI   *Graphical User Interface*.

HEMS   *High-level Entity Management System*   A protocol for managing network elements. This protocol was never widely implemented.

HP   *Hewlett Packard*, Inc.

ICMP   *Internet Communications Message Protocol*   A protocol for communicating basic health, congestion, and path information in an IP infrastructure.

IDNX   A large multiplexer switch produced by Network Equipment Technologies, primarily used to aggregate and split T1s into channels.

IETF   *Internet Engineering Task Force*   A standards body that defines protocols for IP-based networks.

IfOperStatus   A commonly used object in MIB-2 that indicates the operational state of a specific interface or port.

IMPLICIT SEQUENCE   An ASN.1 convention, as defined by the SMI. IMPLICIT SEQUENCEs are used to define an ordered list of objects. They are encoded as various application-specific types.

INS   *International Network Systems*, Inc.   A large network consulting company purchased by Lucent Technologies.

instance   A specific, identifiable, implementation of a managed object. For example, an object may identify IfOperStatus, and its instance would specify the interface or port being described.

INTEGER   An ASN.1 type, as defined by the SMI. INTEGERs are 32-or 64-bit signed numbers.

International Standards Organization   A large standards body whose work includes defining telecommunications protocols to ensure interoperability.

InterfaceCount   A commonly used object in MIB-2, which indicates the total number of supported interfaces, or ports, contained in this device. Note that this number is without regard to their state.

Internet protocol   A protocol for the transmission of datagram based messages, originally developed by the U.S. Department of Defense. It has the capability to dynamically choose the best path for each message (fault tolerant). This standard is now managed by the IETF and serves as the standard for connecting to the global Internet.

Higher layer protocols, such as UDP and TCP, are used to provide additional services and characteristics.

Internet service provider A company or organization that provides access to the global Internet.

IP *See* Internet Protocol.

IpOutNoRoutes A commonly used object in MIB-2 that indicates the total number of IP messages dropped because there was no destination entry in the forwarding table.

ISO *See International Standards Organization.*

ISP *See Internet service provider.*

Keepalives A protocol used by Cisco routers to determine whether a link or interface is correctly passing traffic.

leaf Used in graph theory to denote a node that sits at the extreme edge of a tree (i.e., has no children).

locally ordered Used in graph theory to indicate that paths extending from each node are identified with labels that are unique within the node only; generally used to number the paths, starting with 1, at each node.

MAC *Media Access Control* indicates Layer 2 of the ISO stack.

MacroCorrelation The act of analyzing coincident symptoms based on data that changes infrequently. These symptoms are expected to change on the order of minutes or hours.

manager Used in SNMP to indicate a device that generates requests.

MIB *Management Information Base* A collection of managed objects indicating their unique names and meanings.

MIB-1 The first standard MIB defined by the IETF. All SNMP-compliant devices were required to fully support this.

MIB-2 A revised version of MIB-1, now the current standard in effect. All SNMP-compliant devices were required to fully support this.

MicroCorrelation™ The act of analyzing coincident symptoms based on data that changes frequently (every few seconds). This bottoms up analysis results both in a conclusion and the instantiated values required to take corrective action.

MRTG *Multi Router Traffic Grapher* A program available on the Internet for graphing data collected via SNMP and for producing reports viewable by standard web browsers.

network operations center   A facility used to monitor and manage the health of a network infrastructure.

network service provider   A company or organization that provides access to a private network infrastructure.

NOC   *See* Network Operations Center.

node   Used in graph theory to indicate a point, also called a *vertex*. In networking, this can be any managed element or object.

NoSuchName   An SNMP error indicating that the requested object or instance is not supported.

NSFNet   An IP backbone network, originally funded by the U.S. National Science Foundation to link researchers and computing facilities. This network was built by IBM, MCI, and Merit (University of Michigan) and served as the second generation backbone of the global Internet after DARPANet.

NSP   *See* Network Service Provider.

NULL   An ASN.1 type, as defined by the SMI. NULLs are generally placeholders that contain no information.

object   A uniquely named instrumentation point.

OBJECT IDENTIFIER   An ASN.1 object type, as defined by the SMI. OBJECT IDENTIFIERs provide a unique name, expressed in dotted decimal or text, of an object.

OCTET STRING   An ASN.1 object type, as defined by the SMI. OCTET STRINGs are combinations of 8-bit characters.

OID   *See* OBJECT IDENTIFIER.

OPAQUE   An ASN.1 type, as defined by the SMI. OPAQUE objects are used to wrap complex or constructed objects in a simply encoded type. They are expected to have a predefined meaning to a manager and agent.

out of band   The act of communicating with a managed element without using the infrastructure under management.

packed PDU   An SNMP request or response containing more than one varbind.

packet   A variable-sized message, formatted for transmission by a specific protocol.

padding   Additional bytes that are added to a packet to increase its size to the minimum specified by a given protocol.

parent   Used in graph theory to indicate a vertex, or node, that contains one or more vertices (the children). In a tree structure, a parent may have multiple children, but a child may only have one parent.

path   Used in graph theory to indicate a succession of one or more edges.

pattern stripping   The act of removing extra bits inserted into a data stream to return it to its original form.

pattern stuffing   The act of inserting extra bits into a data stream to ensure that it contains no patterns that have other meanings (such as end of message flags).

PDU   *Protocol Data Unit*   A message formatted with a higher layer protocol (e.g., SNMP).

peer   Used in BGP to indicate another device with which it shares routing updates.

ping   A program that measures response rates and round trip times using the ICMP protocol.

platform   A network management system that hosts a variety of applications.

PVC   *Permanent Virtual Circuit*   A logical point-to-point connection that changes infrequently.

ReadOnly   A MIB designation that indicates this object may be fetched but not set.

reassembly   The act of recombining message fragments back into their original, contiguous form.

RFC   *Request For Comments*   An IETF document that proposes or defines a standard.

RMON   *Remote MONitoring*   The collection of standards that enable the collection of traffic data on remote segments using SNMP.

RMON1   The first RMON standard, used primarily to instrument utilization, capacities, and errors.

RMON2   The second set of RMON standards, adding the capability to look at higher layer protocol information.

root   Used in graph theory to designate the highest level vertex on a tree, one with no parents.

root cause   The use of fault analysis to determine why a problem occurred, in addition to its existence and location.

router   A device that forwards packets based on Layer 3 addresses.

routing   The act of determining and using an optimized forwarding table.

routing loop   An inconsistency between distributed forwarding tables that causes packets to travel through devices that they have already traversed.

routing protocol   Used to create and maintain an optimized Layer 3 forwarding table.

routing update   An update or change in known information used by a routing protocol.

SEQUENCE   An ASN.1 convention, as defined by the SMI. SEQUENCEs are used to define an ordered list of objects.

SEQUENCE OF   An ASN.1 convention, as defined by the SMI. SEQUENCE OFs are used to define an ordered list of objects that repeats one or more times.

session   *See flow.*

SGMP   *Simple Gateway Monitoring Protocol*   The predecessor to SNMP.

SLA   *Service Level Agreement*   A promise or guarantee of minimum performance of an infrastructure.

SMI   *Structure of Management Information*   An IETF standard that defines the allowable subset of ASN.1 to be used by SNMP.

SMIv1   The first standard SMI.

SMIv2   The second standard SMI, primarily allowing the use of 64-bit numbers.

SNMP   *Simple Network Management Protocol*   Used to refer to all versions.

SNMPv1   The original standard SNMP that contains the commands GetRequest, GetNextRequest, SetRequest, GetResponse, and TRAP.

SNMPv2   The collection of proposed standards for the second version of SNMP. Competing standards limited the widespread adoption.

SNMPv3   A collection of standards for the third version of SNMP. This version adds security, reliability, and other features (at the cost of increased complexity). It is not yet widely adopted.

SPX   A protocol layered on Novell's IPX to add reliability and session identification.

subtree   Used in graph theory to indicate a portion of a tree structure.

switch   A device that forwards packets based on Layer 2 addresses.

synthetic transactions   The technique of emulating user traffic to measure infrastructure performance and availability.

SysUpTime   A commonly used object in MIB-2, which indicates the number of TimeTicks that a network management engine has been running.

T1   A full duplex, point-to-point circuit clocked at 1.544Mbps.

target   *See agent*.

TCP   *Transmission Control Protocol*   A protocol layered on IP to add reliability and session management.

Telco   Slang for telephone company.

TimeTicks   An ASN.1 convention, as defined by the SMI. TimeTicks are used to count hundredths of a second.

TLV   *Type, Length, Value*   A tuple indicating the three fields of ASN.1 encoded data.

TooBig   An SNMP error indicating that the received or requested message size exceeds internal limits.

topology analysis   The act of analyzing network fault data to determine the geographic location of a problem.

transmission group   A MIB subtree used to identify objects related to a specific Layer 2 technology.

TRAP   A SNMPv1 message containing asynchronous (unrequested) status information.

tree   A graph theory structure containing no loops.

trouble ticket   Used by a NOC to identify a known problem.

Varbind   *Variable binding*   A pairing of an instantiated OID with a value.

vertex   Used in graph theory for a point connected by an edge (plural vertices); also called a *node*.

VLAN   *Virtual LAN*   The act of emulating a single layer 2 segment over multiple physical segments.

walk, tree   Used in graph theory to indicate the traversal of edges on a tree.

working group   A group chartered by the IETF to study a problem or propose a standard.

APPENDIX A

Following is a sample SNMP packed GET-REQUEST and the corresponding GET-RESPONSE, as captured and substantially decoded by a Network Associates SnifferPro™. Each field is followed by a highlighted portion of the hex packet dump.

```
DLC:  —- DLC Header —-
      DLC:
      DLC:  Frame 3 arrived at  14:21:19.0963; frame size is 246
(00F6 hex) bytes.
      DLC:  Destination = Station Sun    99E6D8
      DLC:  Source      = Station Sun    B083C9
      DLC:  Ethertype   = 0800 (IP)
      DLC:

ADDR  HEX
0000: 08 00 20 99 e6 d8 08 00 20 b0 83 c9 08 00 45 00


IP:  —- IP Header —-
      IP:
      IP: Version = 4, header length = 20 bytes
      IP: Type of service = 00
      IP:       000. ....  = routine
      IP:       ...0 ....  = normal delay
      IP:       .... 0...  = normal throughput
      IP:       .... .0..  = normal reliability
      IP: Total length    = 232 bytes
      IP: Identification  = 51401
      IP: Flags           = 4X
      IP:       .1.. ....  = don't fragment
      IP:       ..0. ....  = last fragment
      IP: Fragment offset = 0 bytes
      IP: Time to live    = 255 seconds/hops
      IP: Protocol        = 17 (UDP)
      IP: Header checksum = F9EF (correct)
      IP: Source address      = [207.17.13.28]
      IP: Destination address = [207.17.13.12]
      IP: No options

ADDR  HEX
0000: 08 00 20 99 e6 d8 08 00 20 b0 83 c9 08 00 45 00
0010: 00 e8 c8 c9 40 00 ff 11 f9 ef cf 11 0d 1c cf 11
0020: 0d 0c 88 a8 00 a1 00 d4 6e 63 30 81 c9 02 01 00


UDP:  —- UDP Header —-
      UDP:
      UDP: Source port      = 34984
      UDP: Destination port = 161 (SNMP)
      UDP: Length           = 212
      UDP: Checksum         = 6E63 (correct)
      UDP: [204 byte(s) of data]
      UDP:
```

```
ADDR  HEX
0000: 08 00 20 99 e6 d8 08 00 20 b0 83 c9 08 00 45 00
0010: 00 e8 c8 c9 40 00 ff 11 f9 ef cf 11 0d 1c cf 11
0020: 0d 0c 88 a8 00 a1 00 d4 6e 63 30 81 c9 02 01 00
```

SNMP: —- Simple Network Management Protocol (Version 1) —-

    SNMP: SEQUENCE

```
ADDR  HEX
0000: 08 00 20 99 e6 d8 08 00 20 b0 83 c9 08 00 45 00
0010: 00 e8 c8 c9 40 00 ff 11 f9 ef cf 11 0d 1c cf 11
0020: 0d 0c 88 a8 00 a1 00 d4 6e 63 30 81 c9 02 01 00
```

SNMP: Version   = 1

```
ADDR  HEX
0000: 08 00 20 99 e6 d8 08 00 20 b0 83 c9 08 00 45 00
0010: 00 e8 c8 c9 40 00 ff 11 f9 ef cf 11 0d 1c cf 11
0020: 0d 0c 88 a8 00 a1 00 d4 6e 63 30 81 c9 02 01 00
```

    SNMP: Community   = public

```
ADDR  HEX
0000: 08 00 20 99 e6 d8 08 00 20 b0 83 c9 08 00 45 00
0010: 00 e8 c8 c9 40 00 ff 11 f9 ef cf 11 0d 1c cf 11
0020: 0d 0c 88 a8 00 a1 00 d4 6e 63 30 81 c9 02 01 00
0030: 04 06 70 75 62 6c 69 63 a0 81 bb 02 04 10 02 75
```

    SNMP: Command   = Get request

```
ADDR  HEX
0000: 08 00 20 99 e6 d8 08 00 20 b0 83 c9 08 00 45 00
0010: 00 e8 c8 c9 40 00 ff 11 f9 ef cf 11 0d 1c cf 11
0020: 0d 0c 88 a8 00 a1 00 d4 6e 63 30 81 c9 02 01 00
0030: 04 06 70 75 62 6c 69 63 a0 81 bb 02 04 10 02 75
```

    SNMP: Request ID   = 268596680

```
ADDR  HEX
0000: 08 00 20 99 e6 d8 08 00 20 b0 83 c9 08 00 45 00
0010: 00 e8 c8 c9 40 00 ff 11 f9 ef cf 11 0d 1c cf 11
0020: 0d 0c 88 a8 00 a1 00 d4 6e 63 30 81 c9 02 01 00
0030: 04 06 70 75 62 6c 69 63 a0 81 bb 02 04 10 02 75
0040: c8 02 01 00 02 01 00 30 81 ac 30 0c 06 08 2b 06
```

    SNMP: Error status = 0 (No error)

```
ADDR  HEX
0000: 08 00 20 99 e6 d8 08 00 20 b0 83 c9 08 00 45 00
0010: 00 e8 c8 c9 40 00 ff 11 f9 ef cf 11 0d 1c cf 11
0020: 0d 0c 88 a8 00 a1 00 d4 6e 63 30 81 c9 02 01 00
0030: 04 06 70 75 62 6c 69 63 a0 81 bb 02 04 10 02 75
0040: c8 02 01 00 02 01 00 30 81 ac 30 0c 06 08 2b 06
```

```
         SNMP: Error index = 0

ADDR  HEX
0000: 08 00 20 99 e6 d8 08 00 20 b0 83 c9 08 00 45 00
0010: 00 e8 c8 c9 40 00 ff 11 f9 ef cf 11 0d 1c cf 11
0020: 0d 0c 88 a8 00 a1 00 d4 6e 63 30 81 c9 02 01 00
0030: 04 06 70 75 62 6c 69 63 a0 81 bb 02 04 10 02 75
0040: c8 02 01 00 02 01 00 30 81 ac 30 0c 06 08 2b 06
```

```
         SNMP: SEQUENCE-OF

ADDR  HEX
0000: 08 00 20 99 e6 d8 08 00 20 b0 83 c9 08 00 45 00
0010: 00 e8 c8 c9 40 00 ff 11 f9 ef cf 11 0d 1c cf 11
0020: 0d 0c 88 a8 00 a1 00 d4 6e 63 30 81 c9 02 01 00
0030: 04 06 70 75 62 6c 69 63 a0 81 bb 02 04 10 02 75
0040: c8 02 01 00 02 01 00 30 81 ac 30 0c 06 08 2b 06
```

```
         SNMP: SEQUENCE
         SNMP: Object = {1.3.6.1.2.1.4.4.0} (ipInHdrErrors.0)
         SNMP: Value = NULL

ADDR  HEX
0000: 08 00 20 99 e6 d8 08 00 20 b0 83 c9 08 00 45 00
0010: 00 e8 c8 c9 40 00 ff 11 f9 ef cf 11 0d 1c cf 11
0020: 0d 0c 88 a8 00 a1 00 d4 6e 63 30 81 c9 02 01 00
0030: 04 06 70 75 62 6c 69 63 a0 81 bb 02 04 10 02 75
0040: c8 02 01 00 02 01 00 30 81 ac 30 0c 06 08 2b 06
0050: 01 02 01 04 04 00 05 00 30 0c 06 08 2b 06 01
```

```
         SNMP: SEQUENCE
         SNMP: Object = {1.3.6.1.2.1.4.5.0} (ipInAddrErrors.0)
         SNMP: Value = NULL

ADDR  HEX
0000: 08 00 20 99 e6 d8 08 00 20 b0 83 c9 08 00 45 00
0010: 00 e8 c8 c9 40 00 ff 11 f9 ef cf 11 0d 1c cf 11
0020: 0d 0c 88 a8 00 a1 00 d4 6e 63 30 81 c9 02 01 00
0030: 04 06 70 75 62 6c 69 63 a0 81 bb 02 04 10 02 75
0040: c8 02 01 00 02 01 00 30 81 ac 30 0c 06 08 2b 06
0050: 01 02 01 04 04 00 05 00 30 0c 06 08 2b 06 01 02
0060: 01 04 05 00 05 00 30 0c 06 08 2b 06 01 02 01 04
```

```
         SNMP: SEQUENCE
         SNMP: Object = {1.3.6.1.2.1.4.7.0} (ipInUnknownProtos.0)
         SNMP: Value = NULL

ADDR  HEX
0000: 08 00 20 99 e6 d8 08 00 20 b0 83 c9 08 00 45 00
0010: 00 e8 c8 c9 40 00 ff 11 f9 ef cf 11 0d 1c cf 11
0020: 0d 0c 88 a8 00 a1 00 d4 6e 63 30 81 c9 02 01 00
0030: 04 06 70 75 62 6c 69 63 a0 81 bb 02 04 10 02 75
0040: c8 02 01 00 02 01 00 30 81 ac 30 0c 06 08 2b 06
0050: 01 02 01 04 04 00 05 00 30 0c 06 08 2b 06 01 02
0060: 01 04 05 00 05 00 30 0c 06 08 2b 06 01 02 01 04
0070: 07 00 05 00 30 0c 06 08 2b 06 01 02 01 04 08 00
```

```
              SNMP: SEQUENCE
              SNMP: Object = {1.3.6.1.2.1.4.8.0} (ipInDiscards.0)
              SNMP: Value  = NULL

     ADDR  HEX
     0000: 08 00 20 99 e6 d8 08 00 20 b0 83 c9 08 00 45 00
     0010: 00 e8 c8 c9 40 00 ff 11 f9 ef cf 11 0d 1c cf 11
     0020: 0d 0c 88 a8 00 a1 00 d4 6e 63 30 81 c9 02 01 00
     0030: 04 06 70 75 62 6c 69 63 a0 81 bb 02 04 10 02 75
     0040: c8 02 01 00 02 01 00 30 81 ac 30 0c 06 08 2b 06
     0050: 01 02 01 04 04 00 05 00 30 0c 06 08 2b 06 01 02
     0060: 01 04 05 00 05 00 30 0c 06 08 2b 06 01 02 01 04
     0070: 07 00 05 00 30 0c 06 08 2b 06 01 02 01 04 08 00
     0080: 05 00 30 0c 06 08 2b 06 01 02 01 04 0b 00 05 00
```

```
              SNMP: SEQUENCE
              SNMP: Object = {1.3.6.1.2.1.4.11.0} (ipOutDiscards.0)
              SNMP: Value  = NULL

     ADDR  HEX
     0000: 08 00 20 99 e6 d8 08 00 20 b0 83 c9 08 00 45 00
     0010: 00 e8 c8 c9 40 00 ff 11 f9 ef cf 11 0d 1c cf 11
     0020: 0d 0c 88 a8 00 a1 00 d4 6e 63 30 81 c9 02 01 00
     0030: 04 06 70 75 62 6c 69 63 a0 81 bb 02 04 10 02 75
     0040: c8 02 01 00 02 01 00 30 81 ac 30 0c 06 08 2b 06
     0050: 01 02 01 04 04 00 05 00 30 0c 06 08 2b 06 01 02
     0060: 01 04 05 00 05 00 30 0c 06 08 2b 06 01 02 01 04
     0070: 07 00 05 00 30 0c 06 08 2b 06 01 02 01 04 08 00
     0080: 05 00 30 0c 06 08 2b 06 01 02 01 04 0b 00 05 00
```

```
              SNMP: SEQUENCE
              SNMP: Object = {1.3.6.1.2.1.4.16.0} (ipReasmFails.0)
              SNMP: Value  = NULL

     ADDR  HEX
     0000: 08 00 20 99 e6 d8 08 00 20 b0 83 c9 08 00 45 00
     0010: 00 e8 c8 c9 40 00 ff 11 f9 ef cf 11 0d 1c cf 11
     0020: 0d 0c 88 a8 00 a1 00 d4 6e 63 30 81 c9 02 01 00
     0030: 04 06 70 75 62 6c 69 63 a0 81 bb 02 04 10 02 75
     0040: c8 02 01 00 02 01 00 30 81 ac 30 0c 06 08 2b 06
     0050: 01 02 01 04 04 00 05 00 30 0c 06 08 2b 06 01 02
     0060: 01 04 05 00 05 00 30 0c 06 08 2b 06 01 02 01 04
     0070: 07 00 05 00 30 0c 06 08 2b 06 01 02 01 04 08 00
     0080: 05 00 30 0c 06 08 2b 06 01 02 01 04 0b 00 05 00
     0090: 30 0c 06 08 2b 06 01 02 01 04 10 00 05 00 30 0c
```

```
              SNMP: SEQUENCE
              SNMP: Object = {1.3.6.1.2.1.4.18.0} (ipFragFails.0)
              SNMP: Value  = NULL

     ADDR  HEX
     0000: 08 00 20 99 e6 d8 08 00 20 b0 83 c9 08 00 45 00
     0010: 00 e8 c8 c9 40 00 ff 11 f9 ef cf 11 0d 1c cf 11
     0020: 0d 0c 88 a8 00 a1 00 d4 6e 63 30 81 c9 02 01 00
     0030: 04 06 70 75 62 6c 69 63 a0 81 bb 02 04 10 02 75
```

```
0040: c8 02 01 00 02 01 00 30 81 ac 30 0c 06 08 2b 06
0050: 01 02 01 04 04 00 05 00 30 0c 06 08 2b 06 01 02
0060: 01 04 05 00 05 00 30 0c 06 08 2b 06 01 02 01 04
0070: 07 00 05 00 30 0c 06 08 2b 06 01 02 01 04 08 00
0080: 05 00 30 0c 06 08 2b 06 01 02 01 04 0b 00 05 00
0090: 30 0c 06 08 2b 06 01 02 01 04 10 00 05 00 30 0c
00a0: 06 08 2b 06 01 02 01 04 12 00 05 00 30 0c 06 08
```

```
SNMP: SEQUENCE
SNMP: Object = {1.3.6.1.2.1.4.23.0} (ipRoutingDiscards.0)
SNMP: Value  = NULL
```

```
ADDR  HEX
0000: 08 00 20 99 e6 d8 08 00 20 b0 83 c9 08 00 45 00
0010: 00 e8 c8 c9 40 00 ff 11 f9 ef cf 11 0d 1c cf 11
0020: 0d 0c 88 a8 00 a1 00 d4 6e 63 30 81 c9 02 01 00
0030: 04 06 70 75 62 6c 69 63 a0 81 bb 02 04 10 02 75
0040: c8 02 01 00 02 01 00 30 81 ac 30 0c 06 08 2b 06
0050: 01 02 01 04 04 00 05 00 30 0c 06 08 2b 06 01 02
0060: 01 04 05 00 05 00 30 0c 06 08 2b 06 01 02 01 04
0070: 07 00 05 00 30 0c 06 08 2b 06 01 02 01 04 08 00
0080: 05 00 30 0c 06 08 2b 06 01 02 01 04 0b 00 05 00
0090: 30 0c 06 08 2b 06 01 02 01 04 10 00 05 00 30 0c
00a0: 06 08 2b 06 01 02 01 04 12 00 05 00 30 0c 06 08
00b0: 2b 06 01 02 01 04 17 00 05 00 30 0c 06 08 2b 06
```

```
SNMP: SEQUENCE
SNMP: Object = {1.3.6.1.2.1.7.2.0} (udpNoPorts.0)
SNMP: Value  = NULL
```

```
ADDR  HEX
0000: 08 00 20 99 e6 d8 08 00 20 b0 83 c9 08 00 45 00
0010: 00 e8 c8 c9 40 00 ff 11 f9 ef cf 11 0d 1c cf 11
0020: 0d 0c 88 a8 00 a1 00 d4 6e 63 30 81 c9 02 01 00
0030: 04 06 70 75 62 6c 69 63 a0 81 bb 02 04 10 02 75
0040: c8 02 01 00 02 01 00 30 81 ac 30 0c 06 08 2b 06
0050: 01 02 01 04 04 00 05 00 30 0c 06 08 2b 06 01 02
0060: 01 04 05 00 05 00 30 0c 06 08 2b 06 01 02 01 04
0070: 07 00 05 00 30 0c 06 08 2b 06 01 02 01 04 08 00
0080: 05 00 30 0c 06 08 2b 06 01 02 01 04 0b 00 05 00
0090: 30 0c 06 08 2b 06 01 02 01 04 10 00 05 00 30 0c
00a0: 06 08 2b 06 01 02 01 04 12 00 05 00 30 0c 06 08
00b0: 2b 06 01 02 01 04 17 00 05 00 30 0c 06 08 2b 06
00c0: 01 02 01 07 02 00 05 00 30 0c 06 08 2b 06 01 02
```

```
SNMP: SEQUENCE
SNMP: Object = {1.3.6.1.2.1.7.3.0} (udpInErrors.0)
SNMP: Value  = NULL
```

```
ADDR  HEX
0000: 08 00 20 99 e6 d8 08 00 20 b0 83 c9 08 00 45 00
0010: 00 e8 c8 c9 40 00 ff 11 f9 ef cf 11 0d 1c cf 11
0020: 0d 0c 88 a8 00 a1 00 d4 6e 63 30 81 c9 02 01 00
0030: 04 06 70 75 62 6c 69 63 a0 81 bb 02 04 10 02 75
```

```
0040: c8 02 01 00 02 01 00 30 81 ac 30 0c 06 08 2b 06
0050: 01 02 01 04 04 00 05 00 30 0c 06 08 2b 06 01 02
0060: 01 04 05 00 05 00 30 0c 06 08 2b 06 01 02 01 04
0070: 07 00 05 00 30 0c 06 08 2b 06 01 02 01 04 08 00
0080: 05 00 30 0c 06 08 2b 06 01 02 01 04 0b 00 05 00
0090: 30 0c 06 08 2b 06 01 02 01 04 10 00 05 00 30 0c
00a0: 06 08 2b 06 01 02 01 04 12 00 05 00 30 0c 06 08
00b0: 2b 06 01 02 01 04 17 00 05 00 30 0c 06 08 2b 06
00c0: 01 02 01 07 02 00 05 00 30 0c 06 08 2b 06 01 02
00d0: 01 07 03 00 05 00 30 0e 06 0a 2b 06 01 02 01 02
```

```
              SNMP: SEQUENCE
              SNMP: Object = {1.3.6.1.2.1.2.2.1.12.2} (ifInNUcastPkts.2)
              SNMP: Value = NULL
```

```
ADDR  HEX
0000: 08 00 20 99 e6 d8 08 00 20 b0 83 c9 08 00 45 00
0010: 00 e8 c8 c9 40 00 ff 11 f9 ef cf 11 0d 1c cf 11
0020: 0d 0c 88 a8 00 a1 00 d4 6e 63 30 81 c9 02 01 00
0030: 04 06 70 75 62 6c 69 63 a0 81 bb 02 04 10 02 75
0040: c8 02 01 00 02 01 00 30 81 ac 30 0c 06 08 2b 06
0050: 01 02 01 04 04 00 05 00 30 0c 06 08 2b 06 01 02
0060: 01 04 05 00 05 00 30 0c 06 08 2b 06 01 02 01 04
0070: 07 00 05 00 30 0c 06 08 2b 06 01 02 01 04 08 00
0080: 05 00 30 0c 06 08 2b 06 01 02 01 04 0b 00 05 00
0090: 30 0c 06 08 2b 06 01 02 01 04 10 00 05 00 30 0c
00a0: 06 08 2b 06 01 02 01 04 12 00 05 00 30 0c 06 08
00b0: 2b 06 01 02 01 04 17 00 05 00 30 0c 06 08 2b 06
00c0: 01 02 01 07 02 00 05 00 30 0c 06 08 2b 06 01 02
00d0: 01 07 03 00 05 00 30 0e 06 0a 2b 06 01 02 01 02
00e0: 02 01 0c 02 05 00 30 0e 06 0a 2b 06 01 02 01 02
00f0: 02 01 12 02 05 00
```

```
              SNMP: SEQUENCE
              SNMP: Object = {1.3.6.1.2.1.2.2.1.18.2} (ifOutNUcastPkts.2)
              SNMP: Value  = NULL
```

```
ADDR  HEX
0000: 08 00 20 99 e6 d8 08 00 20 b0 83 c9 08 00 45 00
0010: 00 e8 c8 c9 40 00 ff 11 f9 ef cf 11 0d 1c cf 11
0020: 0d 0c 88 a8 00 a1 00 d4 6e 63 30 81 c9 02 01 00
0030: 04 06 70 75 62 6c 69 63 a0 81 bb 02 04 10 02 75
0040: c8 02 01 00 02 01 00 30 81 ac 30 0c 06 08 2b 06
0050: 01 02 01 04 04 00 05 00 30 0c 06 08 2b 06 01 02
0060: 01 04 05 00 05 00 30 0c 06 08 2b 06 01 02 01 04
0070: 07 00 05 00 30 0c 06 08 2b 06 01 02 01 04 08 00
0080: 05 00 30 0c 06 08 2b 06 01 02 01 04 0b 00 05 00
0090: 30 0c 06 08 2b 06 01 02 01 04 10 00 05 00 30 0c
00a0: 06 08 2b 06 01 02 01 04 12 00 05 00 30 0c 06 08
00b0: 2b 06 01 02 01 04 17 00 05 00 30 0c 06 08 2b 06
00c0: 01 02 01 07 02 00 05 00 30 0c 06 08 2b 06 01 02
00d0: 01 07 03 00 05 00 30 0e 06 0a 2b 06 01 02 01 02
00e0: 02 01 0c 02 05 00 30 0e 06 0a 2b 06 01 02 01 02
00f0: 02 01 12 02 05 00
```

```
- - - - - - - - - - - - - - - - - - - - - - - - - - - - - - - - - - - - - - - - - - - -
DLC: —- DLC Header —-
      DLC:
      DLC:  Frame 4 arrived at  14:21:19.0986; frame size is 262
      (0106 hex) bytes.
      DLC:  Destination = Station Sun   B083C9
      DLC:  Source      = Station Sun   99E6D8
      DLC:  Ethertype   = 0800 (IP)
      DLC:
```

```
ADDR  HEX
0000:  08 00 20 b0 83 c9 08 00 20 99 e6 d8 08 00 45 00
```

```
IP: —- IP Header —-
     IP:
     IP: Version = 4, header length = 20 bytes
     IP: Type of service = 00
     IP:        000. ....  = routine
     IP:        ...0 ....  = normal delay
     IP:        .... 0...  = normal throughput
     IP:        .... .0..  = normal reliability
     IP: Total length  = 248 bytes
     IP: Identification = 10524
     IP: Flags       = 4X
     IP:        .1.. ....  = don't fragment
     IP:        ..0. ....  = last fragment
     IP: Fragment offset = 0 bytes
     IP: Time to live   = 255 seconds/hops
     IP: Protocol      = 17 (UDP)
     IP: Header checksum = 998D (correct)
     IP: Source address    = [207.17.13.12]
     IP: Destination address = [207.17.13.28]
     IP: No options
     IP:
```

```
ADDR  HEX
0000:  08 00 20 b0 83 c9 08 00 20 99 e6 d8 08 00 45 00
0010:  00 f8 29 1c 40 00 ff 11 99 8d cf 11 0d 0c cf 11
0020:  0d 1c 00 a1 88 a8 00 e4 b7 ab 30 81 d9 02 01 00
```

```
UDP: —- UDP Header —-
      UDP:
      UDP: Source port      = 161 (SNMP)
      UDP: Destination port = 34984
      UDP: Length           = 228
      UDP: Checksum         = B7AB (correct)
      UDP: [220 byte(s) of data]
      UDP:
```

```
ADDR  HEX
0000:  08 00 20 b0 83 c9 08 00 20 99 e6 d8 08 00 45 00
0010:  00 f8 29 1c 40 00 ff 11 99 8d cf 11 0d 0c cf 11
0020:  0d 1c 00 a1 88 a8 00 e4 b7 ab 30 81 d9 02 01 00
```

```
SNMP: —- Simple Network Management Protocol (Version 1) —-
      SNMP: SEQUENCE

ADDR  HEX
0000: 08 00 20 b0 83 c9 08 00 20 99 e6 d8 08 00 45 00
0010: 00 f8 29 1c 40 00 ff 11 99 8d cf 11 0d 0c cf 11
0020: 0d 1c 00 a1 88 a8 00 e4 b7 ab 30 81 d9 02 01 00
```

```
      SNMP: Version      = 1

ADDR  HEX
0000: 08 00 20 b0 83 c9 08 00 20 99 e6 d8 08 00 45 00
0010: 00 f8 29 1c 40 00 ff 11 99 8d cf 11 0d 0c cf 11
0020: 0d 1c 00 a1 88 a8 00 e4 b7 ab 30 81 d9 02 01 00
```

```
      SNMP: Community    = public

ADDR  HEX
0000: 08 00 20 b0 83 c9 08 00 20 99 e6 d8 08 00 45 00
0010: 00 f8 29 1c 40 00 ff 11 99 8d cf 11 0d 0c cf 11
0020: 0d 1c 00 a1 88 a8 00 e4 b7 ab 30 81 d9 02 01 00
0030: 04 06 70 75 62 6c 69 63 a2 81 cb 02 04 10 02 75
```

```
      SNMP: Command      = Get response

ADDR  HEX
0000: 08 00 20 b0 83 c9 08 00 20 99 e6 d8 08 00 45 00
0010: 00 f8 29 1c 40 00 ff 11 99 8d cf 11 0d 0c cf 11
0020: 0d 1c 00 a1 88 a8 00 e4 b7 ab 30 81 d9 02 01 00
0030: 04 06 70 75 62 6c 69 63 a2 81 cb 02 04 10 02 75
```

```
      SNMP: Request ID   = 268596680

ADDR  HEX
0000: 08 00 20 b0 83 c9 08 00 20 99 e6 d8 08 00 45 00
0010: 00 f8 29 1c 40 00 ff 11 99 8d cf 11 0d 0c cf 11
0020: 0d 1c 00 a1 88 a8 00 e4 b7 ab 30 81 d9 02 01 00
0030: 04 06 70 75 62 6c 69 63 a2 81 cb 02 04 10 02 75
0040: c8 02 01 00 02 01 00 30 81 bc 30 0d 06 08 2b 06
```

```
      SNMP: Error status = 0 (No error)

ADDR  HEX
0000: 08 00 20 b0 83 c9 08 00 20 99 e6 d8 08 00 45 00
0010: 00 f8 29 1c 40 00 ff 11 99 8d cf 11 0d 0c cf 11
0020: 0d 1c 00 a1 88 a8 00 e4 b7 ab 30 81 d9 02 01 00
0030: 04 06 70 75 62 6c 69 63 a2 81 cb 02 04 10 02 75
0040: c8 02 01 00 02 01 00 30 81 bc 30 0d 06 08 2b 06
```

```
          SNMP: Error index  = 0

ADDR  HEX
0000: 08 00 20 b0 83 c9 08 00 20 99 e6 d8 08 00 45 00
0010: 00 f8 29 1c 40 00 ff 11 99 8d cf 11 0d 0c cf 11
0020: 0d 1c 00 a1 88 a8 00 e4 b7 ab 30 81 d9 02 01 00
0030: 04 06 70 75 62 6c 69 63 a2 81 cb 02 04 10 02 75
0040: c8 02 01 00 02 01 00 30 81 bc 30 0d 06 08 2b 06


          SNMP: SEQUENCE-OF

ADDR  HEX
0000: 08 00 20 b0 83 c9 08 00 20 99 e6 d8 08 00 45 00
0010: 00 f8 29 1c 40 00 ff 11 99 8d cf 11 0d 0c cf 11
0020: 0d 1c 00 a1 88 a8 00 e4 b7 ab 30 81 d9 02 01 00
0030: 04 06 70 75 62 6c 69 63 a2 81 cb 02 04 10 02 75
0040: c8 02 01 00 02 01 00 30 81 bc 30 0d 06 08 2b 06


          SNMP: SEQUENCE
          SNMP: Object = {1.3.6.1.2.1.4.4.0} (ipInHdrErrors.0)
          SNMP: Value  = 0 datagrams

ADDR  HEX
0000: 08 00 20 b0 83 c9 08 00 20 99 e6 d8 08 00 45 00
0010: 00 f8 29 1c 40 00 ff 11 99 8d cf 11 0d 0c cf 11
0020: 0d 1c 00 a1 88 a8 00 e4 b7 ab 30 81 d9 02 01 00
0030: 04 06 70 75 62 6c 69 63 a2 81 cb 02 04 10 02 75
0040: c8 02 01 00 02 01 00 30 81 bc 30 0d 06 08 2b 06
0050: 01 02 01 04 04 00 41 01 00 30 0d 06 08 2b 06 01


          SNMP: SEQUENCE
          SNMP: Object = {1.3.6.1.2.1.4.5.0} (ipInAddrErrors.0)
          SNMP: Value  = 0 datagrams

ADDR  HEX
0000: 08 00 20 b0 83 c9 08 00 20 99 e6 d8 08 00 45 00
0010: 00 f8 29 1c 40 00 ff 11 99 8d cf 11 0d 0c cf 11
0020: 0d 1c 00 a1 88 a8 00 e4 b7 ab 30 81 d9 02 01 00
0030: 04 06 70 75 62 6c 69 63 a2 81 cb 02 04 10 02 75
0040: c8 02 01 00 02 01 00 30 81 bc 30 0d 06 08 2b 06
0050: 01 02 01 04 04 00 41 01 00 30 0d 06 08 2b 06 01
0060: 02 01 04 05 00 41 01 00 30 0d 06 08 2b 06 01 02


          SNMP: SEQUENCE
          SNMP: Object = {1.3.6.1.2.1.4.7.0} (ipInUnknownProtos.0)
          SNMP: Value  = 0 datagrams

ADDR  HEX
0000: 08 00 20 b0 83 c9 08 00 20 99 e6 d8 08 00 45 00
0010: 00 f8 29 1c 40 00 ff 11 99 8d cf 11 0d 0c cf 11
0020: 0d 1c 00 a1 88 a8 00 e4 b7 ab 30 81 d9 02 01 00
```

```
0030:  04 06 70 75 62 6c 69 63 a2 81 cb 02 04 10 02 75
0040:  c8 02 01 00 02 01 00 30 81 bc 30 0d 06 08 2b 06
0050:  01 02 01 04 04 00 41 01 00 30 0d 06 08 2b 06 01
0060:  02 01 04 05 00 41 01 00 30 0d 06 08 2b 06 01 02
0070:  01 04 07 00 41 01 00 30 0d 06 08 2b 06 01 02 01
```

```
        SNMP: SEQUENCE
        SNMP: Object = {1.3.6.1.2.1.4.8.0} (ipInDiscards.0)
        SNMP: Value  = 0 datagrams
```

```
ADDR  HEX
0000:  08 00 20 b0 83 c9 08 00 20 99 e6 d8 08 00 45 00
0010:  00 f8 29 1c 40 00 ff 11 99 8d cf 11 0d 0c cf 11
0020:  0d 1c 00 a1 88 a8 00 e4 b7 ab 30 81 d9 02 01 00
0030:  04 06 70 75 62 6c 69 63 a2 81 cb 02 04 10 02 75
0040:  c8 02 01 00 02 01 00 30 81 bc 30 0d 06 08 2b 06
0050:  01 02 01 04 04 00 41 01 00 30 0d 06 08 2b 06 01
0060:  02 01 04 05 00 41 01 00 30 0d 06 08 2b 06 01 02
0070:  01 04 07 00 41 01 00 30 0d 06 08 2b 06 01 02 01
0080:  04 08 00 41 01 00 30 0d 06 08 2b 06 01 02 01 04
```

```
        SNMP: SEQUENCE
        SNMP: Object = {1.3.6.1.2.1.4.11.0} (ipOutDiscards.0)
        SNMP: Value  = 0 datagrams
```

```
ADDR  HEX
0000:  08 00 20 b0 83 c9 08 00 20 99 e6 d8 08 00 45 00
0010:  00 f8 29 1c 40 00 ff 11 99 8d cf 11 0d 0c cf 11
0020:  0d 1c 00 a1 88 a8 00 e4 b7 ab 30 81 d9 02 01 00
0030:  04 06 70 75 62 6c 69 63 a2 81 cb 02 04 10 02 75
0040:  c8 02 01 00 02 01 00 30 81 bc 30 0d 06 08 2b 06
0050:  01 02 01 04 04 00 41 01 00 30 0d 06 08 2b 06 01
0060:  02 01 04 05 00 41 01 00 30 0d 06 08 2b 06 01 02
0070:  01 04 07 00 41 01 00 30 0d 06 08 2b 06 01 02 01
0080:  04 08 00 41 01 00 30 0d 06 08 2b 06 01 02 01 04
0090:  0b 00 41 01 00 30 0d 06 08 2b 06 01 02 01 04 10
```

```
        SNMP: SEQUENCE
        SNMP: Object = {1.3.6.1.2.1.4.16.0} (ipReasmFails.0)
        SNMP: Value  = 10
```

```
ADDR  HEX
0000:  08 00 20 b0 83 c9 08 00 20 99 e6 d8 08 00 45 00
0010:  00 f8 29 1c 40 00 ff 11 99 8d cf 11 0d 0c cf 11
0020:  0d 1c 00 a1 88 a8 00 e4 b7 ab 30 81 d9 02 01 00
0030:  04 06 70 75 62 6c 69 63 a2 81 cb 02 04 10 02 75
0040:  c8 02 01 00 02 01 00 30 81 bc 30 0d 06 08 2b 06
0050:  01 02 01 04 04 00 41 01 00 30 0d 06 08 2b 06 01
0060:  02 01 04 05 00 41 01 00 30 0d 06 08 2b 06 01 02
0070:  01 04 07 00 41 01 00 30 0d 06 08 2b 06 01 02 01
0080:  04 08 00 41 01 00 30 0d 06 08 2b 06 01 02 01 04
0090:  0b 00 41 01 00 30 0d 06 08 2b 06 01 02 01 04 10
00a0:  00 41 01 0a 30 0d 06 08 2b 06 01 02 01 04 12 00
```

```
        SNMP: SEQUENCE
        SNMP: Object = {1.3.6.1.2.1.4.18.0} (ipFragFails.0)
        SNMP: Value  = 0 datagrams
```

```
ADDR   HEX
0000:  08 00 20 b0 83 c9 08 00 20 99 e6 d8 08 00 45 00
0010:  00 f8 29 1c 40 00 ff 11 99 8d cf 11 0d 0c cf 11
0020:  0d 1c 00 a1 88 a8 00 e4 b7 ab 30 81 d9 02 01 00
0030:  04 06 70 75 62 6c 69 63 a2 81 cb 02 04 10 02 75
0040:  c8 02 01 00 02 01 00 30 81 bc 30 0d 06 08 2b 06
0050:  01 02 01 04 04 00 41 01 00 30 0d 06 08 2b 06 01
0060:  02 01 04 05 00 41 01 00 30 0d 06 08 2b 06 01 02
0070:  01 04 07 00 41 01 00 30 0d 06 08 2b 06 01 02 01
0080:  04 08 00 41 01 00 30 0d 06 08 2b 06 01 02 01 04
0090:  0b 00 41 01 00 30 0d 06 08 2b 06 01 02 01 04 10
00a0:  00 41 01 0a 30 0d 06 08 2b 06 01 02 01 04 12 00
00b0:  41 01 00 30 0d 06 08 2b 06 01 02 01 04 17 00 41
```

```
SNMP: SEQUENCE
SNMP: Object = {1.3.6.1.2.1.4.23.0} (ip.23.0)
SNMP: Value  = 0 (counter)
```

```
ADDR   HEX
0000:  08 00 20 b0 83 c9 08 00 20 99 e6 d8 08 00 45 00
0010:  00 f8 29 1c 40 00 ff 11 99 8d cf 11 0d 0c cf 11
0020:  0d 1c 00 a1 88 a8 00 e4 b7 ab 30 81 d9 02 01 00
0030:  04 06 70 75 62 6c 69 63 a2 81 cb 02 04 10 02 75
0040:  c8 02 01 00 02 01 00 30 81 bc 30 0d 06 08 2b 06
0050:  01 02 01 04 04 00 41 01 00 30 0d 06 08 2b 06 01
0060:  02 01 04 05 00 41 01 00 30 0d 06 08 2b 06 01 02
0070:  01 04 07 00 41 01 00 30 0d 06 08 2b 06 01 02 01
0080:  04 08 00 41 01 00 30 0d 06 08 2b 06 01 02 01 04
0090:  0b 00 41 01 00 30 0d 06 08 2b 06 01 02 01 04 10
00a0:  00 41 01 0a 30 0d 06 08 2b 06 01 02 01 04 12 00
00b0:  41 01 00 30 0d 06 08 2b 06 01 02 01 04 17 00 41
00c0:  01 00 30 0e 06 08 2b 06 01 02 01 07 02 00 41 02
```

```
SNMP: SEQUENCE
SNMP: Object = {1.3.6.1.2.1.7.2.0} (udpNoPorts.0)
SNMP: Value  = 31771 datagrams
```

```
ADDR   HEX
0000:  08 00 20 b0 83 c9 08 00 20 99 e6 d8 08 00 45 00
0010:  00 f8 29 1c 40 00 ff 11 99 8d cf 11 0d 0c cf 11
0020:  0d 1c 00 a1 88 a8 00 e4 b7 ab 30 81 d9 02 01 00
0030:  04 06 70 75 62 6c 69 63 a2 81 cb 02 04 10 02 75
0040:  c8 02 01 00 02 01 00 30 81 bc 30 0d 06 08 2b 06
0050:  01 02 01 04 04 00 41 01 00 30 0d 06 08 2b 06 01
0060:  02 01 04 05 00 41 01 00 30 0d 06 08 2b 06 01 02
0070:  01 04 07 00 41 01 00 30 0d 06 08 2b 06 01 02 01
0080:  04 08 00 41 01 00 30 0d 06 08 2b 06 01 02 01 04
0090:  0b 00 41 01 00 30 0d 06 08 2b 06 01 02 01 04 10
00a0:  00 41 01 0a 30 0d 06 08 2b 06 01 02 01 04 12 00
00b0:  41 01 00 30 0d 06 08 2b 06 01 02 01 04 17 00 41
00c0:  01 00 30 0e 06 08 2b 06 01 02 01 07 02 00 41 02
00d0:  7c 1b 30 0d 06 08 2b 06 01 02 01 07 03 00 41 01
```

```
SNMP: SEQUENCE
SNMP: Object = {1.3.6.1.2.1.7.3.0} (udpInErrors.0)
SNMP: Value  = 0 datagrams
```

```
ADDR  HEX
0000: 08 00 20 b0 83 c9 08 00 20 99 e6 d8 08 00 45 00
0010: 00 f8 29 1c 40 00 ff 11 99 8d cf 11 0d 0c cf 11
0020: 0d 1c 00 a1 88 a8 00 e4 b7 ab 30 81 d9 02 01 00
0030: 04 06 70 75 62 6c 69 63 a2 81 cb 02 04 10 02 75
0040: c8 02 01 00 02 01 00 30 81 bc 30 0d 06 08 2b 06
0050: 01 02 01 04 04 00 41 01 00 30 0d 06 08 2b 06 01
0060: 02 01 04 05 00 41 01 00 30 0d 06 08 2b 06 01 02
0070: 01 04 07 00 41 01 00 30 0d 06 08 2b 06 01 02 01
0080: 04 08 00 41 01 00 30 0d 06 08 2b 06 01 02 01 04
0090: 0b 00 41 01 00 30 0d 06 08 2b 06 01 02 01 04 10
00a0: 00 41 01 0a 30 0d 06 08 2b 06 01 02 01 04 12 00
00b0: 41 01 00 30 0d 06 08 2b 06 01 02 01 04 17 00 41
00c0: 01 00 30 0e 06 08 2b 06 01 02 01 07 02 00 41 02
00d0: 7c 1b 30 0d 06 08 2b 06 01 02 01 07 03 00 41 01
00e0: 00 30 11 06 0a 2b 06 01 02 01 02 02 01 0c 02 41
```

```
                    SNMP: SEQUENCE
                    SNMP: Object = {1.3.6.1.2.1.2.2.1.12.2} (ifInNUcastPkts.2)
                    SNMP: Value  = 1162608 packets
```

```
ADDR  HEX
0000: 08 00 20 b0 83 c9 08 00 20 99 e6 d8 08 00 45 00
0010: 00 f8 29 1c 40 00 ff 11 99 8d cf 11 0d 0c cf 11
0020: 0d 1c 00 a1 88 a8 00 e4 b7 ab 30 81 d9 02 01 00
0030: 04 06 70 75 62 6c 69 63 a2 81 cb 02 04 10 02 75
0040: c8 02 01 00 02 01 00 30 81 bc 30 0d 06 08 2b 06
0050: 01 02 01 04 04 00 41 01 00 30 0d 06 08 2b 06 01
0060: 02 01 04 05 00 41 01 00 30 0d 06 08 2b 06 01 02
0070: 01 04 07 00 41 01 00 30 0d 06 08 2b 06 01 02 01
0080: 04 08 00 41 01 00 30 0d 06 08 2b 06 01 02 01 04
0090: 0b 00 41 01 00 30 0d 06 08 2b 06 01 02 01 04 10
00a0: 00 41 01 0a 30 0d 06 08 2b 06 01 02 01 04 12 00
00b0: 41 01 00 30 0d 06 08 2b 06 01 02 01 04 17 00 41
00c0: 01 00 30 0e 06 08 2b 06 01 02 01 07 02 00 41 02
00d0: 7c 1b 30 0d 06 08 2b 06 01 02 01 07 03 00 41 01
00e0: 00 30 11 06 0a 2b 06 01 02 01 02 02 01 0c 02 41
00f0: 03 11 bd 70 30 10 06 0a 2b 06 01 02 01 02 02 01
```

```
                    SNMP: SEQUENCE
                    SNMP: Object = {1.3.6.1.2.1.2.2.1.18.2} (ifOutNUcastPkts.2)
                    SNMP: Value  = 19197 packets
```

```
ADDR  HEX
0000: 08 00 20 b0 83 c9 08 00 20 99 e6 d8 08 00 45 00
0010: 00 f8 29 1c 40 00 ff 11 99 8d cf 11 0d 0c cf 11
0020: 0d 1c 00 a1 88 a8 00 e4 b7 ab 30 81 d9 02 01 00
0030: 04 06 70 75 62 6c 69 63 a2 81 cb 02 04 10 02 75
0040: c8 02 01 00 02 01 00 30 81 bc 30 0d 06 08 2b 06
0050: 01 02 01 04 04 00 41 01 00 30 0d 06 08 2b 06 01
0060: 02 01 04 05 00 41 01 00 30 0d 06 08 2b 06 01 02
```

```
0070: 01 04 07 00 41 01 00 30 0d 06 08 2b 06 01 02 01
0080: 04 08 00 41 01 00 30 0d 06 08 2b 06 01 02 01 04
0090: 0b 00 41 01 00 30 0d 06 08 2b 06 01 02 01 04 10
00a0: 00 41 01 0a 30 0d 06 08 2b 06 01 02 01 04 12 00
00b0: 41 01 00 30 0d 06 08 2b 06 01 02 01 04 17 00 41
00c0: 01 00 30 0e 06 08 2b 06 01 02 01 07 02 00 41 02
00d0: 7c 1b 30 0d 06 08 2b 06 01 02 01 07 03 00 41 01
00e0: 00 30 11 06 0a 2b 06 01 02 01 02 02 01 0c 02 41
00f0: 03 11 bd 70 30 10 06 0a 2b 06 01 02 01 02 02 01
0100: 12 02 41 02 4a fd
```

INDEX

A

advanced performance analysis, 64–65
AgentAddress field, PDUs, 21
analysis tools, capacity planning, 40
analysis
   fault (*See also* fault analysis), 44
   performance (*See also* performance
     analysis), 44
ASN.1 (Abstract Syntax Notation 1), 10
   BERs (Basic Encoding Rules), 10
   length fields, 11
   type fields, 11
   value fields, 11
ASPs (Application Service Providers), 45
   performance analysis, 45
ATM, monitoring, 106
attributes
   MIBs
     nodes, 7
     INTEGER, 8
authentication, SNMP, 26
availability measurements, 39

B

BadValue errorStatus, 17
BERs (Basic Encoding Rules), ASN.1, 10
BGP, monitoring, 141
binding instances to objects, 9

box availability, 32
bridges, 802.1d, monitoring, 94

C

CA (Computer Associates), 48
   Unicenter, 48
   Unicenter Framework, 42
cable modems, monitoring, 148
Cabletron/Aprisma Spectrum, 57
capacity planning, 40–42
   management platforms, 43–44
Castle Rock SNMPc, 42
centralized data collection, 67
checking
   infrastructure availability, 37–38
   interface availability, 33
   path availability, 33–35
   service availability, 36
child nodes, MIBs, 6
Cisco NetFlow, 47
Cisco remote source route bridging,
   monitoring, 179
Cisco routers, monitoring, 163
Cisco uBR cable modems,
   monitoring, 188
Cisco VLANs, monitoring, 180
Cisco WSC switches, monitoring, 184
columns, MIB tables, 9
Community field
   PDUs, 21
   SNMP, 16

T

U–V